Team Spirits

The Native American Mascots Controversy

Edited by *C. Richard King*
and *Charles Fruehling Springwood*
Foreword by *Vine Deloria Jr.*

UNIVERSITY OF NEBRASKA PRESS

Lincoln & London

© 2001 by the University of Nebraska Press
All rights reserved
Manufactured in the United States of America

Library of Congress Cataloging-in-Publication Data
King, C. Richard, 1968–
Team spirits : the Native American mascots controversy /
C. Richard King and Charles Fruehling Springwood.
p. cm. Includes bibliographical references and index.
ISBN 0-8032-7798-9 (paperback: alkaline paper)
1. Indians as mascots. 2. Sports team mascots—
Social aspects—United States.
3. Indians of North America—Social conditions—
20th century.
I. Title: Native American mascots controversy.
II. Springwood, Charles Fruehling. III. Title.
GV714.5.K56 2001 306.4′83–dc21
00-059968

MINSTREL SHOW (1993)

•

Dennis Tibbetts (Ojibwe/Shoshone)

Dear Grandfather Redsky:
The university put on a
Minstrel Show today.
The Chi-mookmaan held it in
a stadium of 60,000 people.

The Anishinabe "The People"
The old ones found a place,
a place called White earth,
it became sacred to "The People"
A place for ceremonies.

In the parking lot there were men
with hairy chests, war whooping
and jumping around, without spilling
the drinks they carried in their hands.

The Anishinabe came from great distances,
for the Warrior Ceremony.
In old cars and pick-ups; parking near the forest.
Throughout the night,
there was dancing, songs, and drumming.

They painted their white faces.
They wore feathers in their hair.
They bought little drums
They carried toy tomahawks.

The Keeper of the Sacred Pipe,
starts the ceremony.
Tobacco, fur, feathers, wood, clay.
Facing the four directions, praying the
smoke will guide us to the truth.

They have an authentic white Indian.
Impressive headdress, buckskins, and bare feet.
An imposing warrior, who dances quite a dance,
when the helmets scored a touchdown.

The sweat lodge was crowded
with twelve men.
Heated rocks and steam to purify
these modern Anishinabe warriors.
We are as one, as we feel the earth's heat.

A band played a Hollywood Indian
war song. It stirred their blood.
They war whooped and chopped.
Painted faces and feathered heads.

An elder sang the warrior song:
A warrior is the one;
    who carries the burden of the bones of his people.
A warrior is the one;
    to revenge the wrongs carries out on his people.
A warrior is the one;
    who sacrifices his life for the existence of his people.

They tell me they honor us Grandfather
by remembering our fierceness in battle.
Powerful image makers, more powerful
than cavalry bullets and soldiers' bayonets.

Grandfather Redsky you taught me:
how to believe in my essence,
how to listen to the earth,
how to sing the songs,
how to soar.

If not for that Grandfather Redsky,
    I could not bear this Minstrel Show.

CONTENTS

FOREWORD
•
Vine Deloria Jr.

Sports mascots have come under increasing fire by American Indians as they try to achieve equal status as an identifiable ethnic group within American society. No other group faces this particular problem, and the unique nature of the situation calls for serious deliberations. Why are Indians singled out as a group of people devoid of the sentiments that characterize other groups? No team in any sport has its logo or slogans used to demean another identifiable ethnic, religious, or economic group.

One answer may be the long tradition of virulent racism against the original inhabitants best illustrated in the nursery rhyme "Ten Little Indians," which celebrated the genocide of local Indian tribes in the eastern United States. Some years ago a national publisher released a book of "animals and their children," and prominently displayed among the deer, raccoons, and birds were mother and her child. And when a group of us filed to cancel the trademark of the Washington Redskins, some sportswriters complained that now Bears, Dolphins, and Lions would all complain. This kind of racism is buried so deeply in the American psyche that it may be impossible to resolve. No one seriously holds these views as a conscious part of their understanding of the world. But, in the spur-of-the-moment response, this profound racism rises quickly to consciousness and is expressed before the individual realizes what he or she has said.

With diehard refusal to change the names and logos of sports teams we always hear the justification that the name is being used to "honor" us. This tortured reasoning makes its proponents look

ix

absurd. Obviously if garish costumes, demeaning cheers, and crude logos are the essence of honor, then the various sports halls of fame need to perform drastic surgery on the busts and plaques of their honorees. The excuse, being lame, must conceal something more profound, which cannot or will not be articulated by those people "honoring" us.

American Indians are always presented as something "other," a historical relic or a status, which is beyond the reach of the average person. I think that the romantic image of the Indian has unlimited potential for psychic disruption for two reasons, and that barring a maturing process in American society, we will always face the kind of discrimination represented by derogatory sports names and mascots. The American Indian represents a freedom completely at home with the natural world. This freedom is proper and can be realized occasionally by everyone, but it creates the belief that only Indians experience it continually. Indians thus stand apart from everyone else, and the gulf between them and others is insurmountable.

Equally important, Indians represent the American past, and Europeans and Americans have been fleeing from their own past since the days of discovery and settlement. If whole nations had supplanted the Indian nations, there would have been a simple displacement of populations, and the shared attributes of one nation would have been an adequate substitute for the culture and history of the previous occupants. North America was settled, however, by individuals who were always fleeing civilization and moving west. In spite of the glorious patriotic traditions of the United States, the fact is that people were alone and alienated from the very beginning and remain that way today. The Indian then reminds them that they are not really people of the land but mere usurpers. Now rednecks and peckerwoods can argue this point forever, but in those cold, dark hours of the night when they have to face themselves, the experience of being aliens cannot be overcome.

Progress is being made in many places in this country as school after school, and college after college, changes its name and adopts neutral slogans and mascots. With the increasing number of sports teams changing names, those that remain are on shifting, sinking grounds, and consequently we can now see a determined racism emerging: for example, the Washington Redskins owner, who is adamant about keeping the name. No one realizes the image of Americans seen by the other nations of the world—in the nation's capital the football team has the most derogatory mascot in the world. That alerts statesmen throughout the world that pretty words and solemn pledges do not constitute a reliable basis of trust.

This book covers a wide variety of local situations and gives us more precise information on the struggles all over the country to change the way we do our entertainment business. It is particularly important here to note that much of the problem revolves around a few stubborn people—be they alumni of Illinois or the owner of the Redskins—and that in spite of the good will of many Americans, a few individuals resist change and continue their ignorant ways. That is perhaps the burden of a free society, and it is a shame that we cannot help these people achieve some kind of maturity and social responsibility. We hope this book will energize people to join in the struggle to put derogatory stereotypes behind us.

ACKNOWLEDGMENTS

Writing, scholarship, editing, activism, and cultural critique ultimately are collaborative. This collection, as a product of these processes, depended upon others giving of themselves, offering us their time and ideas, sharing their experiences, and, at times, sacrificing for us. We owe much to our families, friends, colleagues, and students. We have accrued more debts of gratitude than we can ever hope to repay. We wish to thank, first and foremost, the contributors. They patiently endured the travails of publishing, completing polished and insightful essays, perhaps in spite of our efforts.

Countless individuals have enhanced *Team Spirits*, individually and collectively contributing to our efforts in unique ways. Although we cannot reconstruct the full list, we wish to thank the following people for their advice, encouragement, and ideas: Shari Addonizio, Teddy Amoloza, Jim Anderson, Marsha Brofka, Edward Bruner, Paul Bushnell, Cheryl Cole, Karen Conner, Catherine Davids, Philip Deloria, Norman K. Denzin, Robert Eurich, Joe Gone, Brenda Farnell, Allan Hanson, Patti Hartman, Ginna Husting, Ishgooda, Abby Jahiel, Kevin Karpiak, Bill Kelleher, Harvey Klevar, Lyle Lockwood, Shana Marie Basmarion Miller, Patra Noonan, Anthony Paredes, Chris Prendergast, David Prochaska, Renya Ramirez, Debbie Reese, Bob Rinehart, George Rundblad, Joseph Schneider, April Schultz, Jim Sikora, Jim Stanlaw, Rose Stremlau, Lori Stanley, Synthia Sydnor, Chris Thompson, Mike Weis, and Stanford University's archival librarian Patricia White.

Generous institutional support facilitated the completion of this collection. The Mellon Center at Illinois Wesleyan University awarded an Artistic and Scholarly Development grant to Charles

Fruehling Springwood, while the Humanities Center at Drake University also provided financial assistance for this volume. Librarians at both universities, particularly Sue Stroyan, Kris Vogel, and Meg Gunderson, have been invaluable. Editorial assistants Mark Heine, Shelley Manning, and Andrea Wyant offered key support in the preparation of this volume.

C. Richard King wishes to note his particular gratitude to a number of individuals central to his creative endeavors. Most importantly, I want express my deep thanks to my partner, Marcie Gilliland, for her passion, perspective, and presence. Her love and support continually inspire and enlighten. She is the best thing that ever happened to me. And even though they have never thought about mascots, my young daughters, Abigail and Ellory, deserve high praise for encouraging me to relearn the world, reminding me of the importance of play and imagination. My parents and brothers have provided useful suggestions and enduring encouragement. Finally, I thank my coeditor, Charles Fruehling Springwood. His commitment to social justice and intellectual rigor not only makes the arduous process of editing a joy, but also constantly enriches my scholarship.

Charles Fruehling Springwood also wants to express his thanks to several people. My debts of gratitude are enormous and numerous, and they do not always seem to fall into distinct, circumscribed categories such as scholarly, familial, personal, or emotional. Indeed, my relationships with most of those whom I feel compelled to acknowledge in this space transcend categorization. Foremost, I would like to express thanks to my family—in particular, my loving friend and partner, Cheryl Springwood, and our sons, Jacob and Josua. Your companionship enlivens me, every day! The vital support of my parents and extended family members remains priceless. C. Richard King has served faithfully, as a colleague always willing to engage, integrate, critique, synthesize, and deconstruct any scholarly conversation or writing, including my own. His kind friendship has meant more to me than he can know. Irv Epstein and Tom Lutze each have sustained me through a stimulating blend of friendship and rigorous intellectual counsel. Finally, special thanks to Joe Gone and to my brother, Doug Fruehling.

TEAM SPIRITS

Introduction

Imagined Indians, Social Identities, and Activism

•

C. Richard King and Charles Fruehling Springwood

This collection is about Native American mascots and what they
reveal about race, power, and culture. These essays interrogate the
troubling uses of "Indians" in athletics and recent efforts to challenge them. Unlike much popular discourse, this collection is not
content simply to pass moral judgments or identify stereotypes,
although individual essays undertake each of these tasks. Instead,
Team Spirits traces the (re)inventions of self and society through Native American mascots and the cultural artifacts, public sentiments,
and ritual performances—victory dances, school songs, cheers,
chants, drinking games, face painting, shirts, hats, bumper stickers,
and even toilet paper—associated with them. The critical essays in
this volume are unified by a set of questions about representation,
the politics of culture, and identity: What makes it possible for Euro-
Americans to invent such symbols? What historical uses and understandings of Native Americana animate mascots? What does it
mean to "play Indian" at halftime? What broader lessons about
American culture might be discerned from these halftime performances? What do these performances say about the changing role

I

of Native Americans in public culture? How is Native American activism around mascots important to broader understandings of social movements, identity, and community in Native America?

Team Spirits opens a multivocal, interdisciplinary, and transcultural dialogue about the complex history and significance of Native American mascots. Essays written by both academics and activists explore the means and meanings of "playing Indian" in more than a dozen localities. The authors balance a concern for stereotypes about Native Americans with attention to Native Americans as sociopolitical actors contesting and condoning them. Conceiving of mascots as something more than mere entertainment, the contributors detail the complex and contradictory ways in which individuals and institutions have fashioned identity, history, and community through and against them. Significantly, Native American mascots afford a splendid opportunity to explore the construction and contestation of particular versions of race, especially Indianness and whiteness; to highlight the colonial legacies and "postcolonial" predicaments of American culture; and to outline a nuanced account of the changing position of Native Americans in American society from invented icons to embodied actors.

Native American mascots are a pervasive, ubiquitous feature of American culture. Dozens of professional and semi-professional sports teams have (or have had) such monikers. A quarter of a century after Stanford University, the University of Oklahoma, and Dartmouth College retired "their" Indians, according to the National Coalition on Racism in Sports and Media, more than eighty colleges and universities still use Native American mascots (Rodriguez 1998). Innumerable high schools continue to refer to themselves and their sports teams as the Indians, the Redskins, the Braves, the Warriors, or the Red Raiders.

Euro-American individuals and institutions initially imagined themselves as Indians for a myriad of reasons. Whereas some institutions, such as Dartmouth College, had historically defined themselves through a specific relationship with Native Americans, more commonly, especially at public universities, regional histories and the traces of the Native nations that formerly occupied the state inspired students, coaches, and administrators to adopt Indian mascots, as in the University of Utah Running Utes or the University of Illinois Fighting Illini. Elsewhere, elaborations of a historical accident, coincidence, or circumstance seem to account for the beginnings of playing Indian. The students at Simpson College, in Indianola, Iowa, became the Redmen, later adopting a victory cheer known as the "Scalp Song" and using idioms of Indianness in their annual rituals such as homecoming, following remarks that they played like a bunch of red men. Similarly, St. John's University teams were known as the Redmen initially because their uniforms were all red; only later did fans and alumni transform this quirk into a tradition of playing Indian. Whatever the specific origins of these individual icons, Euro-Americans were able to fabricate Native Americans as mascots precisely because of prevailing sociohistorical conditions. That is, a set of social relations and cultural categories made it possible, pleasurable, and powerful for Euro-Americans to incorporate images of Indians in athletic contexts. First, Euro-Americans have always fashioned individual and collective identities for themselves by playing Indian. Native American mascots were an extension of this long tradition. Second, the conquest of Native America simultaneously empowered Euro-Americans to appropriate, invent, and otherwise represent Native Americans and to long for aspects of their cultures that had been destroyed by conquest. Third, with the rise of public culture, the production of Indianness in spectacles, exhibitions, and other sundry entertainments proliferated, offering templates for elaborations in sporting contexts.

Importantly, Native American mascots increasingly have become questionable, contentious, and problematic (Banks 1993; Churchill 1994; Davis 1993; Frazier 1997; Jackson and Lyons 1997; King 1998; King and Springwood forthcoming; Pewewardy 1991; Slowikowski 1993; Springwood and King forthcoming; Vanderford 1996; Wenner 1993). Across the United States and Canada, individuals and organizations, from high school students and teachers to the American Indian Movement and the National Congress of American Indians, passionately and aggressively have contested Native American mascots, forcing public debates and policy changes.

At the professional level, in April 1999, the federal Trademark Trial and Appeal Board voided the trademark rights of the Washington Redskins of the National Football League, finding that the name and logo used by the team were disparaging and hence violated the law (Kelber 1994; Likourezos 1996; Pace 1994; see also Sigelman 1998). The seven prominent Native Americans who brought the case in 1992, including contributors Vine Deloria Jr. and Susan Shown Harjo, hoped that the cancellation of trademark protection would encourage the franchise to drop its derogatory moniker. In an effort to fend off similar claims and defuse criticism, the Cleveland Indians have offered an origin myth of sorts that suggests the name and logo memorialize a past player and thus honor Native Americans more generally (Staurowsky 1998, this volume).

Arguably, collegiate mascots have evoked more debate than their professional counterparts. In the past decade, several colleges and universities have taken great strides in response to public concern. Whereas a handful of institutions, including the University of Utah and Bradley University, have *revised* their use of imagery, many others, including St. John's University, the University of Miami (Ohio), Simpson College, the University of Tennessee at Chattanooga, and Adams State College (Colorado) have *retired* their mascots. Some schools without Native American mascots, such as the University of Wisconsin and the University of Minnesota, have instituted policies prohibiting their athletic departments from scheduling games against institutions with racist icons. At the same time, countless communities and boards of education have confronted the issue. Many have deemed Native American mascots to be discriminatory, opting as the Minnesota State Board of Education and the Los Angeles and Dallas School Districts did, to require that schools change them. Of course, many other schools have retained them, often becoming the site of intense protest and controversy, such as the highly visible struggle continuing to unfold at the University of Illinois at Urbana-Champaign (see King 1998; King and Springwood forthcoming; Prochaska, this volume; Spindel 1997; Springwood and King forthcoming). Not surprisingly, media attention has increased markedly. On the one hand, the media have detailed numerous local and national struggles, while on the other hand, they have taken a leading role in modifying public perceptions of mascots, such as when the *Portland Oregonian* changed its editorial policy and refused to print derogatory team names. In both capacities, they have opened a crucial space of public debate about mascots (see Rosenstein, this volume).

For all of this, Native American mascots remain understudied, too often taken for granted, and rarely questioned by scholars and citizens alike. *Team Spirits* challenges these tendencies, reinterpreting the forgotten histories of many of these "invented" Indians, unraveling their significance for players, coaches, spectators, students, and Native Americans more generally, and, finally, revealing their complicated relevance for an array of postcolonial American social relations and identities.

Compiling a collection of essays that problematizes Native American mascots in particular distinct cases serves a larger strategy. Although each invented and contested mascot discussed here offers an intriguing, unique window into nuanced ways of playing Indian, when taken *together*—along with myriad other examples not analyzed here—we begin to see that no *single* Native American mascot can fully be understood in any context that fails to engage the historical relationships uniting all Native American mascots. These Indian icons are signs, and as signs, the cultural *work* they do is accomplished only within the larger representational system to which they belong. This point is significant to any social critique of Native American mascots—or other postcolonial representations of Indians—since it anticipates the common argument in defense of these "team spirits," which is commonly, "Although many other mascots are indeed racist and insensitive, ours remains dignified and more or less accurate." Such comments solicit support for particular local mascots, suggesting they exist in a semiotic vacuum, poised to be "read" as if they bore no trace of the "conditions of possibility" that motivated the widespread invention of Indian mascots. Of course, the significance of any Native American representation—let alone an athletic mascot—cannot fully be appreciated if it is seen as historically unrelated, in *systematic* tandem with all other similar representations, to the construction and maintenance of non-Indian, imperial identities.

These essays attempt to critique various aspects of Native American mascots, and each critique is inspired by a common notion of power that considers such embodied images to be empowered (albeit contested) *representations*. Public culture is made and remade, sometimes unwittingly, but always contextualized by particular relations of power. The interwoven activities of (re)making, telling, selling, seeing, buying, or wearing images such as mascots are one type of *signifying practice* (Comoroff and Comoroff 1991; Hall 1997; Jordan and Weedon 1995). Signifying practices are those activities, discourses, modes of experience, and social relations that serve both individuals and groups in the dynamic construction of cultural subjectivities and identities. For the arguments in this collection, an understanding of signifying practices as *modes of power* to control space, style, and value and, broadly, to *name* emerges as paramount. As Jordan and Weedon (1995 : 11–15) have argued, colonial relationships are usually enacted by a series of signifying "regimes of naming," such as the power to label or define a group of people in official discourse, as in the figure of the wild Indian, the female hysteric, the African American "mammy"; the power to mimic, as in playing Indian and blackface performances; and the power to tell a story from one's own perspective, such as Thanksgiving.

Native American mascots perpetuate inappropriate, inaccurate, and harmful understandings of living people, their cultures, and their histories (Banks 1993; Churchill 1994; Davis 1993; Frazier 1997; Gone 1999; Jackson and Lyons 1997; King 1998; King and Springwood forthcoming; Pewewardy 1994; Slowikowski 1993; Springwood and King forthcoming; Vanderford 1996; Wenner 1993). Through fragments thought to be Indian—a headdress, tomahawk, war paint, or buckskin—Native American mascots reduce them to a series of well-worn clichés, sideshow props, and racist stereotypes, masking, if not erasing, the complexities of Native American experiences and identities. Halftime performance, fan antics, and mass merchandizing transform somber and reverent artifacts and activities into trivial, shallow, and lifeless forms. Indeed, Native American mascots misappropriate sacred ideas and objects, such as the headdress war bonnet, relocating them in sacrilegious contexts. They misuse and misunderstand the elements of Native American cultures and their symbolic meanings. Importantly, since many Euro-Americans encounter Native Americans *only* as mascots and moving images, these unreal Indians materialize the most base images of Native Americans, presenting them as warriors battling settlers and soldiers, noble savages in touch with nature, uncivilized barbarians opposing the civilized and ultimately triumphant advance of Euro-America.

7

The many invented Indians used in sporting contexts reveal a nuanced system of signs comprising a broad performative space. This space, largely designed by and for a white America, has broad historical dimensions that turn on imaginary images of Native Americans (see Berkhofer 1979; Bird 1996; Dilworth 1996; Drinnon 1980; Mihesuah 1996; Pearce 1988; Steedman 1982). These embodied "Indian" caricatures have been *tropically* produced as, variously, the warring body (Berkhofer 1979; King 1998; Springwood and King forthcoming), the drunken Native (Duran 1996), the dancing Native (Drinnon 1980; Bloom 1996; King and Springwood forthcoming), the sexual Native (van Lent 1996), the magical Native (Colin 1987; Duran 1996), and the maiden Native (Albers and James 1987; Green 1975; Sparks 1995). These Indian mascots conceptually *freeze* Native Americans, reducing them to rigid, flat renderings of their diverse cultures and histories. Moreover, these invented mascots indicate moments of writing and rewriting a Euro-American identity in terms of conquest, hierarchy, and domination. From center courts to athletic turfs, Indian mascots typically stage the historical relations between Native Americans and Euro-Americans as unmarked by violence. Indian mascots are often situated as warlike and bellicose, while others—commonly barefooted and bare-chested—imply a constellation of savagery and sexualized wildness. We suggest that these kinds of images dehumanize and demonize Native Americans, constraining the ability of the non-Indian community to relate to Indians as contemporary, significant, and real human actors. The narratives inscribed by these mascot exhibitions are punctuated by an ambivalence that includes contact, friendship, and subsequent submission. It is a sensual narrative that turns on wildness, sexuality, and savagery, and it is a nostalgic narrative mourning the loss of these once-great warriors and their glorious society. To be sure, the performance seeks on some level to "honor" the Indian, but it does so through unconscious forms, by allowing white America to simultaneously enact its grief for and consecrate the memory of the Indian. It is a celebration of the Indian sacrifice in the name of imperial progress according to the divine plan of Manifest Destiny. It is a celebration of imperial power, then, that ritually incorporates the tragic figure of the Indian into the "imagined community," in Benedict Anderson's (1983) words, of the United States of America. It allows white America to primitively reimagine itself as a partial embodiment of Indianness and, in the process, attempts to psychically and sympathetically join with the Indian in the formation of a "shared" American consciousness. But, as the contributors to the volume demonstrate, it is not a liberating ritual, for it remains comfortably informed by oblique relations of power.

Significantly, then, Native American mascots do not merely craft disparaging images of others but facilitate the dynamic stagings of self. They permit Euro-Americans to construct an individual identity—as fans, athletes, students, citizens, and the like—while solidifying a transcendent sense of community, a unifying communitas. In essence, Native American mascots are masks, which when worn enable Euro-Americans to do and say things they cannot in everyday life, *as though by playing Indian they enter a transformative space of inversion wherein new possibilities of experience reside* (Deloria 1998; Green 1988; Huhndorf 1997; Mechling 1980). For example, on numerous occasions all-male, fraternal clubs have chosen to name and ritually adorn themselves after particular Native American tribes in ways that perhaps allow them to bond at spiritual and emotional levels that—to their non-Indian selves—may seem otherwise unattainable.

Thus, Native American mascots are one instance within a much broader complex of practices of playing Indian. We would argue that in the present moment, such mascots represent the most conspicuous, hotly contested, and broadly consumed form of playing Indian. To fully appreciate the significance of such mascots, the ide-

9

ological and political economy grounding them must be examined. Playing Indian has always opened a space in which to articulate American identities, as illustrated here by a handful of examples. At the (much celebrated and so-called) Boston Tea Party of December 16, 1773, for instance, a group of locals who fashioned themselves as "Indians" by smearing their faces and shouting "war calls" relieved the British ship *Dartmouth* of its East India Company's tea (see Deloria 1998). Later, as the new republic and its citizens searched for symbols and stories through which to create themselves, they invariably poached Native American communities or at least idealized notions of their Indianness. Perhaps most important, as early as the late eighteenth century, was a proliferation across the young nation of fraternal orders—often secret "clubs" joining learned, masculine patriots—(in)vested in invented Indianness (Deloria 1998:46). The importance of these homosocial organizations intensified precisely as industrial modernity reshaped the racial and gender contour of everyday life. If sport promotes contexts in which to negotiate these crises, sporting clubs often enhanced the productivity of play by playing Indian (Davis 1993). Moreover, throughout the nineteenth century, Euro-Americans played at being Indian on stage and in literature, while encouraging Native Americans to enact notions of Indianness at fairs, in museums, and for other public performances. These stagings peaked in their popularity and sophistication in the late nineteenth and early twentieth centuries at world's fairs (Rydell 1984) and in Wild West shows (Moses 1996). Importantly, the increased use of Native American culture to (re)create self and society for fun and profit corresponded with the final stages of the Euro-American subjugation of Native America in which reformers and politicians endeavored through increasingly ambitious programs and policies to assimilate Native Americans and in the process sought to restrict their traditional practices and precepts, particularly dance, ritual, and spirituality. It was in this context of well-worn and accepted patterns of playing Indian, imperial nostalgia, and the imperial momentum to control Indian expression that Euro-Americans began to fashion Native American mascots.

Scholars and Native American activists have invested great energy in constructing a critique of Indian mascots by foregrounding their colonial legacies and deconstructing the stereotypes they embody. Efforts to challenge mascots emerged from a broader movement to reclaim sovereignty, redress historical inequities, and assert a socio-political identity in American public culture (Cornell 1988; Johnson, Nagel, and Champagne 1997; Nagel 1996; Smith and Warrior 1996). Fueled by the civil rights movement, anti-colonial struggles, including opposition to the Vietnam War, and rising demands for self-determination in Native American communities, activists and allies demanded a voice in the representation of Native American cultures throughout popular culture. Importantly, struggles over images, although lacking the violence and spectacle of many earlier interventions, have been among the most visible and arguably the most successful examples of American Indian activism and socio-cultural resurgence. Importantly, efforts to challenge and retire Native American mascots have largely been left out of this history. This is a serious omission remedied by *Team Spirits*. Taken together, the local histories and ethnographies presented by the contributors assemble a history of Indian activism. This history documents the diverse contexts and shared strategies used to challenge and retire mascots, grants access to personal reflections on past and present struggles to eradicate these racist icons, and at points agonizes over the involvement of Native Americans in the creation or continuation of these mascots. Consequently, *Team Spirits* renders a complex, compassionate, and conflicted portrait of Native American actors and activism.

Students and their allies called for the retirement of Native American mascots, rightly highlighting the hurtful images, hateful practices, and hostile learning environments associated with them. Initially, as detailed above, their struggles resulted in a measure of success, forcing the retirement of mascots at Stanford University and Dartmouth College and the alteration of practices at Oklahoma University and Marquette University. Over the next thirty years, activists and organizations have continued to struggle against mascots, using litigation, petitions, and protests. Indeed, during this period, combining sociopolitical intervention with sociohistorical education, they have raised formerly unspeakable and unremarkable issues to the forefront of current debates about public culture. Moreover, as discussed in greater detail above, they have encouraged many colleges, universities, and communities to rethink their uses and understandings of Indianness. The results of these reconsiderations have been quite impressive, as prominent schools have retired or modified "their" Indians.

For all of their success, activism against mascots has met vigorous reactionary responses. Indeed, many Euro-Americans, even well-intentioned ones, and some Native Americans do not understand such criticisms or grasp the significance of implementing such changes. The 1995 World Series clarifies some of the difficulties associated with this counter-hegemonic, anti-imperial sociopolitical movement. When members of the American Indian Movement as well as representatives from other Native American organizations demonstrated with placards and bull horns outside Atlanta's Fulton County Stadium during baseball's 1995 World Series—pitting the Atlanta Braves against the Minnesota Twins—they voiced objections to the Braves' spectators, many of whom carried large, colorful Styrofoam tomahawks to wave during the now famous "chop." These demonstrations apparently caught the attention of Jane Fonda, the one-time activist and movie star, who met with the leaders of some of these groups. After listening to Clyde and Vernon Bellecourt of AIM, she promised that she would no longer do the "tomahawk chop." Braves' fans tend to collectively stand and perform this syncopated chop to stadium organ music—a rhythmic "Indian" beat. The promise of Jane Fonda, married to the team owner, millionaire Ted Turner, was significant. And yet, a few games further into the series, with the Braves "rallying," Fonda stood, along with her husband and some 60,000 other spectators, to do the tomahawk chop. Clearly, Native American activism, for all of its success, continues to struggle against racist ideologies. Taken together, the essays in this volume offer a nuanced interpretation of the intricacies of contesting, changing, and retaining Native American mascots.

In fact, *Team Spirits* documents the spectacular passion with which such mascots are often defended by Euro-Americans and with more troubling ramifications by Native Americans. The collected essays move beyond standard scholarly examination of Indian mascots by confronting the novel, sometimes surprising, relationships that emerged in their defense. As such it poses challenging questions. How is it that groups of Native Americans come to embrace various mascots when others view them as racist? How and in what ways do mascots impact Native American identity? How can one who views Indian mascots as dehumanizing reconcile—in either theoretical or personal terms—such a view with the efforts of some Native people to resurrect or even produce such icons of alterity? Further, the volume explores those moments when non-Indian constituencies of mascot support have strategically pitted some Native Americans against others or have cultivated certain sites of Indian support as "authentic" and thus the final Native voice.

Against the backdrop of whiteness, playing Indian, and recent struggles over public culture, we, as editors of *Team Spirits*, pause to situate ourselves as Euro-American scholars from the midwestern United States, reflecting upon how these positions have shaped our involvement with this project. Indeed, we have both written various chapters of our life history in colonial contexts, inscribing experiences in and through images of Native American cultures and histories. We spent many afternoons, after school, playing "Cowboys and Indians" with other children. We tended to restage generic conflicts confirming our sentiments about "the winning of the West." At times, we acted out spontaneous dramas, assuming the identities of historical and imaginary combatants. Just as commonly, we remade the past with the assistance of action figures by Marx Toys, depicting Custer, Geronimo, or even fictitious persons. Our fathers joined us in Y-Indian Guides, ceremonial gatherings of young boys and their fathers, designed to build our character while playing Indian during campouts. Later yet, we joined the Boy Scouts, and one of us (King) endured a rite of passage to enter The Order of the Arrow. Springwood still remembers the mixture of titillation and fear when, upon visiting Mark Twain's cave in Hannibal, Missouri, as a boy, he heard stories about how Injun Joe "terrorized" Tom Sawyer. These experiences guided us through fields of subjectivity wherein we, too, fashioned ourselves out of imaginary Indians.

As Euro-Americans, then, we edited this collection with a keen awareness that, among the variety of issues *Team Spirits* might engage, it would necessarily examine the concept of American whiteness, as a particular racial identity fashioned throughout U.S. history. The social production of whiteness, which generally has always been linked to images of racial *difference*, has until recently been an unspoken and unnamed practice. Thus, *Team Spirits* reframes understandings of American public culture. Placing stagings and struggles over race, particularly whiteness and Indianness, at the center of America, the assembled essays push discussions of the changing contours of "America" in novel directions. Although scholars have enthusiastically mapped the crystallization of postmodernity (Harvey 1990; Jameson 1991) and even post-America (Brown 1991; Pease 1994), they have largely neglected American empire (but see Kaplan and Pease 1993; King 2000), as well as Native America and its centrality to notions of American and modernity. In contrast, *Team Spirits* directs attention not at the logics of late capitalism nor the dissolution of metanarratives fashioning the frontier or the cold war, but at the creation and re-creation of self and society through (post)imperial idioms. In distinct voices and from divergent vantage points, the contributions construct a complex portrait of the ways in which communities and institutions re-imagine, reconstruct, and recuperate imperial identities, imagined communities, invented histories, and possible worlds.

Team Spirits explores the history and significance of Native American mascots within fifteen distinct sociocultural contexts, offering a comprehensive account of the means and meanings of playing Indian both in the past and in the present. To foreground the central themes and key problems energizing the text, the essays have been organized into five sections addressing, in turn, images of Indianness central to mascots, the creation of whiteness by playing Indian at halftime, efforts to change and retire Native American mascots, forms of interventions available to culture workers, and the complexities and complicities associated with creating and challenging them. The first two parts of the collection play off of one another, establishing a context in which to actively work through resistance to mascots first and then to unfold the complexities of Indianness, identity, and activism.

The collection opens with a series of essays concerned with the uses and understandings of Native American cultures and histories central to the construction of mascots. Throughout, these essays explore the invention and appropriation of Indianness. Native American mascots, the contributors in this section argue, are creatures made up from the imaginations of dominant society and as such are inventions. Such creations often incorporate, borrow, and otherwise misappropriate cultural artifacts that condense the complex social and historical differences among Native Americans into a sense of Indianness—the feather headdress, dancing, war paint, plains attire—to fashion fictions that purport to be authentic. Thus, all of the contributions in this section work through what might be termed stereotypes, images of Indians and the ideologies that make such images possible. Their detailed, critical histories engage not only racist representations of Native Americans but also the manner in which individuals and institutions decontextualize Native American cultures to legitimate these imagined Indians. Each of the essays traces the signifying practices and networks of power in localized contexts, speaking to larger issues of representation, race, and power.

Against this background, the essays in the second section contend that while playing Indian surely animates dangerous and demeaning stereotypes about Native American mascots, it also enacts particular Euro-American identities. Native American mascots stage privileged versions of whiteness. They illuminate the manner in which Euro-Americans understand themselves, importantly creating themselves through renditions of otherness and cultural difference. Native American mascots thus open privileged spaces in which individuals and institutions re-create the white subject. Moreover, for Euro-American fans, alumni, and students, performances mimicking (and mocking) Native Americans bind individuals together, creating shared sentiments and solidarity, while marking the (racialized) limits of the moral community and the terms on which others may enter into it. The contributors in this section deconstruct the reformulation of self and society through imagined Indians, detailing the centrality of the erasure and absorption of

Indianness, the absence of embodied Indians, and the presence of imagined Indians, for the fabrication of individual subjectivities, no less than local, national, and racial identities.

Following the establishment of the ideologies animating mascots and their effects on identities and communities, the essays in the third section examine efforts to contest, challenge, and change Native American mascots. Drawing on individual involvement in local and national movements, each of the authors seeks to illuminate four broad concerns: they briefly unravel the ideologies animating Native American mascots both locally and more generally; they outline the injuries caused by such icons; they trace the strategies used to oppose and usurp the continued use of Native American activism in specific local contexts; and they evaluate the effectiveness of their interventions and their implications. Taken together, their reflections begin to offer a history of Native American activism against mascots and related practices and identities.

Resistance to mascots is not, of course, limited to legal remedies or policy changes. In fact, as the pair of essays in the fourth section demonstrate, individuals and institutions in the culture industries have great potential to effect positive social change. More particularly, the authors outline the ways in which education and the media can make a difference. Culture workers, the authors stress, can alter popular understandings of Native American mascots. In teaching, reporting, writing, and other creative work, they can — nay, they must — fashion counter-pedagogies. The authors advocate using conventional technologies against themselves, to undo prevailing uses and understandings of Indianness. They encourage culture workers, on the one hand, to unravel the stereotypes enabling Native American mascots and, on the other hand, to re-educate the public.

The essays in the final section problematize and extend the preceding arguments. A concern for the complex and often contra-

17

dictory roles played by Native Americans on the topic of mascots unites these papers. The authors examine the performance and construction of Indianness that clash with popular and political assumptions that gloss all Native Americans as opponents of mascots. The essays take up difficult questions about alliances forged between Native American individuals and Euro-American institutions, about the sorts of identities available to Native Americans in contexts in which mascots exist or anti-mascot movements flourish, and about some of the ultimate effects of efforts to retire mascots. The authors explore local contexts in which Native Americans have created or supported mascots, have been ensnared in novel stereotypes as politicos, or have been used as authentic voices to legitimate the continuation of a mascot. Taken together, these sympathetic accounts elaborate the complicities and complexities associated with the hegemonic practices that structure contexts in which predominantly white communities reinvent themselves through imagined Indians.

REFERENCES

Albers, Patricia C., and William R. James. 1987. "Illusion and Illumination: Visual Images of American Indian Women in the West." In *The Women's West*, ed. Susan Armitage and Elizabeth Jameson, pp. 35–50. Norman: University of Oklahoma Press.

Anderson, Benedict. 1983. *Imagined Communities*. New York: Verso.

Banks, Dennis J. 1993. "Tribal Names and Mascots in Sports." *Journal of Sport and Social Issues* 17 : 5–8.

Berkhoffer, Robert F., Jr. 1979. *The White Man's Indian*. New York: Vintage Press.

Bird, S. Elizabeth, ed. 1996. *Dressing in Feathers: The Construction of the Indian in American Popular Culture*. Boulder CO: Westview Press.

Bloom, John. 1996. "There Is Madness in the Air: The 1926 Haskell Homecoming and Popular Representations of Sports in Federal Indian Boarding Schools." In *Dressing in Feathers: The Construction of the*

Indian in American Popular Culture, ed. S. Elizabeth Bird. Boulder CO: Westview Press.

Brown, Bill. 1991. "The Meaning of Baseball in 1992 (with Notes on the Post-American)." *Public Culture* 4(1): 43–69.

Churchill, Ward. 1994. "Let's Spread the Fun Around." In *Indians Are Us? Culture and Genocide in Native North America*, pp. 65–72. Monroe ME: Common Courage Press.

Colin, Susi. 1987. "The Wild Man and the Indian in Early 16th Century Book Illustration." In *Indians and Europe*, ed. C. F. Freest. Herodot, Netherlands: Rader Verlag.

Comoroff, John, and Jean Comoroff. 1991. *From Revolution to Revelation*. Chicago: University of Chicago Press.

Cornell, Stephen. 1988. *The Return of the Native: American Indian Political Resurgence*. Oxford: Oxford University Press.

Davis, Laurel. 1993. "Protest against the Use of Native American Mascots: A Challenge to Traditional, American Identity." *Journal of Sport and Social Issues* 17(1): 9–22.

Deloria, Philip. 1998. *Playing Indian*. New Haven: Yale University Press.

Dilworth, Leah. 1996. *Imagining Indians in the Southwest: Persistent Visions of a Primitive Past*. Washington DC: Smithsonian Institution Press.

Drinnon, Richard. 1980. *Facing West: The Metaphysics of Indian-Hating and Empire-Building*. Minneapolis: University of Minnesota Press.

Duran, Bonnie. 1996. "Indigenous versus Colonial Discourse: Alcohol and American Indian Identity." In *Dressing in Feathers: The Construction of the Indian in American Popular Culture*, ed. S. Elizabeth Bird, pp. 111–28. Boulder CO: Westview Press.

Frazier, Jane. 1997. "'Tomahawkin' the Redskins: 'Indian' Images in Sports and Commerce." In *American Indian Studies: An Interdisciplinary Approach to Contemporary Issues*, ed. Dane Morrison, pp. 337–46. New York: Peter Lang.

Gone, Joseph P. 1999. "Not Enough Indians, Too Many Chiefs: Authority and Performance in the Movement to End Chief Illiniwek." Unpublished manuscript.

Green, Rayna. 1975. "The Pocahontas Perplex: The Image of Indian Women in American Culture." *Massachusetts Review* 16:698–714.

——. 1988. "The Tribe Called Wannabee: Playing Indian in America and Europe." *Folklore* 99:30–55.

Hall, Stuart, ed. 1997. *Representation: Cultural Representations and Signifying Practices*. Thousand Oaks CA: Sage.

Harvey, David. 1990. *The Condition of Postmodernity*. Cambridge MA: Blackwell.

Huhndorf, Shari. 1997. "Playing Indian, Past and Present." In *As We Are Now: Mixblood Essays on Race and Identity*, ed. William S. Penn, pp. 181–98. Berkeley: University of California Press.

Jackson, E. N., and Robert Lyons. 1997. "Perpetuating the Wrong Image of Native Americans." *Journal of Physical Education, Recreation, and Dance* 68(4): 4–5.

Jameson, Fredric. 1991. *Postmodernism, or, the Cultural Logic of Late Capitalism*. Durham NC: Duke University Press.

Johnson, Troy, Joane Nagel, and Duane Champagne, eds. 1997. *American Indian Activism: Alcatraz to the Longest Walk*. Urbana: University of Illinois Press.

Jordan, Glenn, and Chris Weedon. 1995. *Cultural Politics: Class, Gender, Race and the Postmodern World*. Oxford: Blackwell.

Kaplan, Amy, and Donald E. Pease, eds. 1993. *Cultures of United States Imperialism*. Durham NC: Duke University Press.

Kelber, B. C. 1994. "'Scalping the Redskins': Can Trademark Law Start Athletic Teams Bearing Native American Nicknames and Images on the Road to Reform?" *Hamline Law Review* 17:533–588.

King, C. Richard. 1998. "Spectacles, Sports, and Stereotypes: Dis/Playing Chief Illiniwek." In *Colonial Discourse, Collective Memories, and the Exhibition of Native American Cultures and Histories in the Contemporary United States*, ed. C. Richard King, pp. 41–58. New York: Garland.

King, C. Richard, ed. 2000. *Postcolonial America*. Urbana: University of Illinois Press.

King, C. Richard, and Charles Fruehling Springwood. Forthcoming. "Choreographing Colonialism: Athletic Mascots, (Dis)Embodied Indians, and EuroAmerican Subjectivities." In *Cultural Studies: A Research Volume*, vol. 5, ed. Norman Denzin. Stamford CT: JAI Press.

Likourezos, G. 1996. "A Case of First Impression: American Indians Seek Cancellation of the Trademarked Term 'Redskins.'" *Journal of the Patent and Trademark Office Society* 78 : 275–90.

Mechling, Jay. 1980. "'Playing Indian' and the Search for Authenticity in Modern White America." *Prospects* 5 : 17–33.

Mihesuah, Devon A. 1996. *American Indians: Stereotypes and Realities*. Atlanta: Clarity Press.

Moses, L. G. 1996. *Wild West Shows and the Images of American Indians, 1883–1933*. Albuquerque: University of New Mexico Press.

Nagel, Joane. 1996. *American Indian Ethnic Renewal: Red Power and the Resurgence of Identity and Culture*. Oxford: Oxford University Press.

Pace, K. A. 1994. "The Washington Redskins and the Doctrine of Disparagement." *Pepperdine Law Review* 22 : 7–57.

Pearce, Roy Harvey. 1988. *Savagism and Civilization: A Study of the Indian and the American Mind*. Rev. ed. Berkeley: University of California Press.

Pease, Donald E., ed. 1994. *National Identities and Post-Americanist Narratives*. Durham NC: Duke University Press.

Pewewardy, Cornel D. 1991. "Native American Mascots and Imagery: The Struggle of Unlearning Indian Stereotypes." *Journal of Navaho Education* 9(1): 19–23.

Rodriguez, Roberto. 1998. "Plotting the Assassination of Little Red Sambo." *Black Issues in Higher Education* 15(8): 20–24.

Rydell, Robert W. 1984. *All the World's a Fair: Visions of Empire at American International Expositions, 1876–1916*. Chicago: University of Chicago Press.

Sigelman, Lee. 1998. "Hail to the Redskins? Public Reactions to a Racially Insensitive Team Name." *Sociology of Sport Journal* 15 : 317–25.

Slowikowski, Synthia Sydnor. 1993. "Cultural Performances and Sports Mascots." *Journal of Sport and Social Issues* 17(1): 23–33.

Smith, Paul Chaat, and Robert Allen Warrior. 1996. *Like a Hurricane: The Indian Movement from Alcatraz to Wounded Knee.* New York: New Press.

Sparks, Carol Douglas. 1995. "The Land Incarnate: Navajo Women and the Dialogue of Colonialism, 1821–1870." In *Negotiators of Change: Historical Perspectives on Native American Women,* ed. Nancy Shoemaker, pp. 135–56. New York: Routledge.

Spindel, Carol. 1997. "We Honor Your Memory: Chief Illiniwek of the Halftime Illini." *Crab Orchard Review* 3(1): 217–38.

Springwood, Charles Fruehling, and C. Richard King. Forthcoming. "Race, Ritual, and Remembrance Embodied: Manifest Destiny and the Symbolic Sacrifice of 'Chief Illiniwek.'" In *Exercising Power: The Making and Remaking of the Body,* ed. Cheryl Cole, John Loy, and Michael Messner. Albany: SUNY Press.

Staurowsky, Ellen J. 1998. "An Act of Honor or Exploitation? The Cleveland Indians' Use of the Louis Francis Sockalexis Story." *Sociology of Sport Journal* 15(4): 299–316.

Steedman, Raymond William. 1982. *Shadows of the Indian: Stereotypes in American Culture.* Norman: University of Oklahoma Press.

Vanderford, Heather. 1996. "What's in a Name? Heritage or Hatred: The School Mascot Controversy." *Journal of Law and Education* 25 : 381–88.

van Lent, Peter. 1996. "'Her Beautiful Savage': The Current Sexual Image of the Native American Male." In *Dressing in Feathers: The Construction of the Indian in American Popular Culture,* ed. S. Elizabeth Bird, pp. 211–27. Boulder CO: Westview Press.

Wenner, L. 1993. "The Real Red Face of Sports." *Journal of Sport and Social Issues* 17 : 1–4.

PART ONE

Inventions

CHAPTER I

Chief Bill Orange and the Saltine Warrior

A Cultural History of Indian Symbols and Imagery at Syracuse University

•

Donald M. Fisher

Although much of the sport world in the twentieth century has witnessed the widespread practice of appropriating Native American symbols for the masculine, warrior images of sports teams from the professional level to youth leagues, it was Syracuse University that was one of the first institutions to employ such Indian symbols and images. Throughout the late nineteenth and twentieth centuries, Syracuse's Indian mascot was rooted in notions of "noble savagery," the "vanishing Indian," and eventually the Indian as wild creature. This history of an Indian sport mascot demonstrates what Eric Hobsbawm described as the "invention of tradition" during the modern era. Indeed, urban-industrial societies often construct "traditions" to promote cohesion among new social groups, establish status and authority, and instill an ideology justifying a new social order. More often than not, these social and cultural phenomena are recent developments. However, as this overview shows, traditions could very easily be attacked and destroyed as well (Hobsbawm and Ranger 1983).

This essay explores a series of questions centering on the construction, perpetuation, and eventual destruction of two distinct, yet sometimes overlapping, characters: Chief Bill Orange and the Saltine Warrior. Why, for instance, did Syracuse students choose to identify their institution with a militarily defeated Indian population? Why did they appropriate a fictional version of a historic past and invent notions of Indianness to create a social order on campus? What ideological and social purposes did the manufactured images and symbols serve over time? How and why did the Syracuse University community transform these mythological notions into a sports mascot? And finally, why did Chief Bill Orange and the Saltine Warrior eventually disappear from the Syracuse campus?

Located in the heart of central New York, Syracuse University occupies the high ground in the center of the city of Syracuse, and from its founding in 1870, people commonly referred to it as "the hill." Beginning in the late nineteenth century, the new university established mythical ties with the Onondaga people of the Iroquois Confederacy. Sometime around 1525, five Iroquois nations established a political alliance to promote peace among themselves and to project their collective military and economic might against their neighbors. With the arrival of French, Dutch, and English colonists, the confederacy remained an important part of the geopolitical landscape of northeastern North America throughout much of the seventeenth and eighteenth centuries. However, after the American Revolution, the new United States punished most Iroquois peoples for having supported Britain during the war by driving them either into Canada or onto small reservations in New York. The new order of the late eighteenth century forced them into a life of agricultural subsistence and cultural chaos. By the mid-nineteenth century, the indigent status of the Iroquois peoples was a far cry from only a century before.

The rising competitiveness in university recruiting and intercollegiate athletics during the late nineteenth century led the university to create an identity rooted in local Native antiquity. A survey of student yearbooks reveals attitudes toward the Onondaga Indians and the region's physical landscape. In fact, the class of 1884 named this student publication *The Onondagan* "in honor of the tribe and the beautiful valley in which we dwell" (*Onondagan* 1894:11). The frequent use of Indian images and metaphors, allusions to the local landscape's natural beauty, and even an illustration of Natives resting reverentially in front of a distant silhouette of the fine arts building demonstrate a student-generated image centered on Indianness (*Onondagan* 1893:3, 1894:8, 1910:n.p., 1911:n.p.). Undergraduates perceived they had symbolically inherited the lands and noble qualities of Natives. Drawing a Social Darwinian parallel between modern students and Indians from the past, one student explained why the class of 1885 developed "from the lower forms of life" to be among the intellectual and athletic champions in the "survival of the fittest": "Like the Iroquois dominating this country prior to the advent of the European, the long drawn cry and unsheathed tomahawk of the heroes of '85, struck terror wherever it went and effectually quelled the insidious attacks of our foes" (*Onondagan* 1886:32).

Tapping into the nineteenth-century "vanishing Indian" phenomenon, a poet from the class of 1903 observed the "spirits" of dead Indians wept at their own passing and their replacement by whites (*Onondagan* 1912:17). According to her view, the Great Spirit allowed for a racial transferral of wisdom from Indians to Syracuse students, with undergraduate "books of magic" replacing the Indian "warrior's bow" (17, 19). In the context of social evolutionism, the connection made between students and their dead Indian predecessors reinforced a prevailing view of historical progressivism centered on race and class. By establishing an ill-defined historical link between Natives and the university, students validated the belief in the supremacy of particular graduating classes. All undergraduates understood their position within the evolutionary hierarchy of campus social relations. Indeed, although freshmen were obligated to acknowledge their own inferior status, all students and graduates developed pride in the university as well as their elite social condition.

While these annual chronicles of nostalgia employed Indian figures to construct a university identity, a more specific Indian warrior figure materialized when two undergraduates penned a song for a minstrel show in March 1911. The lyrics of "The Saltine Warrior" asserted the glorious battles of the medieval era survived in the form of college football games. "In the days of new when the fights are few," the lyricist from the class of 1913 argued, students needed a heroic figure whose physical strength would crush opponents. Syracuse University's leader on the field should be an Indian figure, "a bold, bad man, Victorious over all." Besides the obvious reference to local Indians, the term "Saltine Warrior" referred to the importance of salt mining in local economic history. Popularized by students, the tune became a permanent addition to the university songbook in 1911 (Evans 1939:202; Thorron 1954).

While students forged a mythological Indian, the athletics program pursued its own identity. University athletes wore the colors pink and blue during the 1870s and 1880s until an English professor and a committee of six undergraduates replaced them with orange, which the Alumni Association ratified on June 24, 1890 (Evans 1939:168). The new color is significant given the early Dutch settlement of colonial New York. According to William Harman van Allen, a member of the class of 1890 who later became a distinguished Episcopal cleric, university trustee, and alumni chapter president, "Orange is peculiarly appropriate for a New York college and Syracuse may adopt as her own motto of the illustrious reigning house of Holland: 'Oranje Booen' [orange over all]" (169). Students incorporated the new color into a personification of the university: "Bill Orange." Akin to Uncle Sam and John Bull, the new campus icon was probably a parody of the monarch William of Orange. Ironically, Syracuse University managed to blend an identity associated with

28

religiously intolerant Protestant Orangemen with misappropriated Native cultural symbols.

Just as Indian imagery and orangeness developed into dominant symbol characteristics, the university's sports teams played against Native squads. In fact, the football team played several games against all-Indian teams, including two against the Onondaga reservation in 1902 and 1903, and nine against the Carlisle Indian Industrial School from 1906 to 1914, while the varsity lacrosse squad maintained a rivalry with the Onondaga Indians throughout the 1910s and 1920s. Reminiscing football players during the late 1930s remembered the Carlisle athletes for their physical toughness despite their smaller bodies, for the trickery employed by their white coach, the legendary Glen "Pop" Warner, and their perceived racial homogeneity. When Carlisle stealthily substituted a healthy Indian coach for an injured player at halftime during one contest, a member of Syracuse's class of 1910 recalled "no one knew the difference as all the Indians looked alike" (Evans 1939:210). Syracusans usually credited their victories to the triumph of white intellect and organization over Indian skill and brute strength (75). Contact between Syracuse undergraduates and Native peoples was generally modest, and the games with live Indians did little to deter members of the university community from mythmaking.

Throughout the 1920s, the link between Native imagery and the university's orange-clad athletes was minimal. However, Indian symbols collided directly with the athletics program beginning in 1931 with the publication of the discovery of archaeological remains during an excavation for a new women's gymnasium site from 1929 to 1931. According to *The Syracuse Orange Peel*, the university's humor magazine, a construction crew unearthed old arrowheads, flint instruments, textile fragments, and beads, which allegedly belonged to sixteenth-century Onondaga Indians. Upon assembling the textile fragments, "campus experts" announced an early Jesuit explorer painted a portrait of an Indian chief, which allegedly indicated a name, conveniently translated from Onondaga into English as "The Salt (or salty) Warrior." The real painter—fine arts professor Hibbardus Kline—coincidentally just happened to have a last name only one letter different from the mythical Jesuit ("True Story" 1931: 11; Reigelhaupt 1976a, 1976b).

The magazine took pride in this discovery as a legitimate, evolutionary link between the modern collegian present and the distant Native past: "Syracuse University now has 'O-gee-ke-da Ho-schen-e-ga-da,' the saltine warrior, Big Chief Bill Orange, with the orange feather in his scalp lock, bringing the fine traditions of his people out of antiquity down to present-day tribes of salty youngsters who people his ancient hunting ground" ("True Story" 1931: 11). Regardless of whether people took the story seriously, or whether they knew it was a joke and went along with it, such was the birth of the legend of Chief Bill Orange. The student body voted to employ this mythological chieftain as a university symbol, and the football team quickly adopted him as their own ("Chief" 1931).

The university community's adoption of Bill Orange was an important event in the mythologization of university images and symbols. By combining a color tied to a Dutch past with symbols associated with local Natives, Syracusans forged a hybrid identity. The concocted kinship between the university and the local Onondaga Indians fabricated a sense of the institution's longevity, an important factor when considering the much older history of Ivy League schools. Part of the prestige of a school such as Harvard was simply the age of the institution, and Syracuse possessed no such legacy. More important, the Indian mascot helped to reinforce notions of race and class superiority by imposing on the student body the doctrine of the inevitability of progress, of Indian savagery giving way to collegian civilization. The university community viewed itself not merely as inherently superior to Indians but also as their noble heirs. Moreover, the symbolic passing of the torch from noble savages to virtuous collegians would mirror the transfer of university traditions among the successive classes of students. This evolutionary hierarchy would culminate with a growing population of alumni, who sought confirmation not only of their right choice in attending Syracuse but also of their elite social class. Ultimately, all students and alumni could exhibit pride in the university and football team.

The university's director of public relations, Burges Johnson, faced criticism regarding the excavation story. Emphasizing the legitimacy of both the painting and the mascot, Johnson avoided confronting the authenticity of the alleged Saltine Warrior excavation: "He has more ancient tradition than the Yale bulldog or the Princeton tiger, or any of the miscellaneous live stock of the State universities" ("Meet" 1931:6–7). Johnson's reference to other institutions and his emphasis on the mascot rather than the excavation is significant. By claiming the Indian was older than other mascots, he sought to elevate the status of Syracuse University. Use of Chief Bill Orange as the Saltine Warrior remained intermittent from 1931 through the Second World War. When he did disappear briefly from campus, some students expressed their grief at the passing of a "tradition." For example, barely three years after the so-called discovery, one student complained about the temporary loss of their Indian: "Perhaps the most picturesque tradition that we have known has been allowed to drift into oblivion, seemingly 'unwept, unhonored, and unsung'" (W. E. A. 1934). Although the university community apparently did not invest a great amount of emotional energy in the Indian mascot during the era of the Great Depression and the war, such was hardly the case after 1945.

Sport enthusiasts fully revitalized the cult of the Saltine Warrior at Syracuse during the 1950s, just as millions of Americans reinvigorated themselves in the mythology of film and television westerns.

In contrast to previous years, when Indian images were largely the product of yearbook editors, student songwriters, and the public relations office, a broader group of undergraduates participated in the construction of the new Indian symbolism. Fraternities, the football team, and cheerleaders all joined to reconceptualize the Saltine Warrior. For instance, the university adopted two inanimate Indian figures in 1951. The first, presented by the class of 1951, was an eight-foot-high, three-thousand-pound bronze statue of an Indian archer. Sculpted by a student whose real-life model came from the local Onondaga reservation, the stationary character pointed his bow upward with his arrow already in flight. Although his resting place would change from time to time, the noble creature always resided near academic buildings (Schmidt 1967; Reilly 1998).

The Pi Lambda fraternity discovered the second inanimate warrior, a five-foot-tall wooden Indian with a raised tomahawk, in Binghamton, New York. A relic from nineteenth-century tobacco stores, the figure quickly came to occupy space next to the Alpha Tau Omega fraternity's cannon at pep rallies and football games. Students used this second warrior to tally football victories, with "scalps in the colors of Syracuse's vanquished opponents" hanging from the wooden Indian's belt ("New Saltine" 1951). This new practice signaled a departure from the primarily revered traits of the warrior. Before and during the era of colonization, scalping allowed Native men to demonstrate their masculinity by acquiring war trophies. English colonists and later generations of literary readers viewed scalping only as an example of wild Indian savagery. By misappropriating a fictional version of a historic practice, Syracuse students chose to emphasize what they believed to be the savage nature of the act. As they moved further away from the Indian symbols of previous decades, wild qualities now came to be associated with the mascot.

Taken together, the two inanimate figures—one majestic for an academic setting, the other wild for the athletic arena—reified an alleged campus "tradition" viewed to be very old. Just as Indian side-kick Tonto secured television audience empathy for the Lone Ranger by fighting injustice on the frontier, the different versions of the Syracuse Indian promoted the unification of the university community behind the football team. Moreover, the Indian mascot continued to validate the evolutionary hierarchy linking the various undergraduate classes and alumni together. Wildness might now be celebrated, but students still understood their world to be built upon the ideas of historical progress as well as race and class superiority.

A human mascot reemerged in 1955 at the suggestion of the football cheerleaders. The latest incarnation of Bill Orange—a man dressed in orange attire walking on ten-foot-high stilts—was scrapped after the character fell ("Saltine Mascot" 1955; "Saltine Warrior" 1962). The first student to play a new Indian version of Bill Orange in 1955 was James Mosher, a Springfield College transfer who had belonged to an Indian dance group that toured the Northeast. According to Mosher, "What most people don't understand is that the Indian dance isn't just a bunch of thoughtless movements, but a story told through the medium of dance" (Dahlman 1955). Despite Mosher's concerns for authenticity, succeeding actor mascots emphasized the perceived wildness associated with Native peoples. For example, even though the new mascot of 1957 claimed to be part Mahican Indian, he was praised for his other qualifications: "loudness, wildness and the choreography of his original act" (Kelly 1957). Mascot selection committees encouraged subsequent warriors to be innovative by choosing from a range of personalities, from "stern and brooding" to "a brave of fire-water frenzy" ("Saltine Warrior" 1962).

By the early 1960s, the mascot apparently developed a complex personality. He could be stoic, brave, and intimidating but also boisterous and enthusiastic. In 1962, university chancellor William Tolley envisioned the campus Indian as a symbolic representation of "the thinker," a warrior who could "attack the problems of the day" or even "chart the future." Tolley also argued the mascot "adds zest and savour to life by laughing, by not taking himself too seriously, by looking for and welcoming the unexpected, and by surprising people by not doing the expected" ("Syracuse" 1962). The chancellor's comments reflected important cultural anxieties of the 1950s and early 1960s. Many college-educated men wanted to find a way to reconcile their notions of middle-class respectability, conformity, and professionalism with the expressive, personality-oriented social skills they developed as fraternity brothers.

The Saltine Warrior's public behavior gradually became more farcical throughout the 1960s, just as many students' belief in order and respectability gave way to greater permissiveness and promiscuity. Students celebrated the wild qualities of the warrior as part of their fraternity subculture. Indeed, the frenzied football mascot mirrored drunken, beer-swilling fraternity partygoers. Melvin Eggers, who performed the duties of professor of economics, department chair, and vice chancellor before serving as university chancellor from 1971 to 1991, remembered the mascot as the personification of the alcohol-consuming fraternities: "In the spirit of libertarians doing their thing as they saw fit, the person of the Saltine Warrior took on more extreme forms of behavior that could be interpreted as making fun of the real thing, whether it be noises or antics of one sort or another. . . . He would take off into the stands and run around making the 'whooping' sounds attributed to Indians and their war dances. He would go through a mock form of native Indian dancing. It was clear that the person doing it didn't know or have any respect for the art form at all" (Eggers 1994). This growing emphasis on the wildness of the Saltine Warrior collided with the changing racial climate of American campus life. Armed with the belief in halting racial injustice, some students and faculty no longer simply questioned the mascot's behavior but rather his existence.

Heightened racial sensitivity during the early 1970s brought about a general denouncement of Native American imagery in sports. For example, the American Indian Center of Cleveland launched a $9 million lawsuit in 1972 against Major League Baseball's Cleveland Indians for its satiric logo ("Warrior's" 1972; Carley 1972). This nationally prominent action prodded Syracuse University's vice president for student affairs, Charles Willie, to urge campus organizations and departments in February 1972 to reevaluate the use of Indian imagery (Antonoff 1972; "Warrior's" 1972). Criticism focused primarily on the exaggerated, wild behavior of the mascot. Ironically, one student who urged caution in retreating from the mascot was an Onondaga Indian on the varsity lacrosse team. Although Ron Hill insisted his fellow tribesmen would "not unite and sweep down on the SU campus, raiding and burning down buildings," he viewed the foolish "goofs" of the mascots as "dehumanizing" (Hill 1972). Meanwhile, as the warrior continued his antics along the sidelines over the next several seasons, the issue simmered.

In March 1976, the university student newspaper exacerbated tensions over the mascot by dropping a not-so-surprising bombshell on readers, revealing the alleged discovery of archaeological remains in 1931 had, indeed, been a ruse. Seaman Jacobs, editor of the *Orange Peel* in 1931, finally confessed Chief Bill Orange was a fabrication. Jacobs apparently took pride in generating the legend: "We were the springboard and we were the first ones to have Indians dressed up at football games" (Reigelhaupt 1976a). His acknowledgment of the hoax implicitly exposed how the few—yearbook writers, songwriters, and then the director of public relations—had manufactured a legend. The revelation then undermined the efforts of the many—undergraduates and alumni—of the last few decades who continued to redefine and defend the Saltine Warrior.

Publication of the details of the hoax and a growing sensitivity to racial issues contributed to an all-out assault on the Saltine Warrior. The matter had intensified by the fall of 1977, when the battle lines over the fate of the mascot became clear. Those who supported the continuation of the Indian included the fraternity community in the vanguard, older alumni, and, according to a newspaper poll, about two-thirds of the undergraduate population (Stashenko 1978). All three groups benefited from the progressive doctrine of race and class centering on the mascot. From their point of view, to attack the Indian was to attack the bonds connecting the students and alumni and, ultimately, the university. By claiming symbols were important in the maintenance of tradition and continuity with the past, these supporters argued the Saltine Warrior served the needs of the community. To destroy the warrior would be to give the university an identity crisis. By ignoring the qualities of wildness that came to define the mascot of more recent years, warrior defenders believed the Indian served as an honorable source of pride, representing only positive traits of Native peoples (Sheflin 1977).

Those who supported the elimination of the Saltine Warrior included small, outspoken groups of Native American students, white students, and faculty. Warrior opponents argued from a position of cultural relativism, claiming race-based stereotypes not only ill-served the interests of racial minorities but made poor university symbols. They claimed the Indian mascot to be a disgraceful, dehumanizing diversion from the university's more authentic sources of pride: excellence in academics and athletics (Thurman 1977; Bernsau 1977; Abernethy 1977). For these opponents, the warrior was a racist reminder of archaic interpretations of the nation's past. Besides criticizing the mascot, an organization of Native American students at the university used the controversy to make the institution reevaluate its relationship with Native peoples by pushing for an extensive agenda including future recruitment of Indian students from reservations, implementation of Native studies courses, and social and cultural programs to increase Native student retention (O'Neill 1977a) Furthermore, warrior opponents maneuvered the university's fraternity community to defend its own social exclusivity.

Caught in the middle of the debate between the friends and foes of the Saltine Warrior was the university administration, especially Vice President of Student Affairs Melvin Mounts. The contending parties reached an impasse in December 1977, when it became apparent the Lambda Chi Alpha fraternity's goal of compromise could not be reconciled with the Native American student declaration they would settle for nothing less than the complete elimination of the mascot (O'Neill 1977b). By mid-January 1978, the arguments of warrior opponents convinced Vice President Mounts to announce the university would discontinue use of the Indian at the end of the spring semester. As compensation, the administration said it would help Lambda Chi Alpha create a replacement (McEnaney 1978).

The decision to abandon the Indian mascot drew immediate criticism from alumni and local sports fans who had never even attended the university. They scoffed at accusations of racism and scolded the institution for yielding to interest groups. Addressing his letter to Vice President Mounts, one angry fan concluded Syracuse was kowtowing to a loud minority interest: "Right on Mel— lead us down the road to elimination of all our old traditions. Let others force us to adapt new ones" (Masters 1978b; Wake 1978; Pike 1978; Collins 1978; Pasho 1978). Although the last student to play the warrior, Andy Burns, commiserated that "I treat the Saltine Warrior as an honor. It's not racism at all," he also indicated his disgust with accusations of racism by saying, "I'm beginning not to like Indians" (Finkel and Stanton 1978:31). These sentiments reveal white disinterest in the views of Indians, anxiety over the loss of white control of imagery, and fear of the undermining of the doctrine of racial hierarchy.

Warrior supporters contended the university eliminated the symbol because of pressure-group politics, but opponents maintained it was abolished because reason, truth, and fairness had prevailed over emotion, fiction, and prejudice (Collins 1978; Onakiwahe 1978). According to the Native student organization leading the attack, "We cannot abandon our responsibilities, one of which is to secure a future for the coming generations" (Onakiwahe 1978). The university's decision to terminate the Saltine Warrior had no immediate impact on the greater Syracuse area. The Syracuse Chiefs minor league baseball team, Onondaga Community College, and area high schools all retained their Indian nicknames and mascots for many years (Fish 1978). The university tried to alleviate fraternity and alumni anxieties at Syracuse when Director of Student Activities Ulysses J. Connor declared a new Roman gladiator mascot would retain the name "Saltine Warrior" (McAlary 1978). As compensation to the fraternities and alumni, the most significant characteristics of the old Indian mascot remained intact: its name, gender, and status as a combatant. Other choices cast aside, including animals, fruit, clown-like characters, and superheroes, reveal the emphasis the mascot selection committee placed on maintaining continuity between the old and new versions of the warrior (McAlary 1978; Salmon 1978).

The debut of the Roman gladiator met with a mixture of cheers and jeers in September 1978 (Salmon 1978). Older alumni resisted the new mascot simply because it was not their Indian. A Greek warrior eventually replaced the Roman in March 1980, but neither mascot attracted much support. Ironically, people ignored the inherent logic of the new characters: the Roman mascot coincided with the widespread use of Latin names for central New York's many cities and towns (e.g., Syracuse, Rome, Cicero, Fabius, Marcellus, Pompey), and the Greek was consistent with university intellectual activity and the nomenclature of the fraternity and sorority system

38

(Sternberg 1979; Gibney 1980a, 1980b; Peel 1981). Regardless of plausible ties, the new mascots lacked the historical and racial appeals of Chief Bill Orange.

With the Indian mascot banned, and the Roman and Greek versions of the Saltine Warrior cast aside, the varsity cheerleaders of the 1981–82 academic year created a new figure to represent the university at athletic events: a giant orange fruit. With full knowledge that central New York is hardly a citrus-producing region, some Syracusans were more than disappointed with the idea of the noncombatant as icon. Expressing the feelings of many angry alumni, one member of the class of 1964 complained, "Tradition be damned seems to be the prevailing attitude" (Brooks 1989). Regardless of the fact that Chief Bill Orange was only a satirical hoax dating back to the Great Depression, many alumni had internalized strong passions about their Indian mascot.

The first two orange mascots were called Clyde and Woody, only to be replaced in 1990 by Otto. Despite losing their Indian, Lambda Chi Alpha continued to control the selection process for those who wore the mascot costume. This fraternity suffered another setback in April 1990 when the Office of Student Affairs broke its mascot selection monopoly, allowing other students to join the fraternity's small team of mascot actors. Since Lambda Chi Alpha did not reflect the general campus population—it was all male, 30 percent of the members were Jewish, and only three nonwhites belonged—the student affairs office believed other students should have an opportunity to portray the mascot (Davis 1990). During the following spring, the all-male, rotating group of performers was joined by its first female. Despite all the obvious differences between the new orange and the old Indian, there was one similarity: both emphasized improvisational wildness.

The new fuzzy sun-kissed orange paraded along the sidelines of football and basketball games during the 1980s and 1990s, and most of the university community learned to accept Chief Bill Orange's replacement. With its mascot having moved from noble savage to cute fruit, the university community experienced tranquility until 1995, when sagging merchandise sales prompted a renewed mascot debate. While the controversy lacked the deeper cultural and social questions of the Indian debate, it nonetheless aroused passions for and against the orange. Those who defended Otto believed the university needed to keep whatever tradition, however recent, was in place at any cost. Otto's defenders recognized the silliness of a citrus fruit mascot more appropriate for Florida, and they also realized the tradition was barely a dozen years old, but they were unwilling to abandon him. Moreover, many Otto sympathizers admired the non-offensive nature of the mascot and his ability to generate interest among children. With university marketing concerns spearheading efforts to eliminate Otto, those who opposed Otto most vehemently believed the character lacked masculine toughness. In other words, the orange fruit was the antithesis of the noble Indian of yesteryear. Seeking to bring an end to an "endless dedication to political correctness" on campus, one member of the class of 1997 said, "If this university is to get serious about athletics and school pride, it needs to get a serious mascot" (Eckhardt 1995).

An eighteen-member committee of faculty, staff, and students, plus three national advertising firms, studied the image problem. Although they considered but discarded the idea of bringing back the Indian version of the Saltine Warrior, they focused on three masculine choices: a wolf, a lion, and a "charge" image using either a buffalo or lightning. Unfortunately for the committee, all three proposed characters generated little public enthusiasm (Kramer 1995). Undergraduates circumvented the efforts of the committee by staging pro-Otto rallies and showing overwhelming support for him in polls conducted by the student newspaper, the public affairs office, and a psychology class (Goble 1995; Wiley 1995). Eventually, in early December 1995, university chancellor Kenneth A. Shaw announced the university would not abide by the committee's recommendation to adopt the wolf, instead choosing the orange fruit.

During the years following the adoption of the orange fruit mascot and through the debate when Otto was almost replaced, alumni and local sports fans never ceased in their calls for the return of the Indian mascot. Instead of merely defending the Indian as a tradition, Saltine Warrior supporters made a new argument: a Native student should receive a scholarship for playing the mascot (Grant 1989; Hart 1991; Kramer 1995; Rapp 1995; Heer 1995). In declaring an Onondaga Indian should portray the mascot rather than a fraternity brother, one local sports fan made a declaration to *Syracuse Herald-Journal* readers: "We all need something we can rally around, and selecting a true Saltine Warrior this way would be a great step toward more unity for all of us" (Grodesky 1988).

These nostalgic calls for a return to the old mascot mirrored some of the deepest cultural and economic problems of the greater Syracuse area. With an economy suffering from chronic deindustrialization, the past seemed to be a golden age when compared to the present. For the Syracuse University community, the apprehensions included the relative newness of the university in the late nineteenth century and the social needs of fraternity brothers and alumni. In vociferously defending the right of a fake Indian to make his home on a gridiron sideline, Indian mascot supporters tried to vindicate a constructed and nebulous set of traditions at Syracuse University. Essentially, Syracuse used the Saltine Warrior to lend a sense of permanency and continuity with the past for a constantly changing student body. That Chief Bill Orange was mythical, even fictional, mattered little to the university community because he served a larger ideological purpose. Although the Indian signified some abstract link with the past, he functioned as a binding force among students, alumni, and faculty. By using a primitive noble savage as their symbol, Syracusans essentially celebrated the perceived superiority of their university and community.

ACKNOWLEDGMENTS
The author thanks the following individuals for reading various versions of this paper: Norman Baker, Robert Wright, Donald Fixico, Eric Gansworth, Ellen Parisi, Jean Turcott, and Ruth Kelly.

REFERENCES

Abernethy, David. 1977. "Saltine Warrior: Discard the Symbol of Racism." *Syracuse Daily Orange*, 17 Nov.

Antonoff, Michael. 1972. "Willie Asks Review of Indian as su Symbol." *Syracuse Daily Orange*, 16 Feb.

Bernsau, Tim. 1977. "Orange Offense." *Syracuse Daily Orange*, 4 Nov.

Brooks, Paul. 1989. "su's Identity Crisis." *Syracuse Post-Standard*, 10 March.

Carley, William M. 1972. "Is Chief Noc-A-Homa Racist? Many Indians Evidently Think He Is." *Wall Street Journal*, 27 Jan.

"Chief of Onondaga." 1931. *Syracuse Daily Orange*, 26 Oct.

Coffee, Thomas. 1978. "Save the Mascot." *Syracuse Daily Orange*, 3 March.

Collins, John R. 1978. "Job for Professor." *Syracuse Post-Standard*, 22 Feb.

Dahlman, Diana. 1955. "Mosher Chosen Warrior, Beginning New Tradition." *Syracuse Daily Orange*, 11 Nov.

Davis, Matt. 1990. "Frat Gets Squeezed Out of Orange." *Syracuse Herald-Journal*, 16 April.

Eckhardt, Kevin. 1995. "Changing the Mascot Will Improve Sales." *Syracuse Daily Orange*, 5 April.

Eggers, Melvin. 1994. Interview with author. Syracuse NY. 20 May.

Evans, Arthur L. 1939. *Fifty Years of Football at Syracuse University, 1889–1939*. Syracuse: Syracuse University Football History Committee.

Finkel, Rachel, and Mike Stanton. 1978. "The Last of the Saltine Warriors." *Vantage*, 22 Feb., 31–33.

Fish, Michael S. 1978. "su Alone in Banning Indian Mascot." *Syracuse Herald-American*, 19 Feb.

Gibney, Roberta. 1980a. "Inter Fraternity Council Supports Proposed Mascot." *Syracuse Daily Orange,* 25 March.

———. 1980b. "SU Greek Mascot Still Waits in the Wings." *Syracuse Daily Orange,* 28 Jan.

Goble, Sandra. 1995. "Hundreds Attend Rally in Support of Mascot." *Syracuse Daily Orange,* 12 Sept.

Grant, G. Edward. 1989. "Saltine Warrior." *Syracuse Herald-Journal,* 16 Nov.

Grodesky, George. 1988. "An Indian Should Represent SU." *Syracuse Herald-Journal,* 18 Nov.

Hart, Ron. 1991. "Former Orange Recounts Life under the Peel." *Syracuse Daily Orange,* 19 March.

Heer, Martha L. 1995. "Students Felt Pride Singing Fight Song." *Syracuse Post-Standard,* 18 Aug.

Hill, Ron. 1972. "Hill on Indian Symbol." *Syracuse Daily Orange,* 21 Feb.

Hobsbawm, Eric, and Terence Ranger, eds. 1983. *The Invention of Tradition.* Cambridge: Cambridge University Press.

Kelly, Shaune. 1957. "Hill 'Warrior' Jigs to Ancient Tune." *Syracuse Daily Orange,* 15 Nov.

Kramer, Lindsay. 1995. "SU Fans Give Wolf Grudging Logo Nod." *Post-Standard,* 18 July.

Masters, Bill. 1978a. "Forgotten Tradition." *Syracuse Daily Orange,* 16 Feb.

———. 1978b. "New Traditions?" *Syracuse Herald-Journal,* 20 Feb.

McAlary, Mike. 1978. "Decision on Mascot Made." *Syracuse Summer Orange,* 27 July.

McEnaney, Maura. 1978. "SU Drops Saltine Warrior." *Syracuse Daily Orange,* 16 Jan.

"Meet . . . Chief O-gee-ke-da Ho-schen-e-ga-da (Alias Bill Orange)." 1931. *Alumni News.* Syracuse University Archives. File on S.U. Traditions—Saltine Warrior. 6–7 Dec.

"New Saltine Warrior to Lead Cheering at Games, Rallies." 1951. *Syracuse Daily Orange,* 25 Sept.

Onakiwahe. 1978. "Indians Reject False Imagery." *Syracuse Post-Standard,* 16 March.

O'Neill, Brian. 1977a. "Native Americans Protest Stereotypes." *Syracuse Daily Orange*, 1 Nov.

———. 1977b. "SU May Decide on Saltine Warrior by Next Week." *Syracuse Daily Orange*, 8 Dec.

Onkwehonweneha. 1978. "Warrior: Based on a Lie." *Syracuse Daily Orange*, 3 March.

The Onondagan. 1886, 1893, 1894, 1910, 1911, 1912. Syracuse University Yearbook.

Pasho, Kathy. 1978. "SU: Stand up." *Syracuse Herald-American*, 26 Feb.

Peel, Bob. 1981. "Pride and Woes of SU's Warrior." *Syracuse Herald-American*, 29 March.

Pike, Wally, Jr. 1978. "Saltine Warrior Next to Leave?" *Syracuse Post-Standard*, 18 Feb.

Rapp, William C., Sr. 1995. "SU Leaders Flunked History over Warrior." *Syracuse Post-Standard*, 31 July.

Reigelhaupt, Barbara. 1976a. "Myth of Saltine Warrior Foolum SU Many Moons." *Syracuse Daily Orange*, 23 March.

———. 1976b. "Students Research Warrior Saga's Origin." *Syracuse Daily Orange*, 23 March.

Reilly, Jim. 1998. "Saltine Warrior Update." *Syracuse Post-Standard*, 8 Sept.

Salmon, Jacqui. 1978. "Roman Saltine Warrior Greeted by Cheers, Jeers." *Syracuse Daily Orange*, 13 Sept.

"Saltine Mascot to Make Debut." 1955. *Syracuse Daily Orange*, 24 Oct.

"Saltine Warrior." 1962. *Syracuse Daily Orange*, 12 Oct.

Schmidt, Bunny. 1967. "SU's Very Own Indian." *Syracuse Daily Orange*, 4 Aug.

Sheflin, Francis. 1977. "A Question of Pride." *Syracuse Daily Orange*, 3 Nov.

Stanton, Mike. 1978. "An SU Mascot for All Men?" *Syracuse Daily Orange*, 13 Sept.

Stashenko, Joel. 1978. "SU Loses a Legend." *Syracuse Daily Orange*, 27 March.

Sternberg, Bill. 1979. "Student Shows Model for New SU Mascot." *Syracuse Post-Standard*, 25 Oct.

"Syracuse—School of Traditions." 1962. *Syracuse Daily Orange*, 24 Sept.

Thorron, N. 1954. "History of the Song, 'Saltine Warrior.'" Syracuse University Archives. File on s.u. Traditions—Saltine Warrior. Sept.

Thurman, Blake. 1977. "Portraying a Myth." *Syracuse Daily Orange*, 8 Nov.

"The True Story of Bill Orange." 1931. *Syracuse Orange Peel.* Syracuse University Archives. File on s.u. Traditions—Saltine Warrior. Oct.

Tucker, James. 1978. "Remove Name." *Syracuse Herald-Journal*, 22 Feb.

Wake, Warren K. 1978. "su Purplemen." *Syracuse Herald-Journal*, 27 Feb.

"Warrior's History Traced through Campus Folklore." 1972. *Syracuse University Record.* 24 Feb.

W. E. A. [writer identified by initials only]. 1934. "The Saltine Warrior." *Syracuse Daily Orange*, 6 Nov.

Wiley, Lauren. 1995. "Chancellor Saves Otto." *Syracuse Daily Orange*, 5 Dec.

Williams, S. Robert. 1995. "Beer-Bellied Orange Doesn't Instill Fear." *Syracuse Post-Standard*, 8 Dec.

CHAPTER 2

Becoming the Indians

Fashioning Arkansas State University's Indians

•

Mary Landreth

Arkansas State University (ASU) began competing in intercollegiate athletics in 1911, using a succession of different nicknames such as the "Aggies" and the "Farmers" throughout the 1920s. As the agricultural school began to place a greater emphasis on college-level curriculum, it sought a new and more attractive nickname for its athletic team, officially adopting the "Indians" in 1931. The expectation was that this new athletic name would foster the ideals of higher learning by alluding to the Indian heritage of the state (Dew 1968:127). The Osages are specifically mentioned in ASU historical records as the Indians "honored" because they "were at war with practically all other tribes of the plains" (*Arkansas State Indians* 1998:112). Later, an Indian Family evolved as the mascot, and a caricature of an Indian wielding a tomahawk and a scalp became the athletic logo. Today, these characters linger, even as the university endeavors to "treat Native Americans with dignity and respect" and to "dignify the role they played" in our history ("ASU to Lower" 1999).

This essay presents an interpretation of the ASU Indians and argues that the images and performances associated with the mascot rely upon well-worn stereotypes that distort the history of both Native Americans and the state. Although a powerful source of identity

46

for fans and athletes, the ASU Indians are mythical, inauthentic, and harmful objectifications. Importantly, many Native Americans feel humiliated by the antics of the university "Indians" (Jon Thomas, personal communication, 4 October 1998). Consequently, ASU disrespects rather than honors Native Americans.

MYTHS

Historical inaccuracies and popular myths about Arkansas and its Native peoples are personified in the ASU Indians. The school's mascots do not reflect the Indian heritage of the state because they have been fashioned to resemble the "Indians" portrayed in western movies. The Native American heritage of the state dates back to the pre-Columbian aboriginals, such as the Temple Mound Culture and their descendants, who were living in large permanent villages when Hernando de Soto explored the state in 1541. But these people had disappeared (most probably due to the diseases introduced into the area by the Spanish) by the time the French began exploring the state and established the first European settlement in Arkansas, the Arkansas Post, in 1586 (Dougan 1994:11-12; Ferguson and Atkinson 1966:2-5, 9-12; Novak and Berry 1997:11-17).

The Quapaws had moved into the Mississippi and Arkansas River valleys by this time and were soon joined by the Choctaws and the Cherokees, who began migrating into the state after the French and Indian War, establishing villages between the Arkansas and Red Rivers. The Cherokees hunted in the Grand Prairie between the Arkansas and White Rivers. This area was the traditional hunting area of the Osages, who lived in southwestern Missouri. Intermittent warfare between the Cherokees and the Osages over these hunting lands continued into the early 1800s (Dougan 1994:11-26; Ferguson and Atkinson 1966:2-12; Novak and Berry 1997:11-37).

The population of Indians in the state increased after the War of 1812 with the migration of the Shawnees, Delawares, and Caddos

47

into Arkansas. The establishment of the Arkansas territorial government in 1819 led to treaties removing all these peoples to Indian Territory (later Oklahoma) by 1833. Thousands of Native Americans traveled through the state during the federal government's removal (known to some tribes such as the Cherokees as the Trail of Tears), with many who were too ill to continue the journey being left behind in Arkansas (Dougan 1994:26–29; Ferguson and Atkinson 1966:56–59; Novak and Berry 1997:11–37).

Clearly, Indians, in the sense of peoples traditionally viewed as "Indians" by white American society, have a very brief history in the state, less than three hundred years, with no permanent villages or activity in the northeastern area where Arkansas State University is located. Moreover, these early inhabitants of Arkansas were primarily peaceful villagers, not the warlike peoples portrayed by the university to inspire aggressive characteristics among the athletic team members.

Despite this lack of a substantial "Indian" history in the state, the Indians as an athletic name to reflect the heritage of Arkansas does correlate with the mythic history of the state. A major theme in Arkansas history, according to the current leading state historian (who happens to teach at ASU), is the taming of a frontier spirit. This theme plays off the existence of the state's unsettled mountain and swamp areas and its common western border with Indian Territory, which ties Arkansas with the nation's "Indian and frontier histories" (Dougan 1994:103). In fact, the town of Fort Smith emerged on the state's border as a major trading center for Arkansas businessmen who received contracts to supply the Indians in the territory. Also, not all Indians stayed in Indian Territory; many of those who left moved into Arkansas, such as Elias Boudinot, who practiced law and edited a newspaper in Fayetteville (Dougan 1994:75–103; Ferguson and Atkinson 1966:56–62). Intermarriage among the Indians and whites subsequently occurred in Fayetteville, and today conversations with

Arkansans suggest that most have an Indian princess, not just an ordinary Indian woman nor an Indian male, somewhere in their ancestry (Paul S. Austin, personal communication, 24 February 1999). The town of Fort Smith also served as the judicial seat for the federal district court for western Arkansas. The appointment of Isaac Parker as federal judge in Fort Smith and his numerous sentences of execution by hanging brought great notoriety to Arkansas in the late 1800s. National newspapers reporting the occasional forays of individuals such as Jesse James and Belle Starr into Arkansas helped to foster the unruly frontier reputation for Arkansas (Dougan 1994: 75-82). This literary image tying Arkansas to Indian Territory and the frontier was later rekindled by the cinema and ingrained in the national consciousness when "Hangin' Judge Parker" was popularized by the motion picture industry in westerns, such as *Hang 'em High* starring Clint Eastwood as a deputy for Judge Parker. Also reinforcing the frontier image of the state and the state's tie to Indian Territory is the quintessential Indian fighter of western movies, John Wayne, playing the part of Rooster Cogburn in the movie *True Grit*, which is based on the novel by Charles Portis, a resident of Arkansas.

Movies and works of literature such as these sustain the Indian frontier image of Arkansas, even though its frontier began to diminish with the various New Deal programs bringing hard-surfaced roads and electricity to most parts of the state in the 1930s (Dougan 1994:80-103; Ferguson and Atkinson 1966:211-13; Novak and Berry 1997:78-80). But increased mobility and the development of urbanity led to a sense of loss for the state's traditions and nostalgia for its frontier past. The need for an economic base in the state combined with this nostalgia to create a tourism business that utilized the scenic forests and wildlife areas with the proliferation of exhibitions of "homesteading skills" and the sale of crafts. The initial commercial success of these frontier-like activities led to expanding

the traditional crafts available for purchase to include "Indian" souvenirs made by "real Indians" because the state had bordered Indian
Territory.

It was at the onset of this tourism era in the early 1930s that Arkansas State University chose the "Indians" for its athletic team
name, consciously connecting the college with the image Arkansas
was projecting to the nation. In this context of nostalgia and tourist
consumption, then, the images of Native Americans that developed
were based not on historical evidence but on popular stereotypes
and misconceptions of Indians and the frontier imagery of the state.

STEREOTYPES

ASU relied on stereotypes about Indians to create its mascots. Although the selection was intended to "honor" all the earliest natives
of the state, the ASU Indians pay tribute to the Osages in particular
because of the misconception that they were "savage warriors" and
in the hope that their legendary aggressive traits could be magically
transferred to the athletic teams. It seemed to matter to no one that
the Osages were only occasional visitors, not early inhabitants of Arkansas. They were chosen by ASU because they were famous for their
consistent conflicts with the Cherokees and other Indians in the
state, people like themselves, over control of the Grand Prairie
hunting lands. The university athletic teams, like the Osages, would
be challenging other teams like themselves on the field and court
during athletic competitions. Also, the emphasis on the Osages as
the Indians being honored expunged the inference of paying tribute to those, such as the Caddos, who combated the white settlement of the state, Indians who killed earlier Arkansans.

ASU's Indian Family of mascots consists of "Chief Big Track," "the
Princess," and "the Brave." The name of the Chief could be "honoring" an actual Osage historical figure. An early Osage leader who led
a group from Missouri to establish a trading center along the Arkan-

sas River in the northwestern portion of Arkansas (on the other side of the state from ASU) for a brief period of time was named Big Track. However, most ASU alumni are not aware of the Chief bearing the name of a real person in Osage history. The university newspaper, the *Herald*, reports that the name came from the Chief "mounting a horse and making a full run around the track every time the football team made a touchdown" ("ASU Re-Establishes" 1996).

More importantly, ASU's Chief Big Track and his male companion, the Brave, do not resemble the traditional Osage males they are supposedly honoring. They do not shave their heads and wear the traditional roach worn by the Osage men. Instead, the Chief wears a feathered headdress like those worn by "Indian chiefs" of the cinema while the Brave wears a long black wig and feathered headband like the majority of Indians in Hollywood's western movies. Furthermore, the Princess does not paint the middle part in her hair with red as the Osage women did. Nor does she wear her hair loosely over her back as was the Osage custom for single women; instead, she wears two braids hanging in front of her shoulders like the Indian females of the cinema.

All three members of the ASU Indian Family, moreover, are attired in costumes representing a miscellanea of Hollywood's typical motion picture Indians. They all wear beads and buckskins. Both males also wear quivers of arrows, and the Brave carries a lance. Face paint is applied freely on the faces of the Family with no regard to the importance and religious significance of colors, designs, and paint. No former Indian residents of Arkansas, or anywhere else for that matter, were ever attired and adorned as is the current ASU Indian Family (Stedman 1998:198).

However, to many Arkansans, choosing Indians as the athletic name with reference to the Osages, while costuming the Indian Family to resemble the Indians of the cinema, is appropriate. Osages are Indians. Indians, in the minds of much of the general public, wear beads, braids, buckskins, and feathered headdresses, ride horses, and brandish bows and lances. This stereotypical mental picture of Indians is not a phenomenon of Arkansas. Rather, a deficient educational system that has been unable or unwilling to teach about Native American cultures and histories, combined with the visual images of these peoples in the media, has created generalizations about Native Americans in the minds of the American public. The essence of these generalizations is that all Indians were alike and that there are no more "real" Indians. Therefore, the perceived extinct Indians are viewed as appropriate mascots for athletic teams because society sees them as the "savages" from the movies with characteristics of ferocity and valor that are desired among athletes competing on the field or court. The war whoops, drum beating, tomahawk chops, and other antics that accompany these mascots reinforce that aggressive nature ascribed to American Natives and are used to stir up the adrenaline of the athletic team and its fans (Stedman 1998).

The Brave in the ASU mascot family represents the savage that is being honored by the athletic name (Lobo and Talbot 1998:103). The black-and-white outrageously painted stripes that reach from his eyes to his jaw, the buckskin trousers and vest, the loin cloth, and the bared chest bring back to life that primitive warrior as much as the name, Brave, which denotes aggressiveness and valor.

This reincarnated savage at ASU football games joins the other two mascots in leading the athletic team onto the field by throwing a lance at the ASU emblem to quiver in the middle of the field while the team charges forth before their fans. The Brave then grabs up this lance and does a war dance amid war whoops from the fans before running to the end zone to throw the lance between the goal posts. The Brave has declared war for the ASU Indians against the "enemy" team. As the teams prepare for the kickoff, the Brave crouches in the end zone to raise another lance and give another war whoop as the game begins. These actions offend Native Americans, who view them as disrespectful of the traditions and symbolism of Native culture. Yet, to the fans, the actions are viewed as merely customary among Indians (like the cavalry commander raising his sword as he orders a charge or the Texans shouting "Remember the Alamo" as they battled the Mexican army for independence) because the Indians in the westerns do it. To the spectators, this action is something Indians do; therefore, it is authentic, and the ASU Indians must include it to honor the Indians.

Throughout the game the mascots circulate in the outfield where a teepee has been erected, but the Brave also sporadically crouches in the end zone and moves to stand before the fans to perform his "war dance" and brandish his lance while whooping the team to victory. This performance is what the fans expect, based on what they know about Indians and how they think Indians behaved, especially the dancing and antics with the lance (Berkhofer 1979:97–101; Stedman 1998:198). Such antics by the Brave encourage individual actions among the more enthusiastic fans sporting feathered headbands so that they will join him in whooping and making chops with their construction paper or plastic tomahawks. This behavior by the fans is thought to encourage more aggressive actions from the ASU athletes on the field (or court) to defeat the enemy and win the game.

The stoic and dignified buckskin-clad Chief standing on the sideline adorned with a feathered headdress re-creates the image of the noble savage who was vanquished by the progress of civilization. Meanwhile, the Princess strolls around the teepee, waving and smiling at the spectators and representing the Indian maid who befriended and helped the white settlers survive and conquer the harshness of the West. Thus, we have the re-creation of the peoples who are really being *honored* by the university when it designates its athletic teams as the Indians: those who relinquished their savage ways and became civilized (Berkhofer 1979:103-14; Lobo and Talbot 1998:175-76; Green 1998:191-94).

In contrast, the Brave resembles many of the animals that so many other teams use as mascots. This warrior mascot, along with the chants of "Scalp the . . . " and "Go Tribe," the war whoops, and the tomahawk chops, inspires and channels the aggression of the team members and the fans against the opposing team. The fabled tenacity and bellicosity of the Indian explain in part why the athletic teams at ASU are named Indians, but ASU also includes the Chief and Princess as mascots dressed in stereotypical costumes and exhibiting nonthreatening behavior to reassert that the truly heroic Indians were those that accepted or succumbed to the progress of civilization.

IDENTITY

The teepee constructed in the outfield at the football games is another aspect of the stereotypes and misconceptions about Indians. All the Indians who lived in Arkansas resided in wooden structures and only utilized the teepee for hunting, but the teepee, of course, is part of the package of Indianness from the Hollywood westerns where *all* Indians lived in teepees. The teepee in the ASU outfield provides the expected backdrop to the Indian Family since it completes the movie set of the frontier. The teepee is also what the fans expect to see because it is what they *know* about Indians. If a replica of an Osage dwelling of wood and foliage was erected in the outfield instead of the teepee, it would be viewed by spectators as inauthentic (Berkhofer 1997:181).

Various other stereotypes based on misconceptions about Indians were incorporated and added to the ASU campus during the 1950s. During the "War Drum Ritual" the freshmen on the football team take shifts of one hour each to beat on an Indian war drum in front of Indian Hall (the ASU gymnasium). The drum ceremony began twenty-four hours before the homecoming kickoff, with the Indian Family riding up to the assembled student body on horseback. This tradition was an imitation of the western movie scenes of Indians dancing and chanting to drums before attacking settlers or the army. The freshmen ball players complained about the ritual because it was such a time-consuming activity. Also, the sororities and fraternities that chose the individuals to be the mascots no longer wanted to be required to select students who were competent at riding horses. This led to the drum ritual being phased out in the mid-1980s (*Arkansas State Indians* 1998:114; Thomas Moore, personal communication, 5 October 1998; Fayeth Hurt, personal communication, 22 February 1999).

The "Jumpin' Joe" caricature also evolved during the 1950s as the ASU athletic logo. Female caricatures followed for the women's athletic teams featuring women dressed in female athletic suits with braided hair and a headband with feather. These caricature logos greatly resemble the caricatures used by other athletic teams with names that evoke the imagery of Native American peoples (*Arkansas State Indians* 1998:112; "Area Rich" 1991). These cartoon depictions of Native Americans, usually with an enlarged nose and angry facial expressions, visually deny the reality of these people as humans, which sustains the misconception that Indians are not people or at least not people still living today. Jumpin' Joe, clenching a scalp in his fist and wielding a tomahawk, also exemplified the myth that all Indians were savages ("Runnin' Joe" 1991; Clements 1992). Jumpin' Joe's successor, "Runnin' Joe" (adopted in 1987) continues to sustain this stereotypical image despite the deletion of the scalp.

Other stereotypical accessories based on misconceptions adhered to by the ASU Indians include a totem pole and an Italian-carved marble Indian statue. The totem pole, by an "Indian carver" in Vancouver, British Columbia, was purchased by the Alpha Omicron Pi sorority and is displayed in the convention center on the ASU cam-

55

pus (Dew 1968: 123). Totem poles are associated with Indians in general, as are bows, arrows, lances, and teepees. Consequently, the Indians of ASU have one to honor the Native peoples who formerly populated the state, no matter how lacking it is in any real connection to Native peoples in the state's history. The marble statue, purchased by the Student Government Association in 1958, resembles the typical cigar store wooden Indian. This marble reproduction of a dignified Indian was nicknamed "Clyde" because of the monument company's name plaque. The student body developed the tradition that freshmen were to tip their beanies every time they passed the statute (Dew 1968: 122–23), resulting in a mockery of the dignity of Native Americans this reproduction attempted to convey. This Indianness continues on the campus with a permanent exhibit of Arkansas and Southwest Indian pottery in the library, even though the historical natives of Arkansas were not of the southwest culture. Also, the names of almost all the buildings and streets on the ASU campus are the English version of Native American tribes.

CHANGE

These embellishments of the university's athletic teams, especially the caricature logo in conjunction with the concept of using people (Native Americans) as mascots, spawned criticisms in 1991 from faculty members. A major emphasis by these faculty members was that the mascot and logo detract from the mission of the university as an institution of higher learning. Faculty argued that the university's endorsement of fabricated images of Indians through these athletic-related displays perpetuated misconceptions and stereotypes antithetical to what the university should represent. The very publicly visible athletics department, according to the concerned faculty, was communicating a symbolic image of the university with the mascots and logo that endangered the public identity of the university as a whole. The faculty passed a resolution that the university replace the disrespectful mascots and logo with more appropriate symbols for an institution of learning (Clements 1992).

Members of the faculty elicited support from the student body, alumni, and community. The editors of the campus and community newspapers were overwhelmed with responses throughout the spring of 1992, some of them in support of the faculty's resolution. One alumnus wrote of his feelings of humiliation and shame at the sight of Jumpin' Joe and the Brave representing their team during a televised ASU game, and he urged an end to this "inappropriate false imitation of a people's culture" ("ASU Mascot" 1992; Paul S. Austin, personal communication, 24 February 1999).

However, most responses viewed the faculty call for a mascot change as an "unwarranted and meddlesome" attack on the traditions of the university. Continuing the attentiveness to tradition that led to Arkansas tourism based on folk culture and crafts, many proudly argued that the Indian Family of ASU had become one of the state's celebrated traditions. Some students responded by attacking the faculty members who asked the university to change the mascot. These attacks included suggesting that these faculty members had ulterior motives, such as to encourage Native Americans to completely forget their past or to rewrite history to depict Indians as "nice and gentle tribes of people who did no harm to anyone." Faculty were also accused of wanting "the name changed in the hopes that people will forget about the Indian culture or way of life altogether" ("Tradition" 1991; "Student" 1991).

These statements by students of an institution of higher learning to justify the athletic team name and mascots exhibit perfectly the rationale behind the faculty's resolution calling for the mascot change. Imitations of Indian rituals by non-Indians wearing feathers and paint are not the means whereby Native Americans preserve their past. Indian mascots and logos are how non-Native peoples view and remember the Native peoples of this nation. The aggressive acts and parodies performed by athletic team mascots and participating fans perpetuate dominant Arkansan (and American) myths that Native Americans were uncivilized peoples constantly involved in warlike activities. These misrepresentations help society to deny the reality that Indians were "nice and gentle" peoples who were forced by non-Indians to engage in warfare to protect their families and homes from destruction. The faculty recommendation that the university cease using Indians as mascots was a conscious effort to protect and preserve the "Indian culture and way of life." The concerned faculty viewed the elimination of the very visible stereotypes exhibited and performed by athletic team mascots and fans as a necessary step toward preservation of both Native culture and respect for Native peoples (Fontana 1998:181; Lobo and Talbot 1998:175–76; William Clements 1992, personal communication, 5 October 1998).

The faculty resolution eventually led to the university replacing Runnin' Joe on its letterheads and other printed materials with a "regal and dignified" Indian head montage with headdress (Moore 1993). Unfortunately, this new logo continues another stereotypical tradition by reinforcing the false image that all Indians are the same and that all Indian males wear feathered headdresses.

The Indian Family was also modified ("ASU Re-establishes" 1996). While the basic stereotypes endure, the Chief no longer mounts his horse and runs the track after every touchdown, but this is due in large part to the new university stadium, which does not contain a track around the field for the infamous ride. The Princess dresses with more modesty now. She wears slacks under the buckskin dress that is split almost to the waist. This change is a direct response to criticisms by Native Americans in the area and others in the community.

The Tia Piah Society (a group of preservationists of Native American culture in nearby Memphis) offered to help the ASU athletic department to dress the mascots in more appropriate dress and to teach the cultural meanings of face painting in accordance with the heritage of former Indian residents of Arkansas. Group members were thanked for their offer, but no major adjustments have been made to the elaborate Hollywood costumes, actions, and painting of the Indian Family. The demeaning stereotypes endure, causing Native American children in the community to ask their parents, "Why do they make Indians look like clowns?" and "Why are they making fun of us?"

Nonetheless, the university has attempted in other ways to draw support for the ASU Indians and the mascots from the Native Americans in the area and the more vocal Tia Piah Society. The university waives out-of-state tuition for Native American students who are descendants of Native societies that once lived in the state ("ASU to Lower" 1999). Also, an annual powwow is now held on the campus, supported by the university and the Tia Piah. The proceeds from this annual event support a scholarship fund for Native American students attending the university (Moore 1997, 1998). The tuition waiver is quite obviously a recruitment ploy aimed at Native Americans. The powwow does enable some teaching of American Native culture, particularly about the dances and the meaning of dance to specific Native cultures. It also reeks of the traditional paternalistic approach that American society has always taken toward the Native peoples. In the past, institutions, both governmental and educational, have consistently defined and controlled what is taught about Native peoples to assure the preservation of the accepted images of Indians. This institutional control keeps the incorrect image intact, perpetuates ignorance, and distorts history to justify the destruction of Native cultures and the continued assimilation of the Native peoples into the mainstream white American society. The encouragement for Native Americans to attend the university due to tuition waivers is part of that continuing assimilation process.

CONCLUSIONS

Robert Berkhofer asserts in *The White Man's Indian* (1979:92) that "the quest for American cultural identity . . . and the fate of the Indian and the frontier . . . were all . . . connected." This connection leads to Native American names and objects of their culture being used as athletic team names and the use of Indians as athletic team mascots. The American public views this as a symbolic immortalizing of the Indian who lived a very simple life of hunting and fishing in harmony with the environment and who was fully self-reliant. This myth earns the Indian respect from today's society, as does the fact that the Indian was the most difficult of our country's enemies to defeat. Our nation was engaged in warfare with the various Native peoples longer than any other people. But the defeat, subsequent incarceration on reservations, and attempted assimilation of the American Indian is tied to our nation's mastering the frontier. The "taming of the frontier," which included conquering and taming the Indian, identifies us as a successful, progressive, and "civilized" nation. Therefore, the Indian athletic team names and mascots are really honoring ourselves, the conquerors. The stereotypes and misconceptions on which they are based perpetuate our myths about ourselves. This is evident in Arkansas, where an early Indian frontier image was created through literary works, and the state's most successful enterprise, tourism, is partially based on the nurturing of this image. Today the successful state-projected portrait (in terms of the reaping of tourist dollars) still relies on the connection between the region and nearby Indian Territory during frontier times. This justifies the sale of pioneer folk culture through exhibitions and craft stalls, including the marketing of the trappings defined as Indian: powwows, war bonnets, teepees, totem poles, tomahawks, feathers, lances, and face paint (Fontana 1998:181). The ASU Indians mirror these trappings and contribute to the success of their marketing.

Indian athletic names and mascots also allow the adult athletes and fans to continue to "play Indian." Adults like to play Indian because the myth has made the Indian a hero, a good "bad guy" — "good" because of the Indian's perceived lifestyle and persistence against white expansion, yet "bad" because he fought against the whites. Also, the mascots are viewed as a way of keeping the Indian alive because we see the Indian as being ultimately defeated, and we do not want to let the Indian of our myth die. We want to keep the Indian myth alive as part of white American history, just as we want to preserve the myths about other parts of our past, such as George Washington and Thomas Jefferson as models of "great" men for our children to look up to as unblemished heroes. In reality, both these men were rebels against their established government and were the owners of other people as slaves. Yet the myth omits these characteristics of the men, just as the Indian myth omits the diversity of cultures and realities of life of the peoples we label as Indians. That is why we do not view today's Native Americans as "Indians." The myth is that there are no more Indians. The Indians were defeated, conquered, and assimilated into our society. Therefore, American society fails to understand that the misconceptions and stereotypes of our nation's Indian myth used in the sports arenas across the nation to laud ourselves disrespect our nation's Native American peoples and distort both their history and ours while "honoring" whites. This distortion of history will continue, and Native Americans (real, living people in today's society) will remain in the past in the consciousness of the public as long as the sports arena is the classroom for teaching about Native peoples and their culture. As the faculty who instigated the resolution to end this demeaning behavior and mis-education at ASU proposed, the most visual and most notable false representations of Native peoples must be removed before the true culture and history of these citizens will be accepted. Yet, like those at Arkansas State University who refused to change the mascots, Americans are adamant about keeping our myths intact. The mascots, like the myths, make us feel good about ourselves (for having successfully conquered the impossible foe, the Indians) so we justify the use of Native American culture through stereotypes and mascots by claiming to be "honoring" the peoples these actions degrade.

REFERENCES

Arkansas State Indians Media Guide. 1998. Jonesboro: ASU Press.

"ASU Mascot Degrading to American Indians." 1992. *Jonesboro Herald,* 7 Feb.

"ASU Re-establishes Indian Family." 1996. *Jonesboro Herald,* 18 Oct.

"ASU to Lower Tuition for Eligible Indians Who Live out of State." 1999. *(Little Rock) Arkansas Democrat-Gazette,* 20 April.

Berkhofer, Robert F., Jr. 1979. *The White Man's Indian: Images of the American Indian from Columbus to the Present.* New York: Longman.

Clements, William M. 1992. Letter to the Faculty Senate. In possession of author. 10 April.

———. 1991. Letter to the editor. In possession of author. 3 Dec.

Dew, Lee A. 1968. *The ASU Story: A History of Arkansas State University, 1909–1967.* Jonesboro: ASU Press.

Dougan, Michael B. 1994. *Arkansas Odyssey: The Saga of Arkansas from Prehistoric Times to the Present.* Little Rock: Rose.

Ferguson, John L., and J. H. Atkinson. 1966. *Historic Arkansas.* Little Rock: Arkansas History Commission.

Fontana, Bernard L. 1998. "Inventing the American Indian." In *Native American Voices,* ed. Susan Lobo and Steve Talbot, pp. 178–82. New York: Longman.

Green, Rayna. 1998. "The Pocahontas Perplex: The Image of Indian Women in American Culture." In *Native American Voices,* ed. Susan

Lobo and Steve Talbot, pp. 182–92. New York: Longman. Originally published in *Massachusetts Review* 16 (1975): 698–714.

Lobo, Susan, and Steve Talbot. 1998. "'The Only Good Indian . . .': Racism, Stereotypes, Discrimination." In *Native American Voices*, ed. Susan Lobo and Steve Talbot, pp. 171–77. New York: Longman.

Moore, Tom. 1998. "Native American Pow Wow." Arizona State University press release. 28 April.

———. 1997. "Pow-Wow Coming to ASU." Arizona State University press release. 3 Sept.

———. 1993. "Logo Changes, Nickname Stays." Arizona State University press release. 15 Oct.

Novak, John, and Fred Berry. 1997. *The History of Arkansas*. Little Rock: Rose.

"Runnin' Joe Reduces Indians to Animals: Professor Suggests Abandoning Mascot for Non-Demeaning Symbol." 1991. *Jonesboro Herald*, 1 Nov.

Stedman, Raymond W. 1998. "Lingering Shadows (Movie Stereotypes)." In *Native American Voices*, ed. Susan Lobo and Steve Talbot, pp. 195–204. New York: Longman.

"Student Disagrees with New Mascot Ideas: More Important Issues Facing Faculty Senate than Running Joe's Successor." 1991. *Jonesboro Herald*, 29 Nov.

"Tradition Already Lost." 1991. *Jonesboro Herald*, 6 Dec.

CHAPTER 3

Wennebojo Meets the Mascot

A Trickster's View of the Central Michigan University Mascot/Logo

•

Richard Clark Eckert

This essay describes an adventure of Wennebojo, the rhetorically explosive and forever elusive trickster of the Anishinaabegs. Tricksters like to play, especially toying with those so serious that they fail to laugh at themselves.

During this adventure Wennebojo travels to Mount Pleasant, Michigan, with the intention of examining the continued use of the "Chippewa" name by Central Michigan University. Wennebojo had heard different things about the Chippewa name still being used at CMU, but he wanted to see for himself.

Wennebojo was curious as to how CMU first used the Chippewa name and how that use and the word's meaning had been transformed and reinvented. Wennebojo was also curious in regard to the continued use of the Chippewa name; he wondered whether CMU had consulted all of the many bands of Chippewa in Michigan, Minnesota, North Dakota, Montana, Wisconsin, and Canada.

On the way to Mount Pleasant Wennebojo stopped and visited his friend Makwa (Bear), who lived on the Isabella Reservation, home of the Saginaw Chippewa Tribe. Makwa came from a traditional family. Some think of him as a clan leader. Makwa stuck his

64

head out the door. A grin came to his face as he recognized Wennebojo. Everyone grins or chuckles when Wennebojo visits. People laugh when saying his name.

"*Boozhoo* [hello]," said Makwa.

"*Aanniin* [hello]," said Wennebojo.

Makwa invited Wennebojo into his home. He brought Wennebojo a cup of "cowboy coffee."

"*Megwitch* [thank you]," said Wennebojo.

The two of them spent hours catching up on old stories. Makwa gave Wennebojo some "Indian tobacco." "*Megwitch*," Wennebojo said as he shook Makwa's hand. Wennebojo sat down and took out a pipe. It was a beautiful pipe with a bowl made of catlanite, or pipestone, and a pipe stem made from sumac. Wennebojo smoked the pipe.

He pulled out his hand drum, sat on the floor with his legs crossed, and began to sing a song. Wennebojo sang a song about going to the lodge of the big bear.

Makwa sighed and said, "Oh, that was a good song, that was a real old Anishinaabeg song. I hadn't heard that song since I was a little child. I remember Grandfather sitting me by a fire near the lake shore and singing that song to me."

Wennebojo let out an otter-like laugh and said, "Brought out the little boy in you—eh?" He followed with otter-like laughs.

Makwa thought to himself. Why is Wennebojo here? Did he trick me already, and I do not even know it? Maybe Wennebojo put some medicine on me to get me to agree with him. I am happy to see him, but I can't wait until he leaves either. He always gets me thinking about things that I wish he hadn't. I should know better than trying to figure out what Wennebojo is thinking. I will ask him.

"What brought you here?" asked Makwa.

Wennebojo replied, "I'm on a mission. I need to question the mascot at CMU."

"How are you going to question the mascot?" Makwa asked.

"Let's go to the game," Wennebojo replied.

"What game?" asked Makwa.

"The CMU women's volleyball game. You drive," responded Wennebojo.

Upon arriving at Rose Arena, Wennebojo observed an electronic scoreboard flashing the words GO CHIPPEWA, followed by CHIPPEWA PRIDE. Wennebojo looked around. There were no mascots running around making foolish idiots of themselves screaming war whoops. The marching band wasn't using any tom-tom rhythms to incite the crowd. None of the CMU cheerleaders or fans sported face paint. There were no caricatures of scalping. No tomahawk chops could be seen anywhere! There weren't any sweatshirts with an Indian profile or spears and feathers. Nothing on the uniforms of the volleyball players even hinted about a history of CMU using a Chippewa mascot, logo, or name. What happened?

For a moment Makwa thought Wennebojo was talking to a manitou, or spirit. Makwa sighed as he realized that Wennebojo was in dialogue with the electronic scoreboard.

"Could you tell me if the electronic words are symbolic of the Chippewas?" Wennebojo asked.

The scoreboard replied by suggesting that Wennebojo go ask the former mascot.

"Where can I find the former mascot?" asked Wennebojo.

"Clarke Historical Library," responded the scoreboard.

So Wennebojo and Makwa left the volleyball game at Rose Arena and walked over to Clarke Historical Library. At the library the receptionist greeted Wennebojo and Makwa by giving them forms to fill out about their research. After completing the paperwork, the two of them waited for the files to arrive. Makwa was told to get rid of his pen. Use pencils only! No request was made of Wennebojo concerning his royal blue "presidential" fountain pen. Looking through the file, Wennebojo located the former mascot.

"Are you the former mascot?" asked Wennebojo.

"I am," said the mascot.

"What happened? Why are you a former mascot and not the current mascot?" asked Wennebojo.

"There is no mascot at CMU anymore," the former mascot replied. Wennebojo looked puzzled. "Tell me, how come the scoreboard flashed GO CHIPPEWA at the volleyball game?" inquired Wennebojo.

"Well," said the former mascot, "the scoreboard is an electronic image, a virtual reality, so to speak. It is a logo. Actually, it isn't even a logo in the dictionary sense. 'Chippewa' is a nickname."

Shaking his head in disbelief, Wennebojo wondered what mental gymnastics had occurred at CMU. There was no Chippewa mascot, perhaps not even a logo. What remained was a nickname whose meaning was understood by few people; even fewer understood how the use of the nickname by CMU was offensive.

Wennebojo thought out loud, "How can I explain to people that 'the meaning of a word is the action it produces'?" (Montagu 1969).

The former mascot began, "I was first introduced to CMU back in 1942 by a member of the coaching staff. I replaced a Bearcat mascot who had replaced a Dragon mascot. I was used for pageantry, but that changed, too. I became a symbol of ferocity, a warlike spirit. I was the CMU Chippewa mascot until 1972. At that point I was transformed into a logo—actually two logos. One logo was a Native American Indian profile. I'm not sure if the profile was from one tribe or a mixture of many tribes. Nor do I have any idea of how authentic I was, but I presume my profile was not of a "real" Indian. The other logo was a combination of a block C with spear points and feathers" (Newsletter CMU 1989; Plachta 1992).

"I didn't notice logos like that today. What happened?" asked Wennebojo.

The former mascot continued, "The two logos were discontinued in March 1989. This resulted from an October 1988 Michigan Civil Rights Commission report that said the use of nicknames, logos, and mascots depicting Native American Indians by Michigan educational institutions was racist. The report cited an article in *Central Michigan Life* entitled 'Torturer.' The article described a CMU wrestler who claimed that if he were an Indian he would take 'great pleasure in collecting enemy scalps and then drinking the blood'" (Newsletter CMU 1989; (MCRC 1988).

Wennebojo gasped as the Mascot said those words. He looked completely disgusted. "Stop! I don't want to hear anymore of that," Wennebojo exclaimed. "You mean to tell me that educated people wrote and read that without objection?" asked Wennebojo.

"Well," replied the former mascot, "the Native students didn't appreciate it much."

"Now wait a second," demanded Wennebojo. "You mean to tell me that the president and the Board of Trustees of CMU supported the Chippewa logo after reading the findings of the MCRC?"

"Yes, the president was aware of the MCRC findings," said the mascot.

"Well, what about the wrestler? You mean to tell me that CMU, an educational institution, didn't have a problem with the 'Torturer'?" asked Wennebojo.

"No problem at all. They encouraged that sort of thing," said the mascot.

"What about non-Native students? Didn't they see a problem with the 'Torturer'?" asked the trickster.

"Not really. Students thought that racism against Native Americans was something of the past. They thought racism had to be like Jim Crow," answered the former mascot (Bobo et al. 1997).

"What else did the commission say?" asked Wennebojo in a very irritated tone.

68

"The commission concluded that the 'use of Indian images is stereotypic, racist, and discriminatory.' The MCRC recommended that 'any use of Indian names, logos and mascots should be discontinued because racial stereotyping of Native Americans is prevalent and destructive'" (MCRC 1900).

"CMU President Jakubauskas responded to the MCRC report by creating a committee to study the issue."

"Wait a second," interrupted Wennebojo, "if they understood the MCRC report, why did CMU think a committee to study the issue was appropriate at all? Why didn't they comply with the recommendations of the commission?"

The former mascot continued, "The nineteen-member committee was composed of students, faculty, alumni, and members of the Saginaw Chippewa Tribe of Michigan," the former mascot responded. "The committee provided the president with recommendations, including retaining the Chippewa nickname. The Native voice on the committee was outvoted" (Newsletter CMU 1989).

The mascot continued, "President Jakubauskas decided upon a three-year trial period. To oversee implementation of the committee's recommendations and the use of the Chippewa name during the trial period, the president set up yet another committee, a Symbol Advisory Committee. At the same time, CMU was negotiating a CMU trademark protection deal with Carnegie Mellon University (which also uses the abbreviation CMU) that included copyrights on the Chippewa name" (Jakubauskas 1989; CMU 1990; Dysinger 1989).

"What did the Symbol Advisory Committee do? Did they do anything?" asked Wennebojo.

The former mascot replied, "The Symbol Advisory Committee met eleven times between June 2, 1989, and May 9, 1990. The committee was formed in the summer of 1989. The defined purpose of the committee was to 'assist in carrying out the recommendations of the Advisory Committee, to eliminate stereotypic images of American Indians associated with the University's Chippewa symbol'" (CMU 1990).

The mascot went on. "The committee focused on removing pictorial representations, changing the name of a dining hall room called Reservation, eliminating tom-tom beats from marching band music, removing a Miami Redskin banner from Finch Fieldhouse, removing the Indian-head profile from ROTC signs on campus, removing a spear displayed on the studio set of the head football coach's television program, discontinuing the use of Chippewa Indian-head logo in the yearbook, educating cheerleaders not to lead "chop" cheers, educating students not to use war whoops and not to wear war paint to athletic events. Local merchants were urged by CMU to discontinue using Native American symbols on products associated with CMU. CMU reminded ABC and ESPN to stop using the old logos as racialized stories were aired by sportscast announcers when CMU beat Michigan State in football" (Goldsmith 1989).

"As another example," the mascot said, "one professor wrote to Vice President James Hill, chair of the Symbol Advisory Committee, and reported seven areas of problems related to the use of the former logos on campus and inappropriate use by local merchants. Some areas on campus, such as the Wellness Resource Center, were cooperative. Others, such as the bookstore, resisted the changes" (Hatch 1989; Rabineau 1989).

"In March 1990," stated the mascot, "CMU intensified efforts to seek the input of local merchants. The problem was they wanted a 'mascot' to sell to the public. One real estate company suggested changing the name from Chippewa to 'Chips' in reference to gambling chips" (Sherwood 1990).

"Did any of those efforts really help anything?" asked Wennebojo.

"Well," continued the former mascot, "by May of 1991 the Affirmative Action Council openly opposed the Chippewa logo. They presented to Jakubauskas eight reasons to drop the logo:

1. It presents a stereotypical image of savage, warlike people.

2. Use of the name of an existing Native American people as the 'mascot' is inherently demeaning to that group.

3. Use of the name of an existing Native American people as the 'mascot' is an affront to the self-esteem of Native American people.

4. Cost should not be a factor in eliminating/changing the name.

5. According to the current plan for Affirmative Action at Central Michigan University discriminatory harassment is unlawful. Racial and ethnic harassment constitutes any intentional, unintentional, physical, verbal, or non-verbal behavior that subjects an individual to an intimidating, hostile, or offensive educational, employment or living environment by a variety of actions.

6. The change in the name was made in 1942 from 'Bearcats' to 'Chippewa.' It was made for pageantry.

7. The Chippewa Tribe did not have input into the name change. The Chippewa Tribe was not consulted. We do not believe the Tribe should be imperiled by being placed in the situation where they bear the burden to change the name.

8. As long as Central keeps the name we have no control of the usage by local merchants.

However, President Jakubauskas decided the three-year trial period would continue" (Gonzales and Newby 1991; Jakubauskas, 1991).

"Shortly thereafter," the former mascot continued, "the Committee to Examine the Use of 'Chippewa' as the university symbol issued a report in which it noted that 'constructive efforts during the trial period had "at best — only limited success." ' The report also indicated that systematic monitoring of abuses had been discontinued for the previous one and one-half years and that cooperation with the Saginaw Chippewa Tribal Council was minimal" (CMU 1992a, 1992b).

Wennebojo asked, "Well, if the Symbol Advisory Committee and the Affirmative Action Council wanted the use of the Chippewa name discontinued, then how did it survive?"

The mascot replied, "Before the three-year trial period was over, the president at CMU resigned. The acting and later official president, Leonard Plachta, supported by the vice president of university relations, sought to retain the logo. There was concern for alumni contributions diminishing if the logo was changed."

"In September 1992, Plachta ignored the recommendations of the Academic Senate and decided to retain the Chippewa name," said the mascot. "Contrary to the findings of the MCRC, the rationale was that 'there is nothing inherently racist or demeaning in using the name of an ethnic group as the nickname for a university — or for a river or city.' Plachta never provided scientific research to support his differences with the MCRC. His decision was immediately voted upon and approved by the Board of Trustees. Some faculty presumed the board made the decision for Plachta" (Plachta 1992).

Puzzled, Wennebojo again interrupted at this point. "Let me see if I understand this right," he said to the former mascot. "The MCRC, the Affirmative Action Council, and the Academic Senate were all recommending that the Chippewa logo be discontinued. Native American students objected to the use of the mascot. Plachta and the Board of Trustees were aware that the MCRC noted that logos using Native American symbols and imagery damages the self-esteem of Indian children."

The former mascot, bowing his head with shame, replied, "That is correct."

"Why in the heck would the president of CMU appeal to ignorance in his decision in favor of the continued use of the Chippewa name?" asked Wennebojo.

"You are expecting the president to be intelligent and act rationally," said the mascot.

"Well, yes," said Wennebojo. "Otherwise we have a president who is locking reason out of a university. I've never known a president of a university to encourage students to be ignorant, except maybe in Alabama or Georgia before the time of *Brown vs. Board of Education*. A president of a university perpetuating ignorance should be a basis from which to force them and trustees supporting them to resign."

"Whoa!" said Makwa. "Don't you think that is a bit strong?"

"No!" said Wennebojo. "Plachta's decision rubs ignorance in the face of all who embrace the motto of enlightenment and have the courage to know," he added emphatically. "Let me ask a few more questions to be certain I understand this correctly. CMU originally had a mascot that was a Dragon. The Dragon became a Bearcat. In 1942 the Bearcat became you, the former Chippewa mascot. You were first used for pageantry and only later for sporting events. After thirty years you became a victim of the 1970s and the civil rights movement and were transformed into a logo."

The former mascot interrupted, "Actually, two logos."

"Okay, two logos," Wennebojo continued. "Sixteen years after you were dropped, the MCRC issued a report that said no to Native nicknames, logos, and mascots. CMU responded by removing spears, chicken feathers, and tom-tom beats, changed the name of a dining room called Reservation, and created a three-year trial period of purging CMU of racial stereotypes. In other words, CMU dropped the mascot, then the logos, yet kept the nickname and called it a logo," said Wennebojo.

"They sure did," said the former mascot.

"CMU decided to retain the logo even though the MCRC identified nicknames, logos, and mascots as perpetuating racial stereotypes. CMU openly uses the word 'Chippewa.' Is that correct?" asked Wennebojo.

"That is true," said the former mascot.

"Didn't the Civil Rights Commission say that continued use would lead to acts of racism against Native American Indians?" asked Wennebojo.

"They certainly did," replied the mascot.

Wennebojo paused for a moment. He asked the mascot, "Which tribes did CMU consult on this issue?"

"What do you mean?" replied the mascot.

Wennebojo, getting a bit impatient, rephrased his question just slightly: "Which tribes did the university ask about the use of the logo?"

"The Saginaw Chippewa Tribe," replied the mascot.

"What other tribes?" asked Wennebojo.

"None that I know of," said the mascot.

"What did the Saginaw Chippewas say?" asked Wennebojo.

"At one point they passed a tribal resolution supporting the use of the nickname" replied the former mascot. "At the same time the MCRC report was coming out, CMU was entertaining the idea of naming the Student Activities Center after the Tribal Council Chief. They were also looking at the idea of giving the Saginaw Chippewa Tribe royalties from the sale of CMU items that had the Chippewa logo on them" (Saginaw 1988; Hill 1992).

Wennebojo looked all the more puzzled. "Weren't there Native American students attending CMU who were from other tribes, such as Sault Sainte Marie, Bay Mills, Lac Vieux Desert, and Keweenaw Bay?"

"Sure," said the mascot, "and a few from Lake Superior bands of Chippewas in Wisconsin and even some from Minnesota, too."

Wennebojo frowned and then asked, "What gave the Saginaw Chippewas the right to speak on behalf of all other Chippewas?"

"What do you mean?" asked the mascot.

"I mean", said Wennebojo, "what gave the Saginaw Chippewa Tribe the right to speak for other Chippewa tribes in Michigan, Wisconsin, Minnesota, Montana, North Dakota, and Canada? What gave them the right to tell CMU anything on behalf of all Chippewas?"

"Nothing gave them that right, but I am not so sure they spoke on behalf of any other tribes," said the former mascot.

"What do you mean?" asked Wennebojo.

"Well, I think CMU presumed that to be true, but the Tribal Council Resolution spoke only for the Saginaw Chippewa Tribe members," said the former mascot.

"There is a sovereignty issue," said Wennebojo.

"Well, not exactly," replied the mascot. "Although the courts have dismissed tribe-against-tribe claims of treaty rights being limited to friendly waters or territories, there simply was no legal obligation for CMU to seek out the opinions of other tribes. In fact, CMU retains the license for the use of the term 'Chippewa.' CMU owns the right to use it and doesn't need permission from any band of Chippewas, let alone all of them—not legally anyway."

Makwa, who was listening attentively to the conversation, interrupted and said, "Hey, not everyone on the reservation agreed with that resolution."

Wennebojo responded by suggesting he and Makwa leave.

"What do you make of all that, Wennebojo?" Makwa asked.

"Let's go back to your place," said Wennebojo.

Makwa put some coffee on the burner and sat quietly. Wennebojo took out his pipe again and smoked it. He spoke. "I was reading a paper called the *University Record* in Ann Arbor. It is a University of Michigan publication for faculty and staff. There was an editorial criticizing Charlene Teters for speaking at the University of Michigan. The editorial asserted, 'some tribes were asking to be remembered in association with universities'" (Simmons 1999).

"Which tribes?" asked Makwa.

"None that I know of," answered Wennebojo. "The author of that editorial also asserted that 'the Chippewas want to be partners with CMU'" (Simmons 1999).

"Where did they get that idea?" asked Makwa. Apparently the Saginaw Public Relations office was claiming that the continued use of the Chippewa symbol by CMU somehow honored Native Americans (Sowmick 1998).

Wennebojo responded, "I also remembered a sporting event contract between CMU and the University of Wisconsin being canceled because of UW policies prohibiting the contracting of sporting events with universities that use Native symbols and imagery. Apparently, CMU entered into a contract with the University of Wisconsin, but the UW had to cancel because the event violated a 1993 Athletic Board policy. The policy explicitly states, 'During the regular season the UW Athletic Department will not schedule any team with a Native American mascot or nickname unless the team is a traditional rival or a conference member'" (Wishaw 1998; University of Wisconsin 1998).

He continued, "I heard that students at CMU now believe that they are no longer allowed to use 'Chippewas,' so they use only 'Chips.' I was told the 'Indian related symbolism' had been dropped. So I grew curious" (Littlefield 1999).

"What have you concluded?" asked Makwa.

"Well," said Wennebojo, "as long as CMU earns revenue from the licensing fees for the use of the Chippewa name and the use of the name damages the self-esteem of Native American Indian children, then it is reasonable to identify such use as exploitative. CMU profits. Native children lose."

He went on, "Although CMU has gone to great lengths to rid itself of a racially stereotypic mascot and logos, ceased to endorse practices of tom-tom beats, got rid of the face paint on cheerleaders, and exposed the chicken feather outfits, the fact remains that MCRC identified the continued use of Indian names by educational institutions to be detrimental to the self-esteem of Native American Indian children. I am not aware of CMU ever citing a study that contradicts the MCRC findings.

"CMU does acknowledge that Indian mascots are inappropriate, but then school officials claim they no longer have a mascot. They argue that CMU is honoring the Chippewa Tribe by using the Chippewa name. One might erroneously presume that the positive changes were somehow initiated by CMU. However, the historical record indicates that CMU habitually resisted changes regarding the mascot and later the logos and now resists efforts to have the use of the Chippewa name discontinued by CMU.

"The president and the Board of Trustees of CMU have blatantly ignored the recommendations of the Affirmative Action Council, the Academic Senate, two different directors of Native American Studies, and Native American students attending CMU. According to one former director of Native American Programs, during the course of his job interview both the provost and the president asked him, if he were to be selected for the job, could he keep his personal opinions to himself, unlike the former director" (Reinhardt 1998).

Wennebojo continued to speak, "While the more overt forms of racism surrounding the mascot and logos have diminished, the covert forms persist with the continued use of the Chippewa name by CMU. Still, the transformations from covert to overt are informative. Recall that the mascot was first adopted for the purpose of pageantry and only later acquired ferocity. Recall that the mascot was dropped in 1972. Yet, in 1988 the 'Torturer' was talking about scalping wrestling opponents.

"As recently as March 1998, alumni were arguing that their

contesting of mascots and logos was 'playing the "race card" in reverse.' Recall the elimination of the logos in favor of using the name only and the resistance to that on campus. The transformations were not smooth. Now they claim to be honoring Chippewa people, though Ojibwes seldom call themselves Chippewas" (van Benschoten 1998).

"Is the tribe really honored? While it is difficult to see how that could be so, there does appear to be a relationship between the Saginaw Chippewa Tribe and CMU. Certainly there is advertising for the Soaring Eagle Casino for fans to notice at sporting events. The problem is that although the earlier tribal council resolution lends support without any pretension of speaking on behalf of other bands of Chippewas, the university and the general public have since interpreted the Saginaw Chippewa voice to speak for all Chippewas."

Wennebojo went on, "Two former directors of Native American Programs at CMU made it clear that the Saginaw Chippewa Tribe does not speak for all Chippewas and certainly not for all Native American Indians. When he was director of the Native American Programs, Martin Reinhardt suggested that the name used by CMU should be 'Saginaw Chippewa' instead of the Chippewa name in general. A member of the Sault Sainte Marie Chippewas, he was highly offended by the continued use of the Chippewa name by CMU" (Reinhardt 1998).

"Where does that leave things?" asked Makwa.

Wennebojo responded, "It is going to be a difficult task to end what the general public sees as a softer and gentler form of racism. Every time we expose racism, the university does not just rewrite the rules — they reinvent what an Indian is and claim they are honoring us. We are not supposed to feel offended. We should be proud.

"The Saginaw Chippewas have apparently decided to support the continued use of the Chippewa name. It is unlikely that other tribal councils are going to openly speak out against that action. The silence of other tribal councils should not be interpreted to mean concurrence or agreement with the resolution passed by the Saginaw Chippewa Tribal Council," Wennebojo cautioned. "Perhaps if we got a grant and started up a wood products company we could have an impact."

Makwa was all confused. "A wood products company, what does that have to do with mascots and logos?" he asked.

Wennebojo responded, "They don't understand how they invent us. We can teach them by reinventing them." Makwa was still confused, but Wennebojo continued, "We can manufacture crucifixes."

"What!" exclaimed Makwa.

"We can make wooden crucifixes that slide open when pulled on both ends, and popcorn springs out sort of like a jack-in-the-box," said Wennebojo.

"You're kidding," insisted Makwa.

"No. I am serious," snapped Wennebojo. "When John Bailey debated the vice president of university of relations over the mascot-logo issue, he brought up that same example. Many non-Indian students were offended. When asked how he could be so insulting, John responded that he was 'honoring' their savior. Some of the students actually understood for the first time. It took others longer to comprehend his point. Some never did get it. I suspect that the use of the Chippewa name by CMU will continue at least until the current president resigns. He has locked reason out of the university," concluded Wennebojo.

"So where are you headed now, Wennebojo?" asked Makwa.

"Oh, I'm going go find some grant applications for you to fill out," he said with a grin as he got into his "rez-rod" and drove away.

REFERENCES

Bobo, Lawrence, et al. 1997. "Laissez-Faire Racism: The Crystalization of a Kinder, Gentler, Antiblack Ideology." In *Racial Attitudes in the 1990s:*

Continuity and Change, ed. Steven A. Tuch and Jack K. Martin. West-port CT: Praeger, 1997.

CMU. 1990. Symbol Advisory Committee Final Report. August 24.

———. 1992a. Central Michigan University Advisory Committee to Ex-amine the Use of the "Chippewa" as a University Symbol. Committee membership list. March.

———. 1992b. Central Michigan University Report of the Advisory Com-mittee to Examine the Use of the Chippewas as the University Sym-bol. 29 May.

Dysinger, Fran, 1989. Memorandum (concerning CMU trademark for lo-gos) from Office of the University Counsel to various directors and media services. 28 March.

Goldsmith, Rae. 1989. Memorandum from Director of Media Relations at CMU to News Director, WBKB-TV, concerning the elimination of ear-lier logos being used by WBKB TV. 17 November.

Gonzales, Laura, and Robert Newby. 1991. Memorandum to President Edward B. Jakubauskas concerning the use of "Chippewas" as the University nickname. 10 May.

Hatch, Roger D. 1989. Memorandum from former advisory commit-tee member to Vice President James Hill concerning continued pres-ence of pictorial representations of Native Americans as CMU sym-bols. 20 October.

Hill, James. 1992. Memorandum from Vice President Tom R. Jones, Cam-pus Recreation Center, regarding renaming of Student Activity Cen-ter. 12 October.

Jakubauskas, E. B. 1991. Memorandum to Affirmative Action Council concerning use of Chippewa name. 17 May.

Littlefield, Alice. 1999. Electronic mail to Richard C. Eckert providing up-date on events at Central Michigan University concerning the use of the Chippewa name. 3 March.

Michigan Civil Rights Commission (MCRC). 1988. Michigan Civil Rights Commission Report on Use of Nicknames, Logos and Mascots Depicting Native American People in Michigan Education Institutions. October.

Montagu, Ashley, ed. 1969. *The Concept of Race.* London: Collier.

NEWSLETTER CMU. 1989. "CMU to Retain Chippewa Name for Three Year Trial Period." 20 March.

Plachta, Leonard. 1992. "President Discusses Reason for Retaining Chippewa Name." *Central Line*, 28 September 1992. Text of President Leonard Plachta's statement on the Chippewa name, 17 September 1992.

Rabineau, Kevin. 1989. Memorandum to Vice President James Hill concerning Wellness Center logo. 16 October.

Reinhardt, Martin. 1998. Memorandum to Affirmative Action Officer concerning the Central Michigan use of the Chippewa name. 7 July.

Saginaw Chippewa Indian Tribe of Michigan. 1988. Resolution 89–007. 7 November.

Sherwood, Doris. 1990. Handwritten note from Mt. Pleasant Realty Inc. to Vice President Jim Hill. Postmarked April 2.

Simmons, Lois D. 1999. "Not All Native Americans Agree with Teters." *University Record* 54 (15 February): 21.

Sowmick, Joseph V. 1998. Editorial. *Central Michigan Life* 79 (4 May).

University of Wisconsin Athletic Board. 1993. "Policy of Native American Logos and Names." Copy of 1993 policy forwarded by electronic mail to Richard C. Eckert, 6 November 1998.

van Benschoten, Rich. 1998. Editorial. *Central Michigan Life* 79 (30 March).

Wishaw, Liz. 1998. "Badgers Shutting Out CMU over Chippewa Nickname." *Central Michigan Life* 79 (17 June): 1.

CHAPTER 4

Sockalexis and the Making of the Myth at the Core of Cleveland's "Indian" Image

•

Ellen J. Staurowsky

Since the reported genesis of the "Indians" name in 1915, Cleveland baseball has become synonymous with culturally appropriated symbols of American Indians. The rate of proliferation of this imagery has increased exponentially as the explosion of media technologies and the creativity of enterprising entrepreneurs have combined to generate consumer enthusiasm for Cleveland memorabilia that regularly places the franchise within the top tier of professional baseball organizations in merchandise sales (King 1994; McNichol 1997; Rosewater 1993). Indicative of the infusion of this imagery into mass consumer culture, the Ohio State Legislature passed a bill into law in December of 1998 that provides for the reproduction of professional sport team logos on motor vehicle license plates ("Professional" 1998). With the passage of this bill, mascot Chief Wahoo can now be bolted onto cars as well as displayed on hundreds of other products as divergent as ice cream, cookies, greeting cards, and children's clothing.

The thirty-year window of time within which the club's economic fate and popular appeal have become ever more inextricably tied to their public "Indian" persona has also been marked by persistent opposition from numerous American Indian groups, along with select members of the media and church groups. Protests launched both in the courts and on the streets have represented attempts to convey the offensiveness of the imagery and its problematic racialized meanings (Banks 1993; Committee 1998b; Means 1995; philncleve 1995; Shepard 1993).

Resistance to the imagery, although generating some understanding at times, has been met more frequently with varying levels of hostility. Those who question the franchise's appropriation of American Indian imagery for racial and ethnic reasons have consistently inspired negative reactions and discouraging treatment. Russell Means, a prominent leader in the American Indian Movement who started his career as an activist in the city of Cleveland, received hate mail when he initiated a lawsuit against the franchise in 1972 alleging libel, slander, and defamation. As Means (1995:155) wrote in his autobiography *Where White Men Fear to Tread*, "That is the only time that has happened during my career as an activist."

In addition to public derision from passersby at staged protests, American Indians opposed to Chief Wahoo and the franchise's Indian imagery have been the targets of attempted censorship, police arrest and detainment, and court action. In December of 1996, a work of public art created by Hachivi Edgar Heap of Birds prompted the Cleveland Institute of Art to consider banning it despite the fact that the piece had been commissioned for an exhibit. The controversial artwork, which some members of the institute's board of directors described as "offensive," was a 25-by-12-foot billboard that featured the phrase "Smile for Racism" next to a portrait resembling Chief Wahoo (Litt 1996a, 1996b, 1997).

Since 1995, the Gateway Economic Development Corporation of Greater Cleveland, the city of Cleveland, and the franchise itself have taken action to prevent demonstrations at Jacobs Field, the home of the ball club. An injunction issued in September of 1995 by Judge John M. Manos of the United States District Court was necessary to protect the rights of protesters to demonstrate in public areas. The provisions in the injunction, however, substantially constrain the activities of demonstrators by restricting protests to two specific locations and limiting the number of protesters to no more than thirty to forty, depending on location. Further, the terms of the injunction stipulate that demonstration planners must provide seven days written notice to Gateway and limit the number of protests to a maximum of four within each month of the baseball season (*Helphrey v. Gateway*; Rollenhagen 1995a, 1995b; "Wahoo" 1995).

Notably, satisfactory compliance with the conditions outlined in the injunction has failed to protect American Indians from being arrested and brought to trial. A total of five individuals were detained or arrested in the fall of 1997 during the American League pennant race and the World Series ("American" 1998; "Cleveland" 1998). On opening day in 1998, four American Indians and one African American were arrested and taken to jail before being released (Scholtz 1998; personal observation and field notes, 10 April 1998).

The kinds of protests that have been orchestrated in response to the actions of the Cleveland baseball franchise are consistent with those occurring throughout the country as part of a larger movement of resistance to athletic team names, logos, mascots, and signifiers (Staurowsky 1999). Despite this record of resistance by American Indians and their supporters, the vast majority of the American public remains largely ambivalent, confused, or hostile to the notion that there are racial implications connected with the imagery so seamlessly interwoven into the fabric of sport entities such as the Cleveland organization. In a study of attitudes about renaming the Washington Redskins organization, Sigelman (1998:317) found that in a time when there is thought to be greater awareness about racial issues, even among groups more inclined to be supportive of the need for social change on racialized issues (racial and ethnic minorities, the more highly educated, and nonfans), their support for changing the Redskins name was "far outweighed by opposition."

The substance of this essay emanates from the dissonance between perspectives of the group of American Indians who regard this imagery as one more offense in a storied history of white offensiveness and insensitivity and the generalized impression that these images are either the reflection of good intentions or are harmless. In studying the club and how it communicates messages about the imagery, we see that this struggle for American Indian legitimacy within the overall confines of this discussion has its roots in the franchise's ability to position itself as an authority that has justifiable and defensible reasons for its appropriation of American Indian imagery through the assertion that the club is named in honor of a Penobscot Indian named Louis Francis Sockalexis.

METHODOLOGY AND THEORETICAL FRAMEWORK

Data analyzed for this project included the franchise's account of how it acquired the name as represented in media guides, team yearbooks, and a publication called *The 1997 Indians Game Face Magazine*, along with renderings and antecedents of the story as they appeared in newspaper articles, discussions on the Internet, and baseball histories published from 1897 to 1997. The story of Louis Francis Sockalexis, as told by the franchise, began in 1897 when Sockalexis signed with the Cleveland Spiders (a National League team) and continues through the present.

The historical claim that Sockalexis originally served as, and remains today, the sole inspiration for Cleveland's "Indian" identity provides access in the present to a past that conceivably might well have been lost otherwise. As a story rooted in the past, it illustrates how the past becomes known. As noted historian David Lowenthal (1995) explains, we access the past through stories told and retold, traditions passed from one generation to the next, and through people and things remembered.

The process described by Lowenthal pervades the club's litera-

ture. According to the organization, the "Indians" name is purportedly intended to introduce fans to the legendary Sockalexis and to
then perpetuate his memory through the reproduction of the story
in the organization's official publications. The club's Indian identity
has become an integral part of the city's identity, forming a shared
tradition around which Clevelanders rally. This fusion of team and
community identity is overpoweringly revealed on opening day in
Cleveland, when people throughout the city literally wear their
loyalties on their sleeves (personal observation and field notes, 10
and 12 April 1999). The question of whether baseball fans and loyal
Clevelanders attach significance and meaning to Sockalexis, however, is one not easily answered.

The Cleveland claim regarding Sockalexis and the source of its
identity illuminates the complexities and difficulties associated
with retrieving the past. As when viewing old scrapbooks with pages
missing, blurred photos, and faded letters, the past is retrieved in
partial and imperfect form. The accounts and reconstructions that
result from the retrieval process are made more imperfect by the limitations of the retrievers themselves (Carnes 1995). Consequently,
the past is a place that can be uncovered, discovered, and recovered
through history and memory, but it is also "in large measure a part
of our own creation, moulded by selective erosion, oblivion and invention" (Lowenthal 1995: inside front cover).

Baseball historian David Voigt cautioned those who wish to ex-
cavate and exhume the past that they must be prepared to deal with
the myths that are a part of a society's folklore. In describing the various functions of myths, he observed that a myth could be "a dramatic story that justifies a popular institution or custom, that seeks
to explain a given practice or value, that articulates a people's
wishful thinking, or that justifies present behavior in terms of what
supposedly happened in the past" (Voigt 1978:94). Myths can be
thought of as a people's world view that rationalizes reality. Until

such time as a myth can no longer inspire faith or trust, it will serve to sustain the existing social order. In turn, as we question myths, the social order itself is then up for question. Recognizing the existence of myth in history allows for a critical distinction to be made. It allows for a consideration of the difference between a story that is "passed on" from one generation to the next and a story that is "passed off" from one generation to the next. An awareness that a historical claim may be nothing more than a tall tale has the potential to alter the behavior of people because "people *act* on the basis of what they believe to be true, not on what they think is fiction" (Hallowell quoted in Bascom 1954:333).

The analytical framework used in the reading and interpretation of the data took into account the possibility that the history as presented in the Cleveland story may have contained an element of invention or distortion or may have experienced erosion as a result of retelling it over time. Further, the claim made by the franchise was evaluated with regard to how closely it aligned with factual details for the purposes of determining where it fell on a continuum between a "true story" and a work of "fiction." Since truth is a social construction that depends in part on one's vantage point, consideration was given to the different vantage points revealed when the story is examined from the perspective of the tellers (the franchise), the believers (the fans and media), and the disbelievers (protesters).

HISTORY FROM WHOSE VANTAGE POINT?

The bulk of sports history has been conveyed to the public through the sports sections of newspapers, with accounts written by sportswriters who did not always place the highest premium on accurate reporting. About the state of sports writing in the late 1930s through the early 1950s, journalism researcher Charles Fountain (1993:257) observed that sportswriters perpetrated what he called "mayhem on American newspaper readers" by producing writing that was "so dense as to be opaque" while it "missed reality by as wide a margin as Runyon-inspired fiction." Whether factually based or the result of imaginative and inventive minds, historical claims form the substance of much of what people believe about their favorite sports and sports heroes (Fountain 1993; Voigt 1978; Wenner 1993).

In the team's press release about the origins of the name and logo, Cleveland shows an awareness of the political cache to be gained from a historical claim. The writers of the press release point out to the readers "that there is historical significance to how the Cleveland baseball franchise became the 'Indians'" ("Name/Logo" 1995).

Whereas the Cleveland team assumes a role very similar to the one Michael Kammen (1991) defines for historians, wherein those who represent history become the "ordained custodians of memory," the controversy surrounding the images themselves raises a question about the historical vantage point from which the Cleveland organization departs and how well Cleveland is executing their custodial responsibilities. Kammen (184–88) notes, for example, that a recurring theme in major episodes in the history of white-Indian relations was the suppression of the truth by whites, "sometimes deliberately and sometimes by apparent inadvertence."

A recognition of the history of white-Indian relations recommends that other vantage points be considered in addition to the one presented by the franchise. Edgar Heap of Birds (1992) urged that the world needed to be examined using a variety of perspectives, not simply the lens of Euro-American male-centered experience, because of the potential to create a paragon of distortion.

The limitations of a Eurocentric world view are brought home as well in the observations of M. Annette Jaimes (1992:1), who writes that messages, in the form of language, literature, symbols, and stereotypes, when "crafted by a dominating culture can be an insidious political force, disinforming people." Similarly, both Pewewardy

(1991) and Hirschfelder (1989) document the role of stereotypes in preventing an authentic understanding of American Indian history and experience and the detrimental impact this kind of stereotyping has had on all children, especially American Indian children.

In her examination of resistance to the elimination of Native American imagery in sport, sociologist Laurel Davis (1993) introduces a parallel consideration. She departs from the observation that the foundation for national and personal identity for many people in the United States is based on a distorted belief that the West was won through the heroic and glorious efforts of men whose ancestry was primarily Euro-American. She asserts that this European- and male-centered perspective hinges on the tendency to think of Native Americans in stereotypical ways. In sport, the stereotype of the revered or feared, although summarily defeated, Indian warrior is a dominant one.

In the book *Fantasies of the Master Race*, Ward Churchill (1992 : 1) addresses the power of stereotypes in perpetuating the genocide of American Indians, stating "The stereotypes assume a documented 'authenticity' in the public consciousness. . . . For stereotyped and stereotyper alike, it becomes dehumanizing and a tool to justify murder under the guise of aesthetic freedom."

In a related argument, historian Laurence Hauptman (1995) points out that the history of the United States most familiar to Americans perpetually represents Indians as obstacles to progress rather than as a complex and diversified group of people who occupied the land ultimately seized under the doctrine of Manifest Destiny. In Hauptman's estimation, "False images of the 'Indian,' whether demeaning or not, are usually simplistic and generally classify the great diversity of Native America into a single entity, obscuring the textures as well as the complexities of the past or present, whether because of convenience, economics, or other reasons" (81).

CLEVELAND'S "INDIANNESS" IN CONTEXT

The dependence of the franchise on a historical context to lend credibility to their story is evidenced in a press release distributed for the purposes of explaining the origin of the name; it reveals that "Any discussion specific to the Cleveland Indians . . . must begin with a history lesson" ("Name/Logo" 1995). History lessons, however, can convey vastly different meanings and understandings, depending on the way in which they are framed and posited.

In presenting its case, the Cleveland franchise uses a basic question and answer format. The question—what is the origin of the nickname? The answer—the name was selected in 1915 to honor Louis Francis Sockalexis. By framing the story in this way, the franchise projects a definitive answer embedded in a story that cannot be told by others and whose origins are quintessentially the intellectual property of the franchise rather than a shared intellectual property that has multiple owners including Louis Francis Sockalexis and American Indians (Staurowsky 1998).

Despite the Cleveland team's efforts to attribute the event of its naming to a single causative factor, the naming of the franchise in 1915 occurred within the context of what was going on in America in the late nineteenth and early twentieth centuries. When viewed from that perspective, it becomes clear that the team was one among many corporate entities that appropriated Native imagery for the purposes of signifying their products. By understanding this broader context, insight can be gained about the circumstances that produced the imagery, what the imagery meant at the time, and subsequent implications for the continued appropriation of the imagery today.

Cleveland's image is one among a vast collection of Blackhawks, Braves, Chiefs, Chieftains, Moccasins, Mohawks, Redmen, Redskins, Savages, Seminoles, and Warriors that populates not only the American sport scene but the American consumer culture in general

(Staurowsky 1996, 1998). About this collection of symbols, American Indian activist Dennis Banks (1997) observed in addressing a rally, "When I first landed in Cincinnati, I thought there weren't any Indians living here. But since noon, I have seen a Cherokee, Navajo, Winnebago, Dakota, Mohawk and a Comanche—And those were just the RV's, trucks, cars and small aircraft!"

As a genre of commodified symbols, Native American sport images are part of a much larger group of product signifiers that emerged during the late nineteenth century to inspire product loyalty and brand recognition in America's newly forming mass consumer culture (Steele 1996). As a characteristic of the era, images of barbarism and conquest in advertising served as an implied affirmation of the civilized status of consumers. Trademarks featuring aboriginal groups colonized by U.S. imperial expansion such as Filipinos, Hawaiians, and Inuits along with African Americans and Indian peoples were infused into the burgeoning American capitalist consumer culture. As a result, material goods became a screen onto which were writ large the signs of otherness that elevated progress over primitivism and civilization over savagery (Coombe 1996).

The location of the moment when images of Native Americans became intertwined with consumer capitalism promoted through the mass media (i.e., the late 1890s) is essential to an understanding of the cultural baggage those images invariably carry with them and pass on from one generation to the next. As early as the 1880s, Moses (1996:4) observes that "most Americans encountered Indians, if at all, as carved statues that adorned shop entrances or as heads in profile impressed on coins."

The social context out of which these images emerge was one in which confusion existed relative to whether American Indians were, in fact, human beings or a lower form of animal, as heard in the common expression of the day: "No Dogs. No Indians" (Leiby 1994; Pewewardy 1991). In 1879, in the civil rights case of *Standing*

Bear v. Crook, Judge Dundy ruled that an Indian was a "person" who had the same rights as anyone from the white race to decline or consent to being transported to areas of the country other than his or her home (Brown 1991). Apart from the immediate impact this decision held for Standing Bear and his people, the Poncas, the case was virtually forgotten as the displacement and relocation of American Indians against their will continued to occur throughout the United States for decades after the 1879 ruling. It is notable that *Standing Bear v. Crook* is only one of several cases from the 1800s where the essential question being disputed was whether American Indians were, in fact, human beings (Lawrence Baca, senior trial attorney, U.S. Department of Justice, personal communication, 10 May 1999).

Ultimately, the connections to westward expansion and the conquering of a continent that form the basis of this imagery reduced Native American experience to that of the idealized fighting warrior on horseback. Through exhibitions at world's fairs and Wild West shows between 1883 and 1933, that image became solidified in the American mind (Moses 1996). Over the span of a century, incarnations of this image reappear in the film genre known as the Western, in product trademarks, and in the use of Native Americans in sport imagery (Bird 1996; Bordewich 1996; Churchill 1992; Coombe 1996; Deloria 1998; Pewewardy 1991).

According to Taussig (1993), the selective cultural amnesia, denial, or ignorance evidenced by many people in the United States regarding the context out of which Native American imagery emerged may be accounted for, in part, by what is called the "mimetic," or imitative, faculty of late-nineteenth-century trademarks. Through a combined process of imitation, contact, and ownership, the commercialized symbols of Native American experience serve as a means of undermining the oppressed group because the symbols become owned and overtaken by the dominant group.

In the case of Native American imagery, the influence of the dominant perspective is seen consistently in marketing and advertising preferences for feathered, war-painted, fighting sport images. The result of mass production and consumption of such images is the creation of distance between the "real" Indian and a manufactured replica of an Indian stereotype. As this cycle of corporate production and mass consumption is repeated, the replica, already degenerative in and of itself, serves to undermine the very people it purports to represent (Staurowsky 1998). The end result is the communication of a value system so thoroughly grounded in a Eurocentric perspective that "even Indian children want to be cowboys" (Jaimes 1992 : 4), or they get the impression that "there aren't any real Indians left" (Bird 1996 : 11).

The mimetic faculty described by Taussig can be found rather easily in sport. From the donning of headdresses, wearing of "war paint," singing of "war chants," and chopping of tomahawks, sports fans regularly engage in an array of imitative, contact, and ownership behaviors (Leiby 1994; Pewewardy 1991; Rosenstein 1997; Specktor 1993). The end result is the systematic and systemic distortion and destruction of deeply significant and spiritual symbols and their associated meanings. As a consequence, things sacred to Indians—such as dancing, the wearing of eagle feathers, and religious chanting—take on a racialized, ethnocentric value structure that codes these behaviors as fun, harmless, and appropriate for fans to engage in en masse at the ball park (Banks 1997; Pewewardy 1991; Rosenstein 1997). Permission is given for the dominant group to determine when traditions and symbols deserve reverence and when those traditions and symbols can be reduced to the quaint and obscure practices of a dead or forgotten people.

Writer Fergus Bordewich (1996) refers to the wholesale transmission of Native American imagery through advertising, media coverage, merchandising, and language as cultural saturation. In an observation about the American public's general lack of awareness or

93

sensitivity to matters pertaining to Native Americans, he noted that "it is almost as if a culture that is literally saturated with allusions to fictional Indians had no interest in living Indians at all" (17). One of the challenges at hand in the examination of the Louis Francis Sockalexis story is to wade through the cultural saturation, which typically produces a surface history, in search of what Rosemary Coombe (1996) described as invisible and unheard referents at the center of the story.

SURFACE HISTORY VERSUS INVISIBLE HISTORY

On the surface, the official story as to how the franchise came to be known as the "Cleveland Indians" begins in 1914. At that time, the team was named the "Naps" after legendary second baseman Napoleon Lajoie. Following a disappointing season at both the gate and in the standings, Lajoie was traded to Philadelphia (Edwards 1915a, 1915b; Evans 1915). With the release of Lajoie, the need arose to rename the franchise (Lewis 1949).

According to a Cleveland Indians press release in which the origin of the name is explained, a claim is made that officials from the club in 1914 contacted a local newspaper to sponsor a naming contest. "The winning selection was the name the 'Indians—in honor of Louis Francis Sockalexis, a Penobscot from Old Town, Maine" ("Name/Logo" 1995). In *The 1999 Cleveland Indians Media Guide*, the unidentified fan believed to have submitted the winning entry is reported to have "explained that it would be a testament to the game's first American Indian" (297).

A critical analysis of the story as produced and distributed by the Cleveland franchise via press releases, media guides, and yearbook entries reveals some informational and contextual gaps that warrant attention. For example, given Cleveland's turbulent newspaper history during that period of time, why is the name of the sponsoring newspaper not mentioned? In a similar vein, at a time when the club was struggling to promote its fan base, why would officials of the team turn to one local newspaper to run a contest rather than involve the three other newspapers in the city? Further, given baseball's pronounced attention to details, statistics, and names, why is there no information about the fan who had been so enamored with Sockalexis that he was remembered fifteen years after finishing a very brief playing career in the major leagues that had been fraught with controversy and misfortune (Staurowsky 1998)?

In order to more fully understand the complexity of the problems associated with this story, consider the claim in light of the time period in which the events are supposed to have occurred. As researcher James Watson (1997) points out, the year 1915 was a scant twenty-five years after the traumatizing and polarizing massacre at Wounded Knee and only six years after Geronimo died as a political prisoner held captive by the United States in Fort Sill, Oklahoma. In effect, at a time when the U.S. government persisted in the implementation of policies designed to strip Native Americans of their culture and their freedom rather than celebrate it, what would be the likelihood that Sockalexis would have been singled out as deserving of honor because of his ethnic heritage and status as one of the first American Indians to play professional baseball?

In an attempt to explore these questions more fully, the sport sections from the *Cleveland Leader*, the *Cleveland News*, the *Cleveland Plain Dealer*, and the *Cleveland Press* from September 1914 through March 1915 were reviewed. Taken as a whole, the account of the renaming of the franchise represented in the articles from that time period differs substantially on several key points from the one presented by the Cleveland organization today. As the professional baseball community readied itself for the upcoming season in January of 1915, the sportswriters in Cleveland were taking note of the departure of the well-liked and much-admired Napoleon Lajoie.

They were also recognizing the necessity for the team to be renamed as a result of Lajoie's leaving town.

On January 6, reports that club president C. W. (Charley) Somers wished to convene a conference of baseball writers for the purpose of selecting a new name appeared in the *Cleveland Plain Dealer* and the *Cleveland Press*. The selection committee was referred to by the informal title of the "nomenclature committee" by a *Plain Dealer* columnist with the pen name of "The Second Cook" (1915). Reports indicated that the committee would meet approximately a week after Somers's announcement and that a name would be selected at that time.

In the days preceding the scheduled meeting, lively banter regarding the renaming of the franchise appeared in the papers. The erroneous notion that the renaming of the franchise was the direct result of a contest may derive from the headline in the *Cleveland Press* that reads, "Fans Will Help Select New Nickname for Naps" (1915). In a solicitation of suggestions from readers to help rename the "Napless-Naps," the *Press* sports editor explained that "Nicknames suggested will be submitted to the committee." Based on reports printed in the *Press* following that invitation, it appears that fans submitted fifty-seven recommendations ("57 Varieties of Names for Naps" 1915).

It is difficult to ascertain from the accounts presented whether there is any link between the suggestions generated through the *Press* solicitation and the eventual selection of the name, although it appears that such a link is improbable. Whereas the contention made by the Cleveland franchise that a fan desired to honor Louis Francis Sockalexis by recommending "Indians" is not impossible, there is a lack of evidentiary foundation in the articles chronicling writer and fan preferences to support such a contention.

In three stories from the *Press* reporting on the results of the fan solicitation, "Indians" does not appear ("Fan Offers" 1915; "Favors"

1915; "57 Varieties" 1915). Consistent with that finding, an early prediction published in the *Cleveland Leader* the morning before the meeting was to take place noted that "the name 'Cleveland Grays' meets with the approval of the club officials and also with the majority of fans who have been asked to voice their opinion on the name" (Swan 1915).

On Sunday, January 17, the *Plain Dealer* ran a large cartoon featuring characters in stereotypical Indian attire, including buckskins, headdresses and feathers, war paint, and moccasins, along with the caption "Ki Yi Waugh Woop! Their Indians!" (Blosser 1915b). Positioned directly below the cartoon is a short account of the outcome of the baseball writers meeting. It noted that "The title of Indians was their [baseball writers'] choice, it having been one of the names applied to the old National League club of Cleveland years ago."

Three aspects of the reporting of the announcement about the new nickname are salient. First, Sockalexis is not mentioned in the notice about the new name. Second, within the *Plain Dealer* announcement, an observation is made that "The nickname, however, is but temporarily bestowed, as the club may so conduct itself during the present season as to earn some other cognomen which may be more appropriate" ("Baseball" 1915). A similar statement had been made in the *Plain Dealer* of January 16, 1915 (p. 13), where it was mentioned that "It is quite possible that merely a temporary name be selected and that the club itself be forced to go out and make its own nickname." These statements do not provide support for the idea that the name was intended to permanently pertain to the team nor to permanently honor Louis Francis Sockalexis. If Sockalexis's name had been discussed at the time the selection took place, it was not deemed worthy of mention within the announcement itself.

Third, there is a palpable shift in the literary energy the writers employ in describing the new nickname that plays off of familiar,

97

stereotypical conceptions about American Indians. Although the *Leader* stories were more modest in form when compared to their competitors' stories at the *Plain Dealer*, the *Leader* nevertheless chose to mark the occasion of the franchise renaming using cartoons as well. In the name announcement in the *Leader*, an "Indian" ballplayer dashes across the column outfitted in headdress and buckskins. With tomahawk in one hand and bat in the other, the "Indian" pursues four white ballplayers from other teams. Within the body of the piece, author Charles W. Swan enthusiastically writes that with the new nickname, "we'll have the Indians on the warpath all the time and eager for scalps to dangle at their belts" ("Indians Replace" 1915).

This substantive shift in the way the ball club is covered, wherein the sleepy prose inspired by the Naps is replaced with both visual and text references to Indian stereotypes, is seen throughout the Cleveland papers in the ensuing days and weeks as the team prepares for spring training. On February 20, 1915, a quarter of the sports page is taken up with a wide-nosed, dark-skinned caricature of a generic Indian with pigtails and a feather. Contained within a grin that literally reaches from ear to ear are the words "Spring Training" (Blosser 1915c). A week later, a team of Indians wrapped in blankets lounges around the train depot watching their "Chief," team manager Birmingham, dance (Blosser 1915a).

The record of the renaming that is found in the sport sections of the day may provide a more logical explanation for why the name was picked than the one posited by the club. Clearly, the new nickname relieved sportswriters of the burden of writing about a lackluster team with a lethargic name. The new nickname presented an opportunity for both the owners and the sportswriters to overhaul the image of the team, using the kind of literary drama and excitement made possible by the "Indians" signifier.

It is notable that in 1897, when Sockalexis was signed by the

Cleveland Spiders, a similar phenomenon occurred in media coverage. Immediately upon the signing of their resident "Indian,"
sportswriters began to make reference to the "Indian's team." This
very quickly was collapsed to the "Indians." Similarly, the literary
devices, metaphors, and cartoons used by the baseball writers in
1915 are identical to those found in 1897 (Staurowsky 1998).

DISCUSSION

As a corporate entity that has asserted a "historical claim," the
Cleveland baseball franchise has used its power of position and
place in the community to persuade the public that the team's appropriation of American Indian imagery is a noble gesture to honor
a noble man. This subtlety is demonstrated in *The 1999 Cleveland Indians Media Guide* in which it is noted that "The memory of Louis
Francis Sockalexis was not forgotten [in 1915]" and "he is still remembered" today (297). The implication, of course, is that he is
remembered because of the efforts of the franchise.

The story loses power, however, when understood as a construction built around either the intentional or unintentional cultiva-
tion of misconceptions, distortions of fact, or misinterpretations.
Those who find Chief Wahoo racist and the use of American Indian
imagery by the franchise offensive see through the mythology upon
which the franchise attempts to legitimate its claim regarding Sockalexis. For protesters, the disbelievers, the telltale signs of the disin-
genuousness of the franchise's motives or the mistake it has made
can be found in the actions of the franchise itself.

The very notion that the Cleveland organization honors Louis
Francis Sockalexis begs to be critically examined. There is a tradition
in baseball, and in our society in general, that when a person is to
be honored through a naming process, the name of that person
appears prominently in association with the identified venue. A
well-known example of this practice is the existence of Babe Ruth

Leagues. Although Cleveland says it honors Louis Francis Sockalexis, his form and name appear infrequently and usually in re-
mote locations at the ball park and in team publications.

A contrast with other occasions when the franchise has sought to
immortalize individuals is helpful in establishing this point. At the
entrance to the stadium, fans are greeted with a statue of revered
pitcher Bob Feller. The stadium itself is named in recognition of Richard Jacobs, the owner of the club. It is noticeable that in both of these
instances, the images used to convey the status and stature of these
individuals connect directly with the individuals they honor. The
statue of Bob Feller is not a caricature; it is a fully embodied portrayal of Feller at the height of his prowess as a ball player. Similarly,
Richard Jacobs's name is always represented in a respectful manner
and always in direct relationship to his position. Given the contention that Louis Francis Sockalexis serves as the only reason for the
franchise's Indian identity, one might wonder why his memory has
not afforded the same kind of respectful treatment if he is genuinely
such an important part of the franchise. Why is Chief Wahoo, a signifier whom longtime Cleveland baseball writer Terry Pluto (1994:
254) describes as a figure who "looks as if he sold his soul for a six-
pack, reinforcing all the old stereotypes," perceived to be a suitable
and appropriate way to honor such an esteemed and highly re-
garded personage in Cleveland baseball tradition who deserves neither to be referred to by name nor represented as a human being?

This evidence of the franchise's suspect commitment to Indians
is seen at several levels. The year 1997 marked the one hundredth
anniversary of Sockalexis playing in the majors. However, despite
the fact that the national spotlight shown brightly on Cleveland in
1997 because of its hosting of the All-Star Game, record-setting attendance, and appearance in the World Series, comparative silence
reigned on this point. Symbolically, this silence was made more profound by the fact that 1997 was also the year when Major League

Baseball was celebrating the fiftieth anniversary of signing Jackie Robinson and the "breaking of the color barrier." Additionally, the three-year record of arrests of American Indians who protest at Jacobs Field, a time frame that coincided with the celebrations that took place in 1997, speaks volumes about the franchise's unwillingness to deal with and listen to the very people they purport to honor (American 1998; "Cleveland Judge" 1998).

As custodian of an intellectual history disseminated to the American public through mass-mediated sources and vehicles, the Cleveland franchise perpetuates a myth about their "Indian" identity that does affect what many people believe about the issue (Staurowsky 1998). The team's success in persuading the public that its motives are pure and sincere because they honor Louis Francis Sockalexis offers many fans, and even some American Indians, permission to believe that the imagery associated with the club is harmless and well intentioned. However, the role the Cleveland story plays in actually promoting intolerance is brought into sharper focus by considering the scene that occurred on April 10, 1998, on opening day in Cleveland. In the course of a demonstration by spectators wearing "Indian" regalia marketed presumably with the purpose of keeping the memory of Louis Francis Sockalexis alive, American Indians were targets of shouted expletives, invectives, and derogatory comments. The scene was made more poignant by the fact that April 10 was also Good Friday and the first day of Passover. The irony of the moment was entirely lost on the spectators involved and may illustrate in ways that nothing else can that the "history lesson" being taught by the franchise is nothing more than a lesson that simply replicates an old pattern of white-Indian relations in general. This revelation suggests that time is long overdue for abandoning the mythology that has sustained this world view (personal observation and field notes, 10 April 1998).

NOTE

The findings reported here have been generated from a study begun in earnest in the spring of 1997. Some portion of the data from the study has already been published in the December 1998 issue of the *Sociology of Sport Journal*. Although the source of the material emanates from the same project, the material presented here is substantially different although certainly connected to the material found in that article. Also, this manuscript started out as a paper entitled "Searching for Sockalexis: Exploring the Myth at the Core of Cleveland's 'Indian' Image," which was presented at the tenth Cooperstown Symposium on Baseball and American Culture in June of 1998. Since that time, the manuscript has been significantly revised.

REFERENCES

1997 Cleveland Indians Media Guide. Cleveland OH: Cleveland Indians.

1998 Cleveland Indians Media Guide. Cleveland OH: Cleveland Indians.

1999 Cleveland Indians Media Guide. Cleveland OH: Cleveland Indians.

"American Indian Movement." 1998. Cleveland OH: American Indian Movement.

Banks, Dennis J. 1993. "Tribal Names and Mascots in Sports." *Journal of Sport and Social Issues* 17 : 5–8.

———. 1997. "Logos and Mascots." *Walk for Justice*. <http://members.aol.com/nowacumig/logos.html> (17 March 2000).

Bascom, William R. 1954. "Four Functions of Folklore." *Journal of American Folklore* 67(266): 333–49.

"Baseball Writers Select 'Indians' as the Best Name to Apply to the Former Naps." 1915. *Cleveland Plain Dealer*, 17 Jan., part 3, 1.

Bird, S. Elizabeth, ed. 1996. *Dressing in Feathers: The Construction of the Indian in American Popular Culture*. Boulder: Westview Press.

Blosser. 1915a. "Hitting the Trail." *Cleveland Plain Dealer*, 27 Feb.

———. 1915b. "Ki Yi Waugh Woop! Their Indians." *Cleveland Plain Dealer*, 17 Jan.

———. 1915c. "A Sign of Spring." *Cleveland Plain Dealer*, 20 Feb.

Bordewich, Fergus M. 1996. *Killing the White Man's Indian: Reinventing Native Americans at the End of the Twentieth Century*. New York: Doubleday.

Brown, Dee. 1991. *Bury My Heart at Wounded Knee*. New York: Henry Holt.

Carnes, Mark, ed. 1995. *Past Imperfect: History According to the Movies*. New York: Henry Holt.

Churchill, Ward. 1992. *Fantasies of the Master Race: Literature, Cinema and the Colonization of American Indians*. Monroe ME: Common Courage Press.

Committee of 500 Years of Dignity and Resistance. 1998a. "Racism and Cleveland Baseball." Cleveland: Committee of 500 Years of Dignity and Resistance.

———. 1998b. "What the Cleveland 'Indians' Name and 'Chief Wahoo' Logo Teach Children." *Newsletter*, 1 Nov.

Coombe, Rosemary J. 1996. "Embodied Trademarks: Mimesis and Alterity on American Commercial Frontiers. *Cultural Anthropology* 11(2): 202–24.

Davis, Laurel. 1993. "Protest against the Use of Native American Mascots: A Challenge to Traditional American Identity." *Journal of Sport and Social Issues* 17 : 9–22.

Deloria, Philip. 1998. *Playing Indian*. New Haven: Yale University Press.

Edwards, Henry P. 1915a. "Birmingham Has Many Problems to Ponder Over. *Cleveland Plain Dealer*, 7 Feb.

———. 1915b. "Recruits Find It Tough Sledding in 1914 Season: Nap Lajoie Figures He Is Still a Fair Man on the Bases." *Cleveland Plain Dealer*, 11 Feb.

Evans, B. 1915. "Recent Deals May Create New Interest in Baseball." *Cleveland Plain Dealer*, 7 Feb.

"Fan Offers Scraps as Team Name." 1915. *Cleveland Press*, n.d.

"Fans Will Help Select New Nickname for Naps." 1915. *Cleveland Press*, 7 Jan., 14.

"Favors Old Nickname." 1915. *Cleveland Press*, 11 Jan., 12.

"57 Varieties of Names for Naps." 1915. *Cleveland Press*, 12 Jan. 12.

Fountain, Charles. 1993. *Sportswriter: The Life and Times of Grantland Rice*. New York: Oxford University Press.

Hauptman, Laurence. 1995. *Tribes and Tribulations: Misconceptions about American Indians and Their Histories*. Albuquerque: University of New Mexico Press.

Heap of Birds, Havichi Edgar. 1992. "In the Annals of the White Man." *http://www.favela.org/frenzy/heapbirds/birds2.html* (April 1998).

Helphrey v Gateway Economic Development Corporation of Greater Cleveland, no. 95-CV-1003.

Hirschfelder, Arlene. 1989. "The Sacred Symbolic Indian Mocks the Native American Reality." *Education and Society* 31.

Jaimes, M. Annette. 1992. "Introduction: Weapons of Genocide." In Ward Churchill, *Fantasies of the Master Race: Literature, Cinema and the Colonization of American Indians*, ed. M. Annette Jaimes. Monroe ME: Common Courage Press.

Kammen, Michael G. 1991. *Mystic Chords of Memory: The Transformation of Tradition in American Culture*. New York: Alfred A. Knopf.

King, James. 1994. "Hitting Gold: Team Souvenirs as Hot as Indians." *Cleveland Plain Dealer*, 17 June, 1A.

Leiby, Richard. 1994. "Bury My Heart at RFK: How the Redskins Got Their Name, and Why Just Maybe It Should Be Changed." *Washington Post*, Nov., F1–F4.

Lewis, Franklin. 1949. *The Cleveland Indians*. New York: G. P. Putnam's Sons.

Litt, Steven. 1996a. "Indian Artist Alleges Censorship." *Cleveland Plain Dealer*, 10 Dec., 1B, 4B.

———. 1996b. "Wahoo Billboard Receives Funding." *Cleveland Plain Dealer*, 12 Dec., 11B.

———. 1997. "Billboards Found for Anti-Wahoo Signs. *Cleveland Plain Dealer*, 30 Jan., 7B.

Lowenthal, David. 1995. *The Past Is a Foreign Country*. New York: Cambridge University Press.

McNichol, Tom. 1997. "A Major-League Insult?" *USA Weekend*, 4 July, 13.

Means, Russell. 1995. *Where White Men Fear to Tread: The Autobiography of Russell Means*. New York: St. Martin's Griffin.

Moses, Lester G. 1996. *Wild West Shows and the Images of American Indians: 1883–1933*. Albuquerque: University of New Mexico Press.

"Name/Logo Issue." 1995. Cleveland Indians, press release, 15 Nov.

Pewewardy, Cornel. 1991. "Native American Mascots and Imagery: The Struggle of Unlearning Indian Stereotypes." *Journal of Navajo Education* 9(1): 19–23.

philncleve. 1995. "Still Not the Real Indians." Posting to NATIVE-L discussion list, which is now inactive. Available at <http://nativenet.uthscsa.edu/archive/nl/9504/0264.html> (17 March 2000).

Pluto, Terry. 1994. *The Curse of Rocky Calavito*. New York: Simon and Schuster.

"Professional Sports Team License Plates." 1999. *Ohio Senate Journal*, 2219–20.

Rollenhagen, Mark. 1995a. "Gateway Indians Concur: Group Can Protest Chief Wahoo Logo. *Cleveland Plain Dealer*, 12 June, 4B.

———. 1995b. "Gateway, Protesters Agree on 2 Sites." *Cleveland Plain Dealer*, 6 May, 2B.

Rosenstein, Jay. 1997. *In Whose Honor? Indian Mascots and Nicknames in Sport*. Ho-ho-kus NJ: New Day Films. Videotape.

Rosewater, Amy. 1993. "Wahoo's Earnings Capped: All Teams Own Piece of Chief." *Cleveland Plain Dealer*, 3 July, 1F.

Scholtz, Karin. 1998. "Wahoo Protesters Burn Effigy, Are Arrested. *Cleveland Plain Dealer*, 11 April, 1B.

"Second Cook." 1915. *Cleveland Plain Dealer*, 9 Jan.

Shepard, Paul. 1993. "Indians Blame Lack of Clout for Wahoo Decision." *Cleveland Plain Dealer*, 11 July, 23.

Sigelman, Lee. 1998. "Hail to the Redskins? Public Reactions to a Racially Insensitive Team Name." *Sociology of Sport Journal* 15(4): 317–25.

Specktor, Mordecai. 1993. "Cleveland Indians: Chief Wahoo's Tribe?" *News from Indian Country*, 15 July, 3.

Staurowsky, Ellen J. 1996. "Tribal Rites." *Ithaca College Quarterly*, spring, 19–21.

———. 1998. "An Act of Honor or Exploitation: The Cleveland Indians' Use of the Louis Francis Sockalexis Story." *Sociology of Sport Journal* 15(4): 299–316.

———. 1999. "American Indian Sport Imagery and the Miseducation of Americans." Unpublished manuscript.

Steele, Jeffrey. 1996. "Reduced to Images: American Indians in Nineteenth-Century Advertising." In *Dressing in Feathers: The Construction of the Indian in American Popular Culture*, ed. S. Elizabeth Bird, pp. 211–27. Boulder: Westview Press.

Swan, C. W. 1915a. "Grays Instead of Naps: Local American League Club Is Christened with a New Nickname." *Cleveland Plain Dealer*, 16 Jan., sports section, 1.

———. 1915b. "Indians Replace Naps." *Cleveland Plain Dealer*, 17 Jan., sports section, 1.

Taussig, Michael. 1993. *Mimesis and Alterity: An Alternative History of the Senses*. New York: Routledge, Chapman and Hall.

United Church of Christ. 1998. "Cleveland Judge Throws Out Case against Anti-'Chief Wahoo' Protesters." Cleveland: United Church of Christ.

Voigt, David Q. 1978. "Myths after Baseball: Notes on Myths in Sports." *Quest* 30: 46–57.

"Wahoo Opponents Want to Protest." 1995. *Cleveland Plain Dealer*, 5 May, 4B.

Watson, James. 1997. "Substituting Myth for History: The Imaginary and Real Origins of the 'Indians' Name for the Cleveland Baseball Team." Unpublished document.

Wenner, Lawrence. 1993. "The Real Red Face of Sports." *Journal of Sport and Social Issues* 17: 1–4.

PART TWO

Whiteness

CHAPTER 5

The Fighting Braves of Michigamua

Adopting the Visage of American Indian Warriors in the Halls of Academia

•

Patrick Russell LeBeau

In 1901, a group of University of Michigan students from the engineering and literary colleges created an Indian tribe and a university club (Temple 1958). Following the historical precedent established by the Sons of Tammany and Sons of Liberty during America's revolutionary past, these heritage-conscious male students chose an appropriate Indian name, Michigamua, for their university-sanctioned tribe and club because the word had an indigenous sound and look (Baraga 1966, 1:153; Blackbird 1977:93; and Vogel 1986:1–5). It established a triple association with Michigan's Indian warriors, the state's oldest university, and the state itself. The allusion to American Indians and patriots allows simultaneous historical resonance with the romantic affection for the savage Indian and the mythic founding, conquest, and settlement of America the beautiful (Horton 1865).

However, their appropriation of an Indian warrior guise worked to negate the existence of federally recognized Indian nations and people residing within the state itself. The rights and privileges afforded the Indians of Michigan by constitutionally protected treaties with the United States government were not worthy of historical investigation by the historically conscious Michigamuas. Instead, they chose to honor their own stereotypical invention for their own patriotic display.

This essay explicates Michigamua's use of Indian warrior imagery and explores the social and moral implications of using such an association for identity and symbolic possession. The essay also chronicles the reactions and actions of Native Americans to the Michigamuas. The protests and the legal sanctions brought against the Michigamuas places their university club into a wider societal context, far beyond the claims of harmless fun and paternal respect offered by its members as defense and justification for their existence on a major U.S. university campus.

CONQUERING HEROES AND THE ONLY GOOD INDIAN

Identifying with Indian warriors offers Michigamua members a way of identifying with American history and American traditions of manhood (Deloria 1998). Indians are indigenous to the North American continent, the United States, and the state of Michigan. Identifying with Indians also creates a natural association with the American landscape. The Michigamuas honor the conquest of Indian nations, the settlement of Indian land, and the courage and perseverance needed to accomplish such an arduous task. Moreover, the founders of Michigamua understood how and why American patriots used the image of Indian warriors as a symbol of America, as a symbol of uniqueness and difference from Europeans, and as a symbol of national identity. Other men's organizations, like the Sons of Liberty, the Sons of Tammany, and the Improved Order of Redmen, preceded Michigamua. The creation of Michigamua followed this well-documented and accepted American tradition of using Indian warriors to promote patriotism and national identity: the Michigamuas merely focused their efforts at the state and university levels.

Naturally, the focus on themselves and their own identity narrows and limits their knowledge of Native Americans. Furthermore, their attention on warfare creates an illusion that Native Americans were displaced, were vanquished, and died due only to warfare. A romantic American history tells a story of honorable warfare. Indians die fighting the expansion of white Europeans, a romantic demise. Young University men can take on the guise of Indian warriors because, they believe, real Indian warriors no longer exist. They have been killed in an act of war on fields of honor, vanquished by a technologically superior and predestined foe. This illusion (and allusion) fosters two lasting impressions: the long history of how Indians lost lands, people, and human rights is simplified and glossed over; and the surviving Indian people are viewed as degenerate descendants of these warrior ideals. With Indian warriors dead and living Native Americans diminished and rendered unimportant, the Michigamuas symbolically emerge to take their place as the rightful inheritors of Michigan's Indian lands, and they become the natural "sons" of its original warrior inhabitants. Indian warrior dress, weapons, and code are not lost to a demoralized and remnant group of survivors but are picked up and donned by descendants of the conquerors. The Michigamua rituals and ceremonies act out the American historical drama in all of its complicated acts of possession and appropriation.

Therefore, the faux Indian warriors of Michigamua could emulate real Indian warriors like the great warrior Tecumseh, once Tecumseh has died and become part of America's heritage. Once dead, Tecumseh could be named the "Greatest Indian," and his likeness, which includes his warrior qualities, could be appropriated for a myriad of uses. Towns, buildings, commercial products, and even children would be named "Tecumseh." Bil Gilbert, who wrote a popular biography of Tecumseh published in 1989, remembers as a child growing up in Monroe County, Michigan, "a hill, lake, grocery store, restaurant, two roads, and a make of combustion engine which bore the name Tecumseh" (Gilbert 1989:334). Henry Thompson Seton explains Tecumseh's virtues: "No one now questions the broad statement that Tecumseh was a great athlete, a great hunter, a great leader, clean, manly, strong, unsordid, courteous, fearless, kindly, gentle with his strength, dignified, silent and friendly, equipped for emergencies, and filled with a religion that consisted not of books and creeds or occasional observances, but of a desire to help those that had need of help" (Rosenthal 1984:65). The Michigamuas follow suit, and they have embraced and appropriated these same warrior virtues and qualities attributed to historical Indian warrior Tecumseh. By joining the ranks of the Michigamuas, twenty-five men every year could become a version of Tecumseh and could become known as one of the "greatest men" to ever graduate from the University of Michigan.

On a more sinister level, the praise of and reverence for dead Indian warriors imply that living Native Americans are somehow lacking in virtue and power. An interpretation of the slogan "the only good Indian is a dead Indian" places the emphasis of "good" on the dead Indian. The dead Indian warrior is not "good" because he is dead but because he is the "ideal" Indian who, regrettably, had to be killed. He dies defending his family, his property, his moral code, and his beliefs. The Indians who are alive are not good in this respect, because they are perceived to have given up or to have run away from an honorable death in battle. The good dead warrior was never a pest that needed eradication but a staunch defender of what he believes is right; he has to be killed to achieve the goals of U.S. settlers, entrepreneurs, and politicians. Emulating an Indian warrior such as the singular Tecumseh is worthwhile because he was "great" and "we shall not look upon his like again," which suggests that living descendants of Tecumseh are not so great or worthwhile (Gilbert 1989:333).

This not so subtle comparative argument suggests living Native

Americans are not what most Americans perceive as the ideal Indian. They are relegated by this comparison to degenerate descendants of a once great and proud race of people, only to be replaced by the likes of the Michigamuas. The continuous association with dead Indians means the only Indians worth honoring or caring about are dead ones. Does this subliminally suggest all the good Indians are dead? What does that say about living Native American people today? In anybody's eyes, can contemporary flesh-and-blood Native Americans ever measure up to anything like a Tecumseh, the romantic warrior ideal?

STAKING OUT AND MARKING
MICHIGAMUA INDIAN TERRITORY

Over the years, Roping Day, a compilation of Michigamua rituals, ceremonies, and traditions, established a yearly reenactment of the conquest of America, the taking of Indian land, and the replacement of Michigan's original inhabitants with a newly ordained and sanctioned male elite ("Unidentified"). Throughout the years, they have consciously, and systematically, staked out their university territory to commemorate these reenactment and recruitment activities.

Michigamua markers existed (and still exist, albeit to lesser extent) in many locations across the University of Michigan's campus (Michigamua, Boxes 1–5). At the university recreation area, a fire pit plaque marked their traditional campgrounds. Nearby, a Michigamua totem pole, presented in commemoration of the fiftieth return of the tribe of 1907, stood to remind everyone of the lore and traditions of this special university club. A Michigamua plaque identifies Michigamua Plaza at the north end of the Michigan Union. On the University Diag, a tomahawk plaque marks the site of Roping Day. Nearby, the Tappan Oak has years of red brick dust from the initiation ceremony embedded within its old bark. (The Tappan Oak is named after the university's first president, Henry Philip Tappan, 1852–63.) The various plaques, the Tappan Oak, the red brick dust embedded in concrete walkways and the Tappan Oak itself, and the many buildings, courtyards, and athletic fields named after Michigamua alumni are the "coded signifiers" because, for many years, the Michigamuas were the only people who could recognize the significance and connection that these signs had to a ninety-eight-year university tradition and secret society.

TAPPING AND ROPING THE WILD WHITE MAN

According to the 1902 Michigamua Charter, the membership of the tribe is meant to represent only the best of the university male community: its top athletes, fraternity leaders, and other members of the literary and engineering colleges with high grade point averages (*Michigamua*, Boxes 1 and 2). To narrow the selection more, tribal membership was limited to twenty-five Fighting Braves, their name for the active group.

The official swearing in follows an officious, and physical, selection process, whereby initiates are "tapped" and told to stand by the Tappan Oak near the Graduate Library on a specified day in the month of May. Roping refers to the ceremonial tying of the initiates to the symbolic oak, followed by a ritualized hazing of the tapped individuals. For example, initiates are stripped of their clothes and painted with red brick dust. After they are given "Indian" names, they smoke the Michigamua peace pipe and listen to the words of their Michigamua elders who share the lore of the tribe ("Unidentified").

In the fall semester of 1951, Alexander "Peace Maker" Ruthven, who served as university president from 1929 to 1951, addressed the gathering of the Michigamuas at the fiftieth anniversary powwow and at the Roping Day activities with these words: "Michigan is characterized by simple intellectual honesty. You are the heart of this institution. It is your influence that has made the University of Michigan . . . not only the greatest university in the world today but, also the greatest University of All Time" ("Fiftieth Anniversary Folder," *Michigamua*, Box 3). Since the inception of Michigamua, members of the tribe pledge to graduate and go forth into the "pale-face" world as proud, loyal, healthy, and successful Americans and to become the wise Old Braves of Michigamua, the Terrible Tribe of Loyal Red Men. The Michigamua "Great Charter" also states that "the object of this tribe shall be to foster loyalty to our Alma Mater and promote good class fellowship" (*Michigamua*, Boxes 1 and 2). In a December 1944 *Tower Talk*, a sachem, or chief, writes: "Must still have um same qualifications as before in order to become young bucks. Michigamua will not lower standards despite the shortage of white males due to World War Two" (*Michigamua*, Box 4).

Qualifications for membership have always been exclusive and strict. Captains of sports teams, leaders of recognized university clubs, groups, and societies, or presidents of the university, athletic directors, and coaches were (and are) the only ones tapped or selected as Honorary Sachems. Honorary Sachems were members of the university community who were never University of Michigan undergraduates or Fighting Braves but who were honored by the Michigamuas. The honor "roped in" or connected university personnel, like university presidents or coaches of university athletic teams, to Michigamua activities and their mission to make the university great. For many years, perhaps until the mid-1960s, most all Michigamua initiates were white males. Even a white male could be kicked out, if he "not take 'um interest in Tribe. He not want 'um to be brave, now he be 'um paleface" (Michigamua, Box 4).

By the 1960s, minority men were selected as initiates, first as "top" athletes and later, in the 1990s, as recognized leaders of minority student organizations. Over the years, civil rights legislation, state laws, and university policies have created changes in Michigamua tapping selections. Minority student organizations have to be recognized as valid leadership organizations, and in the 1999 Tapping, women were included for the first time.

In the late 1980s and most of the 1990s, many Jewish, black, and Hispanic male students have been tapped and roped, and for several critical meetings with Native American students, they have been selected to represent the Michigamuas. They have had to defend exclusion and stereotypical display in exchange for the privilege and status of Michigamua membership. At a postseminar question-and-answer session held January 26, 1999, between the Michigamuas and other university students (sponsored by the Native American Student Organization, NASA), JuJuan Buford questioned a minority member of Michigamua: "How can you call yourself a person of integrity?" Buford, an African American student, could not understand how a minority could be a member of an organization that stereotyped Indians. He went on to say that Michigamua, despite its apparent diversity, is "exclusionist, racist, and detrimental." A member of Michigamua responded to a *Michigan Daily* reporter by saying, "the benefit of [Michigamua] is learning about others, because Michigamua brings together leaders of different campus groups" (*Ann Arbor, Michigan, Daily*, Jan. 27, 1999, 3). Although the Michigamuas tried to tap several Indian students to date, no Native American student has yet agreed to become a member of Michigamua. Andrew Adams, NASA president at the time, was tapped in 1995, but he refused the invitation, citing that Michigamua "exploits Native American traditions" (personal interview, 1999).

INDIGENOUS REPERCUSSIONS

As Native Americans became more a part of the university community as students, faculty, and staff, and when issues of civil rights, equality, and fair play became part of the national consciousness in the late 1960s, the Michigamuas came under attack. Spurred on by the activities of groups such as Probing-the-University (PROBE), a faculty and staff group composed mostly of women, and the Black Action Movement (BAM), Native American students started to become active in the university community themselves (Peckham 1992). In the 1960s and early 1970s, these groups were responsible for collecting and publishing information and data that indicated that the "old-boy" network was alive and well on the University of Michigan campus. Native Americans formed their own group in 1975, called the Native American Student Association. Since then, several complaints have been filed with the U.S. Department of Health, Education and Welfare (HEW) and with the Michigan Civil Rights Commission charging the university with discrimination, racism, and permitting ridicule of Native American cultures (Michigamua, Box 3).

Before Native American students (and the greater Native American community in the state of Michigan) focused their attention on the Michigamuas, they devoted their efforts to treaty rights and repatriation. On August 5, 1971, Paul J. Johnson filed a class action suit: "We the Chippewa, Ottawa, and Pottawotomi are fighting the University of Michigan for educational treaty rights they granted us in 1817, but refused to honor." In this suit, the students cited the 1817 Treaty of Fort Meigs (White 1975). In that treaty, Michigan Indians granted six sections of land that, when later sold, allowed for the establishment of the university. In the *Short History of the University of Michigan*, Wilfred B. Shaw writes that, in 1932, the Regents provided for five scholarships for Native American students in honor of this first benefaction. Michigan's Native Americans felt they deserved universal free tuition as fair compensation for the sale of their land through the Meigs Treaty and the many others that followed. In 1972, Native Americans also demanded that university-owned Native American skeletal remains be returned to Indian communities for reburial.

Eventually, the Native American students detected the presence of the Michigamuas. Despite efforts at secrecy, the Michigamuas were not hard to find; in fact, advertisements of Michigamua activities often appeared in the *Michigan Daily*. Spring initiation rituals put them out in the public eye, especially during the Roping Day Ceremony. Their annual "bar crawls," "bear feasts" at Raderick Farms, dances, "pound um" tables (parties in the Wigwam, located in the tower of the Michigan Union, after university athletic games), and public tapping created many opportunities for detection. Over the years, Native Americans have often seen drunken Michigamua braves, dressed as Indian warriors, on the streets of Ann Arbor. In the fall of 1987, I saw braves swoop down on a couple of university men, knock them down, and drag them into a waiting rental van. I had just witnessed a "tapping."

Once the Michigamuas attracted their attention, Native American students (and NASA) investigated them further. Because the Michigamuas preserved their records and many of their artifacts in the Bentley Historical Library, the official depository for the University of Michigan, Native Americans soon discovered a great deal about the existence and activities of the Michigamuas. Since this revelation, Native American student (and community) response to the Michigamuas has been perennial and vocal. Each generation of NASA has challenged the university to abolish Michigamua's university status and to eliminate all reference to Native American cultures. The university has traditionally ignored the emotional appeal of Native American students and has responded only to legal pressure from state and federal agencies.

In 1972, Victoria Barner filed a complaint with the Michigan Civil Rights Commission for the alleged violation of "Permitting ridicule of culture." She states these facts: Michigamua "holds initiation 'rites' on campus in public each spring which are demeaning and insulting to the Indian culture and heritage. I believe the University has violated my rights and those of other American Indians by permitting our culture to be distorted and ridiculed because of our race and national origin." Through the Office of the General Council, in a letter dated March 27, 1973, the university settled the complaint voluntarily by encouraging Michigamua to eliminate "all public actions" in exchange for the Civil Rights Commission not finding the university engaged in any unlawful discrimination. No other penalty or concession was imposed (*Michigamua*, Box 3).

In 1976, Amy Blumenthal and Anita Tanay filed a complaint with the Office of Civil Rights in the Department of Health, Education and Welfare alleging that the "University's relation with the Michigamua places the University in violation of Title IX" of the Education Amendments Act of 1972 (PL92-318; June 23, 1972). Further, "the membership criteria and functions of Michigamua could present a violation of Title IX." On a visit to the university and to attend the seventy-fifth anniversary Michigamua powwow, former U.S. president and Michigamua Fighting Brave Gerald "Flipp'um Back" Ford was questioned about Title IX and the Michigamuas by a group of Native American students. He responded: "I think there can be some very ridiculous decisions made under Title IX" (*Ann Arbor, Michigan, Daily*, Oct. 17, 1979). This time, the allegations included continued ridicule of culture, violation of the March 27, 1973, agreement, and discrimination against women. Michigamuas, Blumenthal states, also received preferential treatment: free rent for their Wigwam, use of Raderick Farms, use of a university-owned golf course, and "deals" on tickets for athletic events (*Michigamua*, Box 3).

In another complaint filed in 1976, the university was accused of violating Title VI of the Civil Rights Act of 1964 "by denying membership to minorities and ridiculing Native American culture" (PL88-352, July 2, 1964). The university responded by claiming that Michigamua "holds the American Indian in the highest esteem," so

Native Americans are "put to proofs" to establish how Michigamua ridicules Native American culture. The discrimination was easier to counter because, by 1976, more than a few black athletes were Michigamuas. In the portrait of the fiftieth anniversary powwow in 1952, at least two African American males are present. By the 1970s, the percentage of African American Michigamuas had substantially increased. Even William P. Lemmer, university attorney, sarcastically responds to a HEW request to verify minority membership. He cites the Michigamua spokesman, Calvin "Man of Steel" O'Neal, as an example: "Calvin is Black and HEW can verify this through any of your football fans." Further, he claims: "None of the activities of Michigamua can violate Title VI since Michigamua is not a program of the University of Michigan, but is a student group. Nor is any service, financial aid or other benefit denied to anyone by the University. In any case, no one is denied anything, even by Michigamua, because of race, color, or national origin" (*Michigamua*, Box 3). The Michigamuas dodged the Title VI complaint because they had, at times, inducted minorities. They understood, at that time, ridicule of culture was hard to prove. Because, in 1976, the Michigamuas never had a woman member in their seventy-five-year history, they had a harder time avoiding accusations of sex discrimination.

By the end of 1976, John "Drooping Feathers" Feldkamp, university housing director, Henry Johnson, vice president for student services, and Roben "Silver Feathers" Fleming, university president, developed a defense against the Blumenthal Title IX complaint by disavowing any direct relation with the Michigamuas. They also fashioned an argument using *Baird's Manual of American College Fraternities* as a reference (Robson 1968). In so doing, they "reached the conclusion that Michigamua most appropriately fits the definition of a recognition society." This was an important distinction because Senator Birch Bayh had amended the Education Amendments Act of 1972 to exempt social fraternities and sororities, but

Feldkamp, Johnson, and Fleming did not designate Michigamua as such. They left that decision to the HEW. The Office of the General Counsel informed HEW by a letter dated March 8, 1977, of their findings (*Michigamua*, Box 3). Thirty months later, the *Michigan Daily* (Sept. 25, 1979) reported HEW had found the university guilty of sex discrimination.

By December 1979, in order to avert a public lawsuit, the university responded by creating the "Tower Society," which would consist of fifty student leaders drawn from both women and men ("Fact Sheets," undated). Michigamua settled the sex discrimination suit by giving twenty-five women a room of their own on the sixth floor of the Student Union Tower, a room right below the Michigamuas' seventh-floor Wigwam. The top twenty-five women students and "professional women" of the University of Michigan organized a parallel women's club that they named Adara. They, "together with Michigamua, comprise the Tower Society of which one is member for life." The Michigamuas also promised to meet twice a month with the Adara group to plan joint activities, but they would maintain their independence and all-male membership, separate and aside from Adara.

On the other hand, Michigamua Indian rituals and traditions continued in their time-honored fashion, if the publishing of their *1988 Directory of the Tribe of Michigamua* is any indication. Members merely kept their most blatant activities out of the public eye. Secrecy prevented a timely and direct scrutiny of the Michigamuas; however, published accounts of powwows, Roping Day ceremonies, dances, and reports on key Michigamua Fighting Braves and Old Braves appeared regularly in issues of *Tower Talk*, registration forms, announcements, programs, and other mailings (*Michigamua*, Box 4). Periodically, the Michigamuas deposited these records and a portion of their more topical correspondences at the Bentley Historical Library. Clearly, throughout the 1980s, they believed their activities were private and their own concern, despite persistent pressure from successive NASA groups. They knew they were more powerful than NASA, and other concerned Native Americans on and off campus, because their large, active, respectable, and renowned alumni held powerful positions in federal, state, university, and private institutions. Many of the Michigamuas, frankly, did not believe Native Americans could be insulted by the organization's existence or by their activities. They truly believed in the righteousness of their purpose and actions as a sanctioned student group. Laying aside the complaints of Native American students, the Michigamuas believed they served the University of Michigan by "enhancing its reputation and purpose at every opportunity and in all fields of endeavor." Apparently, from a Michigamua perspective, what Native Americans thought did not, in any way, effect the university's reputation. Besides, they did not believe dressing as Indians and engaging in faux ritual practices as stereotypical or harmful.

In October of 1988, the Michigan Department of Civil Rights published *Report on Use of Nicknames, Logos and Mascots Depicting Native American People in Michigan Education Institutions*. The Michigamuas now appeared in an official report, and the stated policy of the Michigan Department of Civil Rights was to instruct them on the destructive and denigrating power of Indian stereotypes. The report called for the immediate survey of Michigan's institutions to find out the extent of use of Indian names, logos, and mascots. It recommended discontinuing "any use of Indian names, logos and mascots . . . because racial stereotyping of Native Americans is prevalent and destructive." The report provided the factual base to make these accusations as well as appendixes of supporting documentation. If, after one year, stereotyping was found to continue, then the commission could consider the "receipt and investigation of formal complaints from Indian students or groups alleging that use of names or logos violate the Elliot-Larsen Civil Rights Act." The university and Michigamua were forced to take this state initiative seriously because Native American students now had a way of proving ridicule of culture.

In 1989, again to avoid a public lawsuit, the Michigamua sachem and a member of Michigamua's Old Braves Council signed an agreement with the Native American student complainant, the chair of the University of Michigan's Minority Affairs Commission, and the student discrimination policy administrator. President "Fish'um puck out of net" Sharples shared the content of the agreement with the Nation of Michigamua in a December 1989 *Tower Talk* under the subheadings "Report to All Members of Michigamua" and "President's Report" (Michigamua, Box 4). He warned: "The conditions of this agreement will almost assuredly appear overly restrictive to most older members of Michigamua. . . . To be more specific, Michigamua is dropping all references to Native American society and culture." Sharples stressed the urgency of changing the traditions and practices but did not advocate any specific time line. He used phrases such as Michigamua "has recently been forced" and "because of pressures from the University and the university community" but ended his commentary by stating: "This was a decision that Michigamua made on its own, we certainly were not pressured." Then, a few lines later, he reverted to Michigamua Indian talk and announced the April 21, 1990, Rope Day Ceremonies held at Raderick Farms.

However, the Michigamuas recognized the need for drastic change to assure their survival. The urgency to make those changes, though so eloquently addressed in *Tower Talk*, was hampered by a painful transition period. Plans for changing the nomenclature surrounding the organization and the replacement of such practical items as their tomahawk membership pin took time. Meanwhile, many of the traditions continued contrary to the signed agreement. Scattered reports by Native American students and Michigamua documents indicate that some of Michigamua Indian rituals were still practiced well into the mid-1990s (*Michigamua*, Boxes 3 and 4).

In 1997, after three years of negotiations, members of NASA received three undated handouts entitled "The University of Michigan Tower Society, Fact Sheet," "Adara of the University of Michigan, Fact Sheet," and "Michigamua, 'Fightin' Like Hell Since 1902,' Fact Sheet." Together, the fact sheets constitute a statement of compliance and change; they are meant to demonstrate the diversity of its membership and the elimination of most of the references to Native Americans and Native American culture. For example, "tribe" is changed to "pride"; "Fighting Braves" has been changed to "Fighting Wolves"; and "Old Braves" has been changed to "Old Wolves." The names of great Michigamua men, like "Yost," "Matthaei," and "Temple" have become the titles of Michigamua officers and replace "Wiskinkee of the Bellowing Bears," "Wampum Chief," and "Medicine Man." Also, university president James B. Angell (1871–1909) has been honored. The Michigamuas have adopted "Angell" and "Honorary Angell" to replace "Sachem" and "Honorary Sachem." In the 1901–02 school year, President Angell was the first university president to sanction the activities of the Michigamuas. Obviously, as well, readers of the fact sheets are to understand that Michigamua is only one-half of a larger organization called the Tower Society and that Adara is the other half.

Between April and October 1997, NASA students met with Michigamua three times. The purpose of the meetings from the Michigamua perspective was to assure NASA that Michigamua no longer uses, or engages in, its previous versions of Native American traditions and practices. Michigamua claimed to have "eradicate[d] this identity from our organizational structure." NASA members wanted more evidence than "facts sheets," and they also advocated the removal of various Michigamua landmarks around campus. As of December 1998, the Michigamuas have given NASA members (and this author) access to the seventh floor Wigwam, now called the Meeting Room. They have changed their membership pin from a tomahawk to a flame with five stars. They have removed the fire pit plaque at the university recreation area and the tomahawk plaque from the University Diag. The totem pole, at the recreation area, was removed at great cost to the university. They have given their Indian-designed and -decorated drum heads and drum mallets to the Bentley Historical Library and the drum frame to NASA "for disposal." Other Michigamua Indian paraphernalia and artifacts, including the pipe, have mysteriously vanished. Current Michigamua Fighting Wolves claim no knowledge of these lost or misplaced items.

LASTING IMPRESSIONS: NAME AND NAMING

Although the Michigamuas have done much to eradicate Indian identity from their organization, they steadfastly refuse to give up their name or to eliminate all reference to Native American culture and traditions. The sophomoric and transparent changes to "pride" and totemic symbols and language still suggest a strong tie to the image of Indian tribes and traditions. Joseph Anthony Reilly, a NASA member from 1996 to the present, stated: "They make these changes only to protect themselves from legal prosecution. Their strong opposition to changing their name makes me think they truly do not want to give up the basis of their organization, which from its foundation has been based upon racist and elitist ideals" (*Ann Arbor, Michigan, Daily*, Jan. 27, 1999, 3).

In their own fact sheet, the Michigamuas admit the name "remains the only element of the group with any Native American connotations." They cite the 1989 agreement as a justification for allowing its use, yet only one Native American student signed that agreement. The Michigamuas use the plural, Native Americans, to imply a greater, if not universal, sanction. NASA and other concerned Native Americans believe the name has too much history and association with the stereotypical display of Indian culture and customs, but that history and association are exactly why the Michigamuas want to keep the name.

The "only element" claim is faulty as well. They still practice the "naming" of initiates. They say this cannot be construed as Native American because the "Indian talk" elements of former naming practices are no longer used. Again, this style of naming is so much a part of "playing Indian" that saying it is not so is not enough to be convincing, especially to Native Americans.

Many other residual elements of pseudo-Indian culture remain in their newly named meeting room. For example, war memorials, display cases with membership pins of deceased Michigamuas, portraits and other photographs, and the overall wigwam facade still have strong references to stereotypical Indian images, despite the fact that some honor Michigamua dead. What they do suggest is the strong traditions the Michigamuas have generated over the years, and they provide a reason why current Michigamuas want to maintain, through their name, a direct link to their heritage and traditions.

For Native Americans, the name "Michigamua" creates a lasting impression of power and elitism and reminds them of the arrogance of the Michigamuas to have claimed to honor or revere Indian culture and traditions. Native American dead are not so honored. Memorials to the original inhabitants of Michigan were never erected. The Michigamuas have never supported Native American youth through scholarships or any other activity. They have never bought books on Native American subject matters and deposited them in the university library. They have never engaged in the recruitment of Native American students. They have never supported or helped Native Americans in any way. And when they were confronted with the power and harm of Indian logos, mascots, and play, they have ducked the issue and fought for their own personal survival.

REFERENCES

1988 Directory of the Tribe of Michigamua. Michigamua Collection, Printed material, Box 4.

Adams, Andrew, III (NASA member 1999). Personal interviews with author, Ann Arbor, Jan. through Feb. 1999.

Baraga, Frederick. 1966. *A Dictionary of the Otchipwe Language, Explained in English.* New ed. 2 vols. in 1. Minneapolis: Ross & Haines.

Blackbird, Andrew J. 1977. *History of the Ottawa and Chippewa Indians of Michigan.* 1887. Reprint, Petoskey MI: Little Traverse Regional Historical Society.

Deloria, Philip. 1998. *Playing Indian.* New Haven: Yale University Press.

"Fact Sheets" and other NASA documents and resources. Office of Multi-Ethnic Affairs, University of Michigan.

Gilbert, Bil. 1989. *God Gave Us This Country: Tekamthi and the First American Civil War.* New York: Anchor Books.

Horton, R. G. 1865. *History of Tammany Society, or Columbian Order.* New York: Tammany Society.

"Life Goes to an Honor Society's Tribal Rites: Redmen at Michigan Initiate New Braves with Noble Savagery." *Life* (June 7, 1954): 189–94.

Michigamua. Bentley Historical Library, University of Michigan. Call number: 87248 BiMu F412. The collection is contained in five boxes under six topic headings: Box 1: Chronological Tribe Files; Box 2: Meeting Minutes; Box 3: Topical Files and Visual Materials (tribe photos); Box 4: Printed Materials and William F. Temple's short history, "The Founding of Michigamua"; and Box 5: Visual Matter (mostly photographic portraits).

Michigan Civil Rights Commission. 1988. *Report on Use of Nicknames, Logos and Mascots Depicting Native American People in Michigan Education Institutions.* Lansing: Department of Civil Rights. John Roy Castillo, Director.

Peckham, Howard H. 1992. *The Making of the University of Michigan, 1817–1992.* Ann Arbor: University of Michigan, Bentley Historical Library.

Reilly, Joe A. (NASA member from 1996 to present). Personal interviews with author, Ann Arbor, Jan. through Feb. 1999.

Robson, John, ed. 1968. *Baird's Manual of American College Fraternities*. 18th ed. Menasha WI: George Banta.

Rosenthal, Michael. 1984. *The Character Factory: Baden-Powell and the Origins of the Boy Scout Movement*. New York: Pantheon Books.

Shah, Rahul M. Personal interview with author, Ann Arbor, Jan. 26, 1999. (Shah was a Fighting Wolf of the 1998–99 pride and is a member of Michigamua for life.)

Shaw, Wilfred B. 1934. *A Short History of the University of Michigan*. Ann Arbor: George Wahr.

Temple, William F. 1958. *The Founding of Michigamua*. Michigamua Collection, Printed material, Box 4.

Title VI of the *Civil Rights Act of 1964* (PL88-352; July 2, 1964). *U.S. Statutes at Large* 78: 252-53.

Title IX of the *Education Amendments Act of 1972* (PL92-318: June 23, 1972). *U.S. Statutes at Large* 86: 304-12.

"Unidentified Michigamua 1939 Initiation." *Motion Picture*, 1 reel, 181 feet (16-mm reference print): 9059 AaZ. (Librarians have also created a 15-minute compilation of various film clips showing several Roping Day Ceremonies from approximately 1939 to 1961. The 1939 clip shows President Ruthven meeting with the Michigamua Fighting Braves and smoking the Michigamua peace pipe.)

Vogel, Virgil J. 1986. *Indian Names in Michigan*. Ann Arbor: University of Michigan Press.

White, Elmer E. *U of M Is Indian Land*, 1975 Update (pamphlet, Committee to Uphold the Fort Meigs Treaty, 1975). Bentley Historical Library, University of Michigan (F1 mu A6) or Special Collections, Graduate Library, University of Michigan (Labadie/Pamphlets/Minorities/19283).

CHAPTER 6

The Best Offense . . .

Dissociation, Desire, and the Defense of the Florida State University Seminoles

•

C. Richard King and Charles Fruehling Springwood

To commemorate the appearance of the University of Tennessee in the National Championship Game at the 1999 Fiesta Bowl, the *Knoxville Sentinel* produced a special section. Emblazoned on the front was a (supposedly) humorous cartoon by R. Daniel Proctor dramatizing the pending competition between the University of Tennessee Volunteers and the Florida State University Seminoles. At the center of the cartoon, a train driven by the Volunteer in a coonskin cap plows into a buffoonish caricature of a generic Indian. As he flies through the air, the Seminole exclaims, "Paleface speak with forked tongue! This land is ours as long as grass grows and river flows . . . Oof!" The Volunteer retorts, "I got news, pal . . . This is a desert. And we're painting it orange!" Beneath this hateful drama, parodying the genocide, lies, and destruction associated with the conquest of North America, Smokey, a canine mascot associated with the University of Tennessee, and a busty Tennessee fan speed down Interstate 10, here dubbed "The New and Improved Trail of Tears." They sing, "Oh give me land, lots o' land, full of starry skies above . . . don't de-fence me in."

Proctor depicts the impending game between the University of Tennessee and Florida State University as an interracial conflict, projecting the desired outcome through a popular, if misleading, pastiche of the past. As he imagines the glories of his team, the conquering Volunteers, he parodies, even mocks, Native Americans. The disrespectful and dehumanizing qualities of the image lay bare the practices and precepts animating Native American mascots. In fact, the image directs attention to those contexts in which individuals and institutions defend their uses of Indianness as expressions of honor, reverence, and tradition and, more particularly, to Florida State University, the institution denigrated in Proctor's cartoon.

While the cartoonist might be admonished for his insensitivity, it can be argued that Florida State University itself is guilty of propagating precisely the kind of environment in which Native Americans are likely to be "playfully" victimized by such forms of symbolic violence. The same year, 1947, that the public institution previously known as the Florida State College for Women became Florida State University, the student body voted to identify its athletic teams with the name "Seminoles," and "the student newspaper, *The Florida Flambeau*, carried a logo in its masthead illustrated with the profile of a Seminole man in a turban and kerchief" (Addonizio 1998:93). As we detail below, the Seminole "signs and symbols" created by Florida State University to inspire its athletes and supporters became increasingly elaborate and stereotypically flattened. Throughout the 1980s and 1990s, and continuing into the new millennium, the predominant spectacle at the start of Florida State University home football games is the entrance of a male student—wearing moccasins, a tasseled leather "Indian" outfit, face paint, and a large bandanna, hoisting a large feathered lance—who "charges down the field riding an appaloosa horse named Renegade and hurls a flaming lance at midfield" (Florida State University

2000). The student "Indian" represents Chief Osceola, the famous Seminole who led an armed resistance against the United States in the 1830s.

This highly polished performance of Indianness turns on the traditional archetypes of masculinity, fierceness, and bellicosity, themes common to nearly all the Native American mascots examined in this volume and themes understandably desired by aggressive athletic teams. Florida State University's Chief Osceola and Renegade inscribe a context that, indeed, openly invites violent-spirited salvos such as the Proctor cartoon. For example, Bobby Bowden, the celebrity coach of the perennial powerhouse Florida State football team, adds the slogan "Scalp 'Em" to his autographs. By the late 1980s, a Florida State cheerleading group, the Marching Chiefs, and the student body had perfected what the university itself calls the "war chant," and what others have embraced (and criticized) nationally as the "tomahawk chop," a repetitious arm motion meant to symbolize the movement of a tomahawk.

Obviously, Florida State University's history of appropriating Seminole icons and inventing performances conveys a traditional set of stereotypes of Native Americans. These practices also underscore the production of whiteness. They foreground desires for impulses, experiences, and affects between and beyond the boundaries of the mundane, highlighting the dissociated identities and communities made possible in the liminal space of imagined Indianness. Importantly, the existence of Chief Osceola and the various ways in which he has been rendered by Florida State University is not just about redness and whiteness but also reveals the significance of blackness. Consequently, in this essay we move beyond an analysis of familiar stereotypes to explore the ways in which Chief Osceola—from his lived, historical existence as a Seminole leader to his role as a contemporary college football cheerleader on horseback—has served as a canvas for the (re-)creation of white identities and racial hierarchies.

Our argument unfolds through an interpretive history. We begin with a brief overview of the Seminoles, noting their ethnogenesis, resistance, and removal. Against this background, we sketch the establishment of the Seminoles as the fight name of Florida State University in 1947, discussing its early efforts to create a mascot. Next, we turn to the enshrinement of Osceola as the Seminoles' mascot after 1978 and more recent efforts to defend Florida State University's uses of Indianness. This account offers a foundation on which to consider the racial hierarchy animated by Native American mascots, particularly in the American South.

THE EMERGENT SEMINOLE

Seminole is an English translation of a Creek (or Muskogee) transliteration of the Spanish word *cimarrón*, meaning "wild" or "untamed." Whereas the Spanish had originally used the term to describe the peoples they encountered and struggled with in the Southeast, Native Americans in the middle of the eighteenth century borrowed the term to communicate to the British that they were a distinct people (Wright 1986:4). As the naming of the Seminoles underscores, they offer a classic example of ethnogenesis, or the formation of a new people or ethnic group. In short, the Seminoles emerged, according to Sturtevant (1971:93; see also Sattler 1996), "in response to European pressure, for the tribe is an entirely post-European phenomenon." The Seminoles, then, both as the imagined Indians staged by Florida State University and the embodied Indians who are enrolled members of either the Seminole Tribe of Florida or the much larger Seminole Nation of Oklahoma, were generated, were fashioned, took shape, or (in popular scholarly parlance) were invented under colonial conditions not of their own making. To appreciate the complex uses and understandings of Indianness animating the Florida State University Seminoles, one must apprehend the creation, attempted destruction, resistance, and persistence of the Seminoles.

Disease, raids by slavers, military conflicts between indigenous groups, and the imperial intrigues of European powers had largely depopulated northern Florida by the early eighteenth century (Milanich 1998:171–75). Lower Creeks, often at the behest of the Spanish, migrated into this area, providing a buffer zone between the Spanish and the English and their Native American allies. Initially, these communities lived their lives as they had before emigrating — for example, building communities around central square grounds, playing stickball, ceremonially imbibing black drink, subsisting on horticulture supplemented by hunting, participating in intricate trade networks, and owning slaves. Each Lower Creek town maintained a unique identity and established loose regional alliances while retaining their allegiance to the Creek Confederacy, perhaps as late as the American Revolutionary War. Over the course of the eighteenth century, other tribes, fleeing armed conflict and slavery, moved south as well. During this period, the Lower Creek incorporated Apalachis, Yamasees, Hitchitis, and others following the Yamasees War of 1715; escaped slaves; and Upper Creeks following the Red Stick War of 1813–14. For much of the eighteenth century, the transplanted peoples in these mestizo communities conceived of themselves as Creeks, but increasingly, in response to changing sociopolitical conditions as well as European and later Euro-American perceptions that the Indians of Florida were a unique, discrete group, one of the Five Civilized Tribes, they came to understand themselves as a distinct people, the Seminoles.

After the Revolutionary War, and particularly in the nineteenth century, the Seminole presence proved problematic for the new republic. White southerners in Georgia, Alabama, and the Carolinas were hungry for land and concerned about slaves escaping to communities in Florida. The federal government, which acquired the territory from Spain, in turn sought to manage the escalating cultural, economic, and political tensions by removing the Seminoles to west of the Mississippi. During the first half of the nineteenth century, the United States waged three costly wars against the Seminoles.

In 1817, misunderstandings, charges and countercharges of theft, violation, and unjustified attacks, and nagging questions about runaway slaves escalated into the First Seminole War. Led by Andrew Jackson, U.S. troops swept across Florida the following spring, destroying a number of African American and Native American communities and capturing Spanish fortifications at Pensacola and St. Marks. Although the Spanish ceded Florida to the United States during peace negotiations in 1819, the federal government did not make peace with the Seminoles until nearly five years after the conflict. In 1823, a portion of the Seminoles signed the Treaty of Moultrie Creek, requiring that they settle on a four-million-acre reservation in central Florida in exchange for annual food and cash payments.

A decade later, in 1832, a segment of the Seminoles agreed to the terms of the Treaty of Payne's Landing and endorsed their removal to Indian Territory. A number of Seminoles balked at both the content of the agreement negotiated at Payne's Landing and the conditions under which it was negotiated. Rather than migrate, they actively resisted U.S. efforts to remove them, provoking the Second Seminole War (1835–42). Under the leadership of the much celebrated Osceola, Jumper, Alligator, Wildcat, and others, the overmatched Seminoles waged a rather successful guerrilla war, receding deep into the Florida interior. After a seven-year campaign, costing in excess of $30 million, the federal government unilaterally declared victory. At the close of the Second Seminole War, the U.S. government had forcibly relocated more than thirty-five hundred Seminoles west of the Mississippi, leaving behind fewer than five hundred renegades in Florida swamps.

In the 1850s, tensions between the Seminole remnants and Euro-American settlers and government agents resulted in the Third Seminole War (1855–58). During the short-lived conflict, U.S. troops concentrated their efforts on locating small, scattered Seminole encampments in the southern swamps. Although the troops were moderately successful in this venture, removing additional Seminoles, several hundred lingered in Florida.

After the Civil War, which had devastated the relocated Seminoles in Oklahoma as a result of internal divisions over slavery and an external alliance with the Confederacy, governmental programs and policies increasingly sought to incorporate members of the Native nation into American society. In contrast, in the half-century following the Third Seminole War, the undefeated remnants left behind survived on the margins of Floridian (and American) life, relying almost exclusively on "traditional" subsistence strategies and social institutions. Then, the establishment of reservations, combined with the pressures of development, particularly the draining of the swamps, compelled many Seminoles to enter mainstream white society. Importantly, during this period, many Seminoles integrated themselves into the tourist industry (Mechling 1996, West 1981), offering, if not embracing, Euro-American uses and understandings of Indianness. In 1957 the federal government officially recognized the Seminole Tribe of Florida. Today, the Seminoles live on five reservations in Florida, one reservation in Oklahoma, and in urban and rural areas throughout the country. They continue to participate in the tourist trade and agriculture and most recently have established a vibrant gaming industry in Florida.

INVENTING THE SEMINOLES

After World War II, a number of a veterans returning to Tallahassee wished to attend college. The needs of these soldiers served as the impetus for the Florida State College for Women to open its doors to men in 1947 (Hartung 1998). Becoming a coeducational campus, the new Florida State University entered into a process that would eventually transform it into a nationally recognized public university. Central to its national reputation has been its emergence as an acknowledged powerhouse in collegiate athletics, particularly in football. In fact, Florida State University now regularly vies for the national championship in football and, to the delight of a national television audience, annually revives its rivalry with the University of Florida.

It was in this not atypical collegiate context that Florida State University began to refashion itself as numerous other institutions had. In part due to the university's desire to capitalize on the (imagined) identity of a regionally significant Native American society, the moniker "Seminoles" was formally adopted by students following a campus-wide competition. "Seminoles" was chosen over a range of alternatives, including Crackers, Statesmen, Tarpons, and Fighting Warriors (Addonizio 1998:93). Apparently, the name was the consensus favorite among the football players, who made certain of the outcome by stuffing the ballot box (McGrotha 1987). From the outset, neither a formal nor a de facto relationship existed between the university and the Seminole Tribe of Florida, although by the 1970s an ongoing, mutual conversation between tribal representatives and school administrators had emerged. But attempts were made by the university to inscribe the very early FSU Seminole tradition as "authentic," as illustrated, for example, by the patchwork skirts worn by FSU cheerleaders in the 1950s. These skirts were "made by members of the *real* Seminole tribe of Florida" (Addonizio 1998:93, emphasis added).

Choosing and retaining a mascot proved more difficult. A series of imagined Indians, actual and planned-but-rejected incarnations, evolved during the latter half of the twentieth century. Although cartoon caricatures of a Seminole figure or, even, of Chief Osceola appeared variously in campus literature and newspapers, the presence of an embodied mascot, or mascots, was unknown until the late 1950s. In 1958, Sammy Seminole became the first figure to perform as a football team mascot. He would lead the FSU team onto the field and follow with a series of back flips. During the game, he was an all-purpose cheerleader and acrobat. The carnivalesque role was played by a number of male students from the gymnastics and circus programs. The Sammy Seminole costume consisted of a breechcloth and a single feather. The practice ended in 1968, possibly due, in part, to budgetary constraints (see Ensley 1997), but according to other news reports, the presence of a Sammy Seminole figure was swiftly reestablished at football games, although not— apparently—under the sponsorship of the gymnastics program (Stacey 1970).

Even more carnivalesque than Sammy Seminole was FSU's Chief Fullabull, who emerged as the mascot at home basketball games, apparently in the late 1960s. Little documentation exists that details the nature of these performances. According to FSU anthropologist Anthony Paredes, the mascot ran around performing silly stunts and clownlike routines (personal communication, August 1999). Shari Addonizio (1998:94) reports that his antics upset members of the campus organization American Indian Fellowship, who in concert with the support of other campus groups and "off campus Seminole people" had Chief Fullabull eliminated and, ultimately, replaced by a figure in Seminole apparel known as the "spirit chief" or "Yahola." The first effort to "rehabilitate" Chief Fullabull, however, failed. The individual portraying Chief Fullabull at the time, Jack Stacy, apparently enjoyed great control over the tradition because, unilaterally, he changed "his" name to Chief Wampumstompum (Rutland 1970). Of course, this change did nothing to appease those complaining that Chief Fullabull was derogatory; later, the name "Yahola" was adopted.

Thus, during the 1960s, one Sammy Seminole was replaced by another at football games, and a Chief Fullabull was incarnated on the basketball court and underwent a series of "rehabilitations" in response. Meanwhile, a lesser-known FSU logo had been "invented" in 1965 by an FSU design and metalsmithing instructor, Fred Metzke. The figure portrayed in the logo was a dancing, ax-wielding, feathered "Indian" named "Savage Sam." He was replaced in the early 1970s by the present logo incarnation, a silhouette of a Native figure (see Lindstrom 1982).

As noted previously, the current and widely popular incarnation of FSU "Seminole Pride" consists of the home football game performances of a student portraying Chief Osceola, atop an Appaloosa named Renegade. The tradition was created in 1978 by Bill Durham, a Tallahassee businessman and FSU alumnus, with the support of Ann Bowden, spouse of the football coach. Durham actually conceptualized the notion of a Seminole mascot on horseback in 1962, when he was elected to the FSU Homecoming Court (Coale 1996). But in 1978 he was better positioned to enact his dream, and he provided the horse and the attire. The support of Bowden proved critical in securing various permits and approvals to have a live horse on the football field.

The first appearance of Chief Osceola on horseback took place at the Florida State University–Oklahoma State University game on September 16, 1978. Details of the performance have changed over the years, and the process has become more refined and more closely monitored by school officials. A self-proclaimed student of Seminole culture, Durham orchestrates all aspects of the contemporary Osceola-Renegade tradition. He trains a number of Appaloosas for the performances and selects the student riders himself. Only one Chief Osceola impersonator serves the role at any given time, and to date, there have been ten such riders. In order to earn the honor, which is accompanied by a $1,200 annual scholarship, students must have a 3.0 grade point average, display a high moral character, and serve a two-year apprenticeship. The Chief Osceola performer must ride bareback while carrying a twenty-eight-pound flaming spear. Near the end of the horse's gallop, the rider must urge the animal to rear up on its hind legs, striking a dramatic, defiant posture. Chief Osceola is required to remain "in character," affecting a solemn, bellicose persona. He is forbidden from smiling or responding directly to the audience (see Coale 1996).

The appropriation and elaboration of the Florida State Seminoles, as well as the performances, costumes, and figures invented to represent them, turn on a complex dialectic of desire and dissociation in which Euro-Americans (and, to a lesser extent, Native Americans) embrace difference, while refusing its significance, and claim Indianness, while erasing embodied Indians. To be sure, the tensions and articulations at Florida State University fit within a rich tradition already well established in American culture by 1947; however, the preoccupation of students, alumni, and fans with Osceola make the stagings and effects of the FSU Seminoles unique.

Osceola has long fascinated Euro-Americans (Perdue 1992; Wickman 1991). Beginning in the Second Seminole War, largely as a result of his position on removal and his exploits in battle, Osceola enjoyed great popularity, gaining prominence and influence that eclipsed most traditional leaders. He became a darling of the American news media for his committed resistance to American encroachment, his uncompromising action, and his bravery in battle. A number of (largely fictional) biographies portrayed his life, and George Catlin rushed to South Carolina to paint the war leader after his surrender in 1837. Upon his death in 1838, Osceola's personal belongings were stolen; his head was taken as a trophy and was later displayed in a museum in New York. Euro-Americans literally appropriated Osceola, making him their own. Then, as now, the repossession of Osceola has turned on erasure and control: romantic renderings of the Seminole war leader do not stress hybridity—he was a mixed-blood, born to an English father and a Creek mother—but purity; they do not foreground his polygyny, religious practices, or other features of his everyday life, but his more fantastic actions during a time of crisis; they do not reflect his complex engagements with American culture but offer a singular and flat vision of his ferocious rebellion. Importantly, for all of the revisioning, Osceola remains "a multifaceted symbol . . . the war hero, the worthy opponent, the 'savage,' the past" (Perdue 1992 : 488); he simultaneously encoded narratives of the hostility and backwardness of Indians, the romance of their (failed) opposition, the honor of conquest, the propriety of removal, and the Manifest Destiny of American civilization in the face of savagery. At FSU, Euro-American enactments of Osceola, their interpretations of who he is and what he means, remain polysemic and ambivalent. Put simply, they fashion Indians and Indianness in fairly formulaic terms, while locating whites and whiteness, what it means to be a white American.

When Osceola leads the FSU football players onto the field, he signifies armed resistance, bravery, and savagery, and his appearance builds on the prevailing understandings of Indianness that construct Native Americans as aggressive, hostile, and even violent. Although numerous other attributes would evoke qualities esteemed on the playing field, violence, competition, and force are invested in the FSU athletic symbol. When read against past and present representations of Native Americans within American popular culture, this association becomes clear: it draws upon the Euro-American knowledge of Native American cultures, misconceptions that paint them as savage warriors removed from the mores of civilization and constantly eager for combat. To characterize the indigenous Seminole people or any other Native nation of North America as warlike or bellicose dehumanizes and demonizes them. More importantly, it disregards both their cultures and their histories. It reduces them to a single aspect of life, namely war, ignoring the numerous other experiences and activities more valued than war.

Thus Osceola, as portrayed at FSU, offers a stereotypical representation of Native American cultures and histories informed by racist notions and romantic sentiments. In fact, we would argue, the FSU icon represents a generic Indianness as much as it signifies the Seminole people as such. This sentiment undoubtedly derives from the cinematic and literary images of Native Americans most familiar to Euro-Americans. On film, according to Bataille and Silet (1980:xvi), "The Indian—no tribe, no identity, almost always male—was either noble . . . or bloodthirsty and vicious. There were certainly variations on the stereotype—the drunken Indian, the heathen, the lazy native—but still it was a picture of a creature less than human." Chief Osceola, then, not unlike its cinematic and literary kin, depends upon the dominant tendency to reduce all Native Americans to dehumanizing representations.

Within the limited space of the Indian warrior, Chief Osceola astride Renegade inscribes a complex, even ambivalent, narrative revolving around desire and dissociation. It conjures an archetype, seeking the wildness and savagery at the core of the naming of the Seminoles and white perceptions of them over the past three centuries. At FSU, the administration, fans, and athletes long for the attributes of the untamed other, particularly autonomy, individuality, defiance, and aggression, crafting rituals that enable them to imitate, materialize, and assume these qualities. That this archetypal, untamed other has been authenticated, really invented, by Euro-

Americans, for Euro-Americans, only enhances the allure of the FSU Seminoles. The distance of time and the removal of imagination have domesticated Osceola, facilitating Euro-American identification and affiliation. Even more significant, the defeat and removal of the Seminoles make them safe, desirable. "In the defeat of Osceola," as Perdue (1992: 484) asserts, "the quintessential 'savage,' Anglo-Americans confirmed that they were right: Failure to become 'civilized' resulted in death, albeit a heroic and romantic death." The performances of Chief Osceola do not so much celebrate his demise as lament it; they imprint a nostalgic drama through which they mourn the passing of a once-great and proud people who honorably and unsuccessfully defended their way of life against all odds. The honor and longing attached to these rites of incorporation enable supporters of FSU to fix the Seminoles as noble savages, enjoy the spoils of subjugation, and embrace Indianness without encountering Indians. Through its stagings, FSU claims Indianness as a right of conquest, grounding white institutions and identities in the domesticated difference projected onto Osceola.

The identification and dissociation circulating as Osceola explodes onto the field merge in the stands where thousands of people invoke signs and gestures associated with Indianness to cheer their Seminoles to victory. As players and fans gaze at the spectacle of a young Euro-American student wielding a flaming spear, galloping bareback to the center of the football field in the persona of an imagined Seminole warrior, they cross into a liminal space where they too "play Indian." This is illustrated, for example, by the FSU war chant, which originated in 1984 during a game against Auburn University. The Marching Chiefs (the FSU marching band) began to perform this cheer. Several students behind the band joined in, and in subsequent games, more spectators participated and even added the now infamous chopping motion symbolic of swinging a tomahawk. It is confirmed by an official student athletic booster organi-

142

zation, the Scalphunters, as well as the more informal actions of individual fans, who dress in paint and feathers and yell war whoops. Such fantastic antics allow the non-Indian audiences to momentarily transform themselves into a partial embodiment of Indianness. They foster a form of communitas in which the boundaries and distinctions of everyday life collapse, giving way to a shared sentiment and identity (Turner 1978). For the duration of the game, those who opt into the ritual become Seminoles.

ENTRENCHED INDIANNESS

As the FSU Seminole name, logo, and mascot have become increasingly controversial and contested in recent decades, a more sustained effort has emerged among campus administrators and supporters to engage members of the Seminole Tribe of Florida. Other than some early attempts to contextualize the FSU logo and mascot with minimal degrees of "authenticity," the evolution of the Seminole icon, in all of its incarnations, has been chaotic and, until recently, did not involve members of the Seminole Nation. But by the 1980s and more publicly in the 1990s, once the university realized that some support for the embattled mascot did, in fact, exist among Florida Seminoles, it has embraced this backing with enthusiasm. In fact, for FSU fans and administrators, these voices of the Florida Seminole Tribe have seemingly come to symbolize *the* authentic authority on the mascot issue. The consent of the Seminole Tribe of Florida, in fact, is touted by the university as shield against criticisms from other Native American organizations and tribes.

A strategic relationship has emerged in which the Florida Seminoles serve to lend a legitimacy to the FSU name and mascot. This Seminole-FSU relationship is of paramount significance, for it reveals a new turn in a long history of "invented" constructions (by both Seminoles and non-Indian people) of the Seminole figure in popular discourse, especially in terms of the idea of "Florida." Jay

143

Mechling (1996:149) revealed how both Florida and the Seminoles—for centuries—have been "locked in a dialectic dance of interpreting each other." He argued that "The Seminoles played a key symbolic role in the social construction of the meanings of Florida though tourism, and the touristic visit is the quintessential act in the modern search for 'authenticity' and identity." Further, he insisted, although real Seminole people do exist, "it is also true that there are real historical circumstances and real institutions that work to determine how a person constructs his or her life as a Seminole." The circumstances under which FSU has engaged, staged, and coaxed contemporary members of the Florida Seminole tribe conform to this older pattern of cultural appropriation.

Supporters of the FSU Seminoles and the Chief Osceola mascot now include official representatives of the Florida Seminole Tribe. Indeed, James E. Billie, chair of the Seminole Tribe of Florida, has repeatedly stated that neither he nor the tribe has any objection to the use of the FSU name, logo, or mascot. As criticisms of the FSU Seminole mascot mounted in the 1980s, administrators purportedly sought the advice of Florida tribal members, and since that time, the regional Seminole voice repeatedly has been invoked as representing the authentic, and thus legitimate, opinion regarding the mascot issue.

The current university Web site (Florida State University 2000), for example, claims that, "The clothing and rigging that Chief Osceola and Renegade wear were designed and approved by the Seminole Indian Tribe of Florida." On the same Web site appears a statement written by former FSU president Dale W. Lick (1993) in which he defends the use of the Seminole iconography. "Recent critics have complained that the use of Indian symbolism is derogatory. Any symbol can be misused and become derogatory. This, however, has never been the intention at Florida State. Over the years we have worked closely with the Seminole Tribe of Florida to ensure the dignity and propriety of the various Seminole symbols we use." He does not, however, indicate the length or nature of this relationship.

Lick then proceeds to essentially deflect blame for certain elements of the FSU mascot culture. "Some traditions we cannot control. For instance, in the early 1980s, when our band, the Marching Chiefs, began the now famous arm motion while singing the 'war chant,' who knew that a few years later the gesture would be picked up by other team's fans and named the 'tomahawk chop?' It's a term we did not choose and officially do not use." Who *knew*, indeed? At the very end of the statement, Lick writes, "Our good relationship with the Seminole Tribe of Florida is one we have cultivated carefully and one we hope to maintain, to the benefit of both the Seminoles of our state and university." He closes by quoting Chief Billie, who says that his people are proud to be Seminoles and are proud of the FSU Seminoles.

In 1995, in response to a George Vecsey (1995) column in the *New York Times* that was critical of the FSU mascot tradition and Indian mascots more generally, the new university president, Talbot D'Alemberte, felt obliged to author a public defense. In his response (D'Alemberte 1995), he describes how FSU has consistently invited Seminole leaders to campus events. "Your column acknowledges that we have always invited Seminoles, including the Chiefs, to our games, but the way you phrase it (that FSU 'always trots out some real Seminoles') is insulting. . . . We do not trot out anyone. We invite Seminoles and they often accept." D'Alemberte, too, cites Chief James E. Billie.

Some critics are skeptical of the Florida Seminole support, which apparently does not involve direct financial reward for the tribe. However, the existence of the Osceola mascot and the Seminole trademark, owned by FSU, apparently earns the university as much as $1.8 million annually. Yet, Chief Billie has worked hard to involve his tribe in a number of economic ventures within the state, including the establishment of Seminole gambling casinos in Tampa, Hollywood, Brighton, and Immokalee. In essence, Billie is a politician, and he has many friends among state legislators in Florida. St. Petersburg journalist Jeff Testerman (1998) even suggested that tribal support for the FSU mascot served Billie well in terms of political advantage. Certainly, a number of faithful FSU alumni serve in the legislature. At any rate, a carefully constructed system of mutual self-promotion has emerged in the context of the FSU–Florida Seminoles friendship.

Tellingly, concern for Seminole involvement and Native responses to Chief Osceola apparently were never of interest to FSU supporters until the mascot became contested. Of further importance is the fact that none of the four Seminole tribes of Oklahoma nor any other well-known Seminole members have endorsed the FSU situation. In fact, Seminole Michael Haney is prominent among a national group of Native Americans who have protested the Indian mascots for many schools and franchises, including FSU. To further complicate matters, the Seminole Tribe of Florida apparently signed a National Congress of American Indians statement condemning Indian mascots. The precise nature of the FSU relationship to the tribe presents another complication, since it has never been spelled out in any detail by either party. For example, nobody associated with FSU whom the authors contacted can state exactly when a formal consultation with the Florida Seminoles was started. And although the FSU Athletic Department Web site claims that the Seminole leaders have worked closely with the university, this is never spelled out. Local journalists informed the authors that, indeed, very little interaction occurs, that Chief Osceola creator Bill Durham is in control of all aspects of the mascot performance, and that he seeks only token approval from Chief Billie.

Under pressure, Chief Billie recently agreed to conduct a tribal referendum on the FSU mascot controversy, although no details regarding such a vote have yet been forthcoming. A vote could prove to be significant, however, and it might rectify the perception held by some, including the authors, that the nature of the FSU–Florida Seminole relationship bears resemblance to the common pattern of the way the U.S. government negotiated treaties with Native Americans. The past practice of negotiating treaties with one or even a few Native representatives, often under awkward circumstances, appears—on the surface, at least—to have been replaced with a practice of negotiating mascot approval with a few tribal representatives, with perhaps questionable motivations.

As troubling as the mascot may be, the fact that a portion of the Seminole community in Florida should find the image of the defiant Osceola appealing, even politically advantageous, conforms to a narrative pattern identified by Mechling (1996), who suggests that a series of stages characterizes the representation of the Seminoles. The first stage located the Seminoles as "noble savages at one with nature," and a number of tourist Seminole villages existed where one could witness a Native wrestle an alligator. Although the nineteenth-century Seminoles did utilize alligator meat and skins, they did not, in fact, traditionally wrestle alligators. A later stage characterized the Seminoles as "noble children of the swamp, but also as people who could pick and choose from modern conveniences without jeopardizing the virtues of their traditional ways." In the current stage of Seminole imaging, according to Mechling (1996:153), the "Seminoles 'interpret back' by gaining control of their own representations, yet these self-representations seem trapped by the narrative conventions of the first two stages." Perhaps the Florida Seminoles' relationship with FSU's Chief Osceola and his Renegade are indicative of having become ensnared in older, stereotypical narratives of Seminole-ness. Or, perhaps Chief Billie, who himself once wrestled alligators for tourists, is merely being pragmatic, seeking to utilize whichever spaces of representation are opened up by the dominant public culture for the Seminole peoples.

To many supporters of mascots, the security of ideological hegemony and deep narrative structures is not enough; they desire legal certainty and control. In March of 1999, Florida State University alumnus Jim King was able to enact his love for his alma mater in a unique fashion. Rather than paint his face or wear a T-shirt, King— who also happens to be a Republican state senator—proposed an amendment to a minor bill in the Florida legislature to name various state buildings. If it had passed, the bill would have made it law that FSU sports teams continue to be known as the Seminoles. It also would have mandated that the mascot be "Chief Osceola atop an appaloosa horse." "For those of us," explained King, "who are of the garnet and gold persuasion [school colors] it is time, in fact it is long past time, for us to defend the heritage that is Florida State University" ("Legislature" 1999). The house speaker, Republican John Thrasher, also an FSU booster, readily accepted King's amendment to the bill (SB 2244). The Florida Senate passed the bill by a vote of 30–0, but it failed to become law when the Florida House session ended without the house having taken any action. The reason for its ultimate failure may have been the actions of two state representatives, alumni of rival Florida universities, who attached additional amendments to the bill. King and Thrasher, at that point, decided to let the session end without a final vote. The bill is likely to be reintroduced again. In our opinion, this kind of legislation, which was similar to an attempt to make Chief Illiniwek's existence mandated by Illinois law (see Springwood and King forthcoming), represents the very worst sort of effort to silence dissent. It embodies a fear of the potential outcomes of a democratic process. Indeed, it is a blatant misuse of legislative power. Yet, representatives of the Seminole Tribe of Florida publicly did not object to the bill.

RED, WHITE, AND BLACK

The Florida State University Seminoles not only vividly illustrate the uses of Indianness and the fashioning of whiteness commonly associated with Native American mascots, but they also reveal the centrality of blackness to the racial spectacles animated when whites play Indian at halftime as well. The image discussed at the outset of this essay begins to reveal the entanglements of red, white, and black. Although central to the 1999 Fiesta Bowl, oddly absent from this depiction is the African American athlete, student, or fan. We do not direct attention to this absence because we believe the inclusion of African Americans would improve it. Rather, we highlight this erasure because it mirrors current understandings of Native American mascots and points to the embedded racial hierarchy legitimating such athletic icons.

Interpretations of Native American mascots, whether condemning or celebrating them, almost invariably turn on rather narrow interpretations of race, history, and culture. Frequently, discussions hinge on understandings of Indianness; they debate images and intentions, noting perhaps the emergence of novel Indian agency and identities. Less common, particularly among defenders of mascots, is a concern for whiteness. African Americans (and other peoples of color) have no place in the current discussion of Native American mascots. This is an odd absence, given the presence of blacks and blackness. African Americans are fans of teams with such mascots; they are students, alumni, faculty, and staff members of institutions employing such symbols; and, on occasion, they have created and challenged Native American mascots as well. More important, they are athletes, central to the success, marketing, and revenues of big-time college sports. The erased presence of blacks and blackness complicates the racial hierarchies structured by and structuring Native American mascots.

Historically, redness, whiteness, and blackness have played off

149

one another to give material expression to racial ideologies and hierarchies. Nowhere has this been truer than in the American South, marked as it was by the traumas of slavery, warfare, and removal as well as more mundane "problems" like miscegenation and acculturation. During the nineteenth century, precisely as they forcibly removed Native Americans, Euro-Americans painted their adversaries in rather romantic terms, stressing their bravery in battle, fidelity to place and people, and commitment to freedom. These renderings were not simply expressions of what Renato Rosaldo (1989) has described as "imperialist nostalgia," or longing for what one has destroyed, but they were also self-portraits that were made all the more heroic, honorable, and powerful by their association with noble savages. According to Joel Martin (1996:139), "romantic Indians were used to support the southern hegemonic class and its ideology. White patrician slave holders were men of honor: They should be in charge." These idealized images had implications, in turn, for popular understandings of African Americans. The romanticized Indian "provided a damning contrast to the African captive, who, according to white authors, loved bondage. . . . Antebellum literature typically portrayed Africans as happy in their captivity, obedient as dogs, eager to play their roles in the greater southern play. Romantic and rebellious Indians served to dramatize by contrast the docility of Blacks" (139). Redness, whiteness, and blackness, then, worked in concert to establish an intricate racial hierarchy.

At the end of the twentieth century, in the context of postsegregation sports, racial stratification persists in more ambivalent forms (King and Springwood forthcoming). Too often today, redness, whiteness, and blackness, in spite of significant modifications, perpetuate racial ideologies and asymmetries, particularly at schools with Native American mascots. At Florida State University the contours of this racial hierarchy are plain. At the risk of simplifying, the overall ranking calls for whites to be in charge; the conquered and

removed Indians should be revered for the ferocity of their historical resistance; and blacks, applauded, if not celebrated, for their exploits on the playing field, should be appreciative of the progress
and opportunities of post–civil rights America. The structures and
sentiments resonating within this context are more complex, more
conflicted. Euro-Americans occupy positions of prestige and privilege as coaches, administrators, entrepreneurs, politicians, and cultural workers. They play Indian and they play football. They cheer,
idealize, even idolize, African American athletes, while performing
the tomahawk chop and dressing in feathers and paint. In stark contrast, Native Americans are largely absent, save for a handful of fans
and students. They materialize at Florida State University home
games most conspicuously in the form of a celebrated mascot enacted by a Euro-American student. The bellicosity, violence, and
wildness of their invented Indian entertains, nay excites, the undu-
lating crowd of primarily white spectators, channeling power to
those who appropriate and mimic Osceola as a trophy, as a totem.
Importantly, the free, unconquered, and heroic warrior is ultimately safe, first, because he was subdued by whites, second, because this is a romantic rendering of the white man's Indian (Perdue
1992), and third, because the Seminole Tribe of Florida endorses it.
African Americans likewise are the center of the desires and aspira-
tions of white public culture. They are not totems, but athletes,
playing a key role in the success of Florida State University over the
past two decades. Not surprisingly, an African American student has
never been selected to represent Chief Osceola, for this is an exclusive space, where redness is engaged by whiteness. At the same time,
even though they have an important presence as fans, students, and
alumni, African Americans hold few positions of authority in
coaching or administration. Many would argue that the prominence of African American athletes corresponds with their physical
superiority. This popular interpretation does much to silently rein-

state racial stratification: the physicality of blacks explains their athletic abilities and their inability to succeed in other pursuits, because, as the story goes, they lack industry, intelligence, or character; consequently, it also justifies the continued control whites exercise over public culture and black bodies. Romantic readings of redness further denigrate blackness. Whereas the Seminoles fought passionately only to be subdued, resisting incorporation regardless of the costs, African Americans, evidenced by their presence on the football field, eagerly have embraced assimilation, acquiescing before white power for personal gain. In the end, blackness and Indianness, taken together, endow white individuals and institutions with identities, power, and meaning.

CONCLUSIONS

In 1993, Shayne Osceola graduated from Florida State University. His accomplishment was remarkable not only because he was the first Seminole to earn a bachelor's degree at the institution but also because he is the great-great-great-great-grandson of Osceola. In agreement with the official position of the Seminole Tribe of Florida, he endorsed the FSU Seminoles as a tribute, honoring his people and their defiance. In fact, he excused, if not embraced, the fan antics that were associated with his esteemed ancestor: "I never took the Tomahawk Chop so seriously I could be offended by it. I never thought about it as anything but a bunch of kids out there having a good time—and I was one of them" (Wheat 1993). In this essay, we have taken the tomahawk chop, the war chant, and the tradition of playing Indian at FSU very seriously, finding that it is much more than kids having fun. We have analyzed the invention and defense of the Seminoles, probing the uses and understandings of Indians and Indianness, the formulation of whiteness, and the racial hierarchies structuring and structured by the mascot.

Indeed, in contrast with the sentiments of Shayne Osceola and other supporters of the Seminoles, both on the field and in the stands, playing Indian at FSU may be a good time for some, but it does not promote empathy, understanding, or respect. Instead, as fans applaud and enact Indianness, they perpetuate stereotypes, foster spaces of terror, warp social relations, and ultimately injure embodied people, especially Native Americans. To offer but one poignant example, Kiowa tribe member Joe Quetone, executive director of the Florida Governor's Council on Indian Affairs, graduated from FSU. He described an experience he had in the middle 1990s, when he and his son attended a Seminole football game. As some students ran through the stands sporting war paint, loincloths, and feathers and carrying tomahawks, Quetone and his son observed a man sitting nearby turn to a little boy next to him and say, referring to the students, "Those are real Indians down there. You'd better be good, or they'll come up and scalp you" (Whitley 1999). This episode shocks and saddens, clarifying the asymmetry, privilege, and terror that saturate Native American mascots at FSU and beyond. It vividly illustrates popular prejudices about Indians emergent around mascots and the role such icons play in perpetuating them. At the same time, it underscores the ease with which Euro-American individuals and institutions appropriate and remake Indians in their own image, literally becoming the real thing as they displace the cultures and histories of Native America. It summarizes in a very poignant fashion a key point of this essay: the Florida State Seminoles do not pay tribute to the Seminoles, nor honor their independent spirit; instead, they display both contemporary and historical leaders, especially Osceola, as trophies and talismans, precisely because they enact racial difference and structure a troubling racial hierarchy.

We want to close our discussion by returning to Osceola. We end by turning the dominant imagination against the self, asking a series of undecidable questions: How would Osceola interpret the

Florida State University Seminoles? Would he recognize himself in the performances of Chief Osceola? What would he make of the Euro-Americans playing Indian at midfield and throughout the stadium? Would he be surprised, flattered, amused, insulted? How would he respond to the fact that descendants of the Seminoles who successfully resisted relocation west now support such spectacles? Would he charge them with complicity? And what sort of conversation might he and his great-great-great-great-grandson have about mascots, race, and power? Although we cannot answer any of these questions for him, we would like to think that he would challenge the Seminole Tribe of Florida and Florida State University to stop playing Indian and engage the difficult postcolonial conditions that have made it possible.

REFERENCES

Addonizio, Shari. 1998. Osceola's Public Life: Two Images of the Seminole Hero. In *Dimensions of Native America: The Contact Zone*, pp. 90–95. Catalogue. Tallahassee: Florida State University, Museum of Fine Arts.

Bataille, Gretchen M., and Charles L. P. Silet. 1980. *The Pretend Indians: Images of Native Americans in the Movies*. Ames: Iowa State University Press.

Coale, Phil. 1996. "FSU Sports Enduring Symbol in Renegade and Chief Osceola." *Tallahassee Democrat*, 26 Nov., 1B.

D'Alemberte, Talbot "Sandy." 1995. "We Honor the Seminole Legend." *www.fsu.edu/~fstime/FS-Times/Volume1/Issue5/legend.html* (20 March 2000).

Ensley, Gerald. 1997. "Sammy Seminole: A Step Closer to Osceola." *Tallahassee Democrat*, 1 Nov., 11E.

Florida State University. 2000. "Chief Osceola and Renegade." *FSU Traditions. www.fansonly.com/schools/fsu/trads/fsu-trads-osceola.html* (20 March 2000).

Hartung, Ron. 1998. "Welcome Back, Men of '46, and Please Note . . ." *Tallahassee Democrat*, 15 Oct., 1C.

King, C. Richard, and Charles Fruehling Springwood. Forthcoming. *Race as Spectacle in College Sport*. Albany: State University of New York Press.

"Legislature: Senate Votes to Put Seminoles Nickname into Law." 1999. *Naples, Florida, News*. 1 May.

Lick, Dale W. 1993. "Seminoles: Heroic Symbol at Florida State." FSU Traditions. *www.fansonly.com/schools/fsu/trads/fsu-trads-seminoles.html* (20 March 2000). Reprinted from *USA Today*, 18 May 1993.

Lindstrom, Andy. 1982. "Artist, FSU Boosters at Peace after 'Savage Sam' War." *Tallahassee Democrat*, 19 September.

Martin, Joel. 1996. " 'My Grandmother Was a Cherokee Princess': Representations of Indians in Southern History." In S. Elizabeth Bird, ed. *Dressing in Feathers: The Construction of the Indian in American Popular Culture*, pp. 129–47. Boulder: Westview Press.

McGrotha, Bill. 1987. *Seminoles! The First Forty Years*. Tallahassee: Tallahassee Democrat.

McReynolds, Edwin C. 1957. *The Seminoles*. Norman: University of Oklahoma Press.

Mechling, Jay. 1996. "Florida Seminoles and the Marketing of the Last Frontier." In *Dressing in Feathers: The Construction of the Indian in American Popular Culture*, ed. S. Elizabeth Bird, pp. 149–66. Boulder: Westview Press.

Milanich, Jerald T. 1998. *Florida's Indians from Ancient Times to the Present*. Gainesville: University Press of Florida.

Perdue, Theda. 1992. "Osceola: The White Man's Indian." *Florida Historical Quarterly* 70(4):475–88.

Rosaldo, Renato. 1989. *Culture and Truth*. Boston: Beacon Press.

Rutland, Jannetta. 1970. "Indians Upset over Name of Spirit Chief." *Tallahassee, Florida, Flambeau*, 12 Oct.

Sattler, Richard A. 1996. "Remnants, Renegades, and Runaways: Seminole Ethnogenesis Reconsidered." In *History, Power, and Identity: Eth-*

nogenesis in the Americas, 1492–1992, ed. Jonathan D. Hill, pp. 36–69. Iowa City: University of Iowa Press.

Springwood, Charles Fruehling, and C. Richard King. Forthcoming. "Race, Ritual, and Remembrance Embodied: Manifest Destiny and the Symbolic Sacrifice of 'Chief Illiniwek.'" In *Exercising Power: The Making and Remaking of the Body*, ed. Cheryl Cole, John W. Loy, and Michael A. Messner. Albany: State University of New York Press.

Stacey, Jack. 1970. "Basketball Chief Chooses Yahola as Indian Name" (letter to editor). *Tallahassee, Florida, Flambeau*, 14 Oct.

Sturtevant, William C. 1971. "Creek into Seminole." In *North American Indians in Historical Perspective*, ed. Eleanor B. Leacock and Nancy O. Lurie, pp. 92–128. New York: Random House.

Testerman, Jeff. 1998. "Chief Speaks on Tribe's Past, Future." *St. Petersburg Times*, 13 Oct., 1B.

Turner, Victor W. 1978. *The Ritual Process*. Harmondsworth, England: Penguin.

Vescey, George. 1995. "No Race of People Should Be a Mascot." *New York Times*, 19 Oct.

West, Patsy. 1981. "The Miami Indian Attractions: A History and Analysis of a Transitional Mikasuli Seminole Environment." *Florida Anthropologist* 34(4): 200–224.

Wheat, Jack. 1993. "Graduate Is Seminole by Birth—and by FSU Diploma." *Tallahassee Democrat*, 19 Dec., 1B.

Whitley, David. 1999. "Noles Facing Politically Correct Times." *Tampa Tribune*, 21 April, Sports 1.

Wickman, Patricia R. 1991. *Osceola's Legacy*. Tuscaloosa: University of Alabama Press.

Wright, J. Leitch, Jr. 1986. *Creeks and Seminoles: The Destruction and Regeneration of the Muscogulge People*. Lincoln: University of Nebraska Press.

CHAPTER 7

At Home in Illinois

Presence of Chief Illiniwek, Absence of Native Americans

•

David Prochaska

No place exerts its full influence upon a newcomer until the old inhabitant is dead or absorbed. —D. H. Lawrence, *Studies in Classic American Literature*

ABSENCE OF AMERICAN INDIANS

I begin with a historical outline of Native Americans in Illinois (Hauser 1976; Hickey 1989; Hoxie and Iverson 1998; Temple 1958; Tregillis 1991; White 1991; Whitney 1976; Wolf 1982):

700–1250: Mississippian mound-building culture centered at Cahokia.

ca. 1650: Illiniwek, a loose confederation of Algonquian-speaking ethnic groups inhabiting present-day Illinois and parts of Wisconsin, Iowa, and Missouri. *Ilaniawaki*, now pronounced "Illiniwek," became the French *Illinois* and means "the real or original ones." Included Kaskaskias, Tamaroas, Cahokias, Peorias, Michigamias, Moingwenas. Subsistence economy based on hunting and gathering, fishing, pottery, garden agriculture in yearly cycle. Corn most important. Longhouses lodged several kin-related families. Perhaps 60 small, circular villages.

1673: Looking for passage to India, Jesuit Jacques Marquette accompanied fur trader Louis Joliet down Mississippi River. Met Kaskaskia on Illinois River. Fur trade alters subsistence economy. French fur traders build trading posts. Iroquois confederacy arrives from east, drives Illiniwek off land and to west. Dramatic population decline. As population diminishes, Tamaroas and Michigamias combine with Kaskaskias; Cahokias with Peorias.

1756: War between French and British begins. Illiniwek ally with French, Iroquois with British. In India, British defeat of French at Battle of Plassey paves way for British takeover of south Asian subcontinent.

1763: British defeat French, gain control of Illinois.

1765: Last Indian resistance to British defeated at Fort de Chartres, southwestern Illinois. French surrender all land east of Mississippi River. Illiniwek population continues decline. Many already west of Mississippi.

1803: Treaty at Vincennes with Kaskaskias, part of Illiniwek. Land rights exchanged for two reservations. Illiniwek no longer play significant historical role in Illinois.

1818: Illinois becomes state. Treaty of Edwardsville with Peorias, then living in Missouri, for reservation there.

1830: Indian Removal Act forces all Indians west of Mississippi River.

1832: Kaskaskias sign another treaty, leave Illinois, settle with Peorias, already in Kansas.

1854: Peorias and Kaskaskias combine with Weas and Miamis, later move to northeastern Oklahoma. Today officially known as Peoria Indian Tribe of Oklahoma with tribal offices in Miami, Oklahoma.

1876: Battle of Little Bighorn.

Native American history of places like Champaign-Urbana has been written until recently in terms of "heroic victims," as "people who are heroic precisely because they have been victimized" (Root 1997: 227). Conversely, the history of the whites with whom the Natives came into contact has generally been cast in a "triumphalist" mode. Thus, "Manifest Destiny" implies that it was somehow the telelogical destiny of whites to win out over Natives as the continent was colonized from "sea to shining sea." In turn, this constitutes a major component of American "exceptionalism," a larger complex of attitudes according to which American history differs from other western history, like that of Europe, because its relative isolation conduced to "democracy"; the relatively greater role played by women and children produced a more "egalitarian" society; independent farmers rather than peasants worked the land; a frontier was gradually "tamed" over time; and a *mentalité* developed that was less "socialistic" and more religious than in Europe (Horsman 1981; Kammen 1997:169–98; Slotkin 1985; Veysey 1979; Wilentz 1984).

I take exception to American "exceptionalism." The notion of settler colonialism accounts for the historical facts better and provides a more plausible explanation of continental American expansion. Settler colonialism in world history constitutes a subtype of formal empire (Prochaska 1990). As opposed to informal empire characterized by indirect political control and increasing economic control, formal empire features direct political and economic control of large numbers of indigenous peoples by small numbers of colonials. As a variant of formal empire, settler colonialism can be usefully conceptualized in turn as a spectrum of historical cases. At one end, small numbers of Native inhabitants were decimated by settlers due to diseases and wars of conquest (Canada, Australia, United States). At the other end, indigenous populations survived settler conquest, began increasing in number rapidly, increasingly clashed with settlers over land rights, resource control, social status, and cultural differences, and during the period of decolonialization often developed violent nationalist, anti-colonial movements (Algeria, Kenya, Zimbabwe, South Africa). The case of the United States clearly fits the former end of the spectrum of settler colonialism.

History is, however, not simply what happened, but the representation of what happened. Dominant representations of Native-settler historical encounters in places like Champaign-Urbana have tended until recently to play up white settlers and downplay, even erase, Native Americans in subtle and not so subtle ways. For example, "prehistory" and "history" are terms used to denote the period before and after written sources are available on Native American groups, which for the Illiniwek is 1673, the date of Marquette's journal. Yet "prehistory" connotes "no history," which is patent historical nonsense. Another example is the corollary of settler colonialism according to which the indigenous inhabitants (Australian aborigines, New Zealand Maoris, Native Americans) were members of a "vanishing" race destined to die out. In 1886 it was argued, "No Peoria of pure blood is [probably] now living" (quoted in King and Springwood forthcoming). In 1916, after conducting three weeks of fieldwork among the Confederated Peoria Tribe, Truman Michelson, a University of Illinois student, concluded that "There probably [are] no absolutely pure blooded Peoria Indians left" (quoted in Springwood and King forthcoming). The Native American population had, in fact, declined precipitously since European contact, but in 1890 it bottomed out at 250,000, and by 1960 it had increased to more than 500,000 (Thornton 1987; Hoxie 1994:159).

In these and other ways settler colonial history codes Native Americans as absent whereas, in fact, they are present. Carlos Montezuma is perhaps the single most illustrious Native American to graduate from the University of Illinois (Montezuma 1888, 1907; Hoxie 1998; Iverson 1982).

Montezuma (1866?–1923) born Yavapai group, Arizona. Age six kid-napped by Pima Indians. Mother left reservation looking for him, mur-dered by army scout. Sold to traveling photographer, Carlos Gentile, for $30. Named for Aztec leader Montezuma. Lived Brooklyn, Chicago, Galesburg IL. Moved to Urbana-Champaign 1879, lived with local preacher, William Steadman. Graduated University of Illinois 1884. Received medical degree Chicago. Doctor in Indian Service and private practice, Chicago. Prominent proponent of assimilation. Harsh critic of Bureau of Indian Affairs. Influential native American leader. Founded newsletter, Wassaja, *his Apache name.*

It seems that the world will never get rid of fakers . . . there have been and are, a great many people using the Indians as their mas-cot. . . . These imposters are generally in business of some sort that requires Indianism, such as imitating the songs and dances of by-gone days . . . do they do any good? . . . they do more harm than good to the Indian people. . . . Anyone who poses as an Indian does not help the Indians. (Montezuma 1921:3)

Montezuma became a nationally prominent Indian leader in the first decades of the twentieth century. His career spanned the early period of Indian reform when initial leadership of whites gave way to indigenous Native Americans such as Charles Eastman and Mon-tezuma (Hoxie 1994, 1998).

"Playing cultural politics for social and political ends, Arthur C. Parker, Charles A. Eastman, Sun Bear, and others found themselves acting In-dian, mimicking white mimickings of Indianness" (Deloria 1998:189).

Uncomfortable thought: Does this also apply to Carlos Mon-tezuma?

In places like Champaign-Urbana, Native Americans may seem absent, but they are there if you look for them.

In 1982 UNESCO declared Cahokia Mounds a World Heritage Site, one of only a handful located in the United States. In 1989 the state of Illi-

161

nois opened an $8.2 million Interpretive Center. In 2000 people have taken to driving their off-road vehicles on the mounds. The Illinois Historic Preservation Agency, which manages the site, promises to beef up security.

PRESENCE OF CHIEF ILLINIWEK

I begin with a historical outline of Chief Illiniwek (Bial 1993, 1994; Spindel 1997; Solberg 1968; Springwood and King forthcoming):

1818: Illinois becomes a state.

1830s: first white settlers arrive in Champaign County.

1833: Champaign County formed with Urbana as county seat.

1854: Railroad arrives, Champaign grows up around it, two miles west of Urbana. Champaign and Urbana referred to as the "Twin Cities."

1862: Morrill Act grants 30,000 acres "unappropriated" federal land to states for each member of Congress, or scrip for other federal land, in turn sold. Used to found land-grant colleges. Federal lands sometimes not vacant; Indians removed by treaty or conquest.

1868: University of Illinois founded, sited between Champaign and Urbana. Funded by sale of 480,000 acres through Morrill Act (16 Congress members). Act required military tactics taught.

1876: Battle of Little Bighorn.

1926–30: Lester Leutwiler and Webber Borchers invent Chief Illiniwek. Leutwiler, Illinois student and former member, Urbana Boy Scout Troop 6, wearing "authentic Indian attire he had made for himself to demonstrate Indian dancing," played Chief Illiniwek during Illinois-Pennsylvania halftime. After dance, Leutwiler met drum major playing William Penn at centerfield, smoked peace pipe, and "walked arm in arm across the field to a deafening ovation" ("Chief Illiniwek" n.d.). In 1928 two new marches written for University Band, "Pride of the Illini March" and "March of the Illini," were added to alma mater, "Hail to the Orange," and telescoped together to form the trilogy "Three in One," still used today ("University of Illinois" 1993). Webber Borchers, second Chief Illiniwek and former Boy Scout, declared intention in 1929 to obtain "a real Indian outfit" so "that a tradition could be established." In 1930 Borchers bought Chief Illiniwek regalia at Pine Ridge Reservation, South Dakota, made by "an old Indian woman" who told him "that she as a girl, had helped mutilate the dead of Custer after the battle of the Little Bighorn" (Borchers 1959).

1926–1988: Heyday of Chief Illiniwek. University athletic lettermen called "Tribe of Illini." Junior honorary society called "Sachem." New members inducted at night by old ones wearing Indian blankets, smoking peace pipes. For the "Fighting Illini Scholarship Fund," $100 donations merit membership in the Tomahawk Club, for $250 the Brave Club, for $500 the Warrior Club, for $1,000 the Chief Club, and for $3,000 the Tribal Council. Squanto, longtime Illinois Agronomy Department symbol, depicted as a cartoon caricature with a hooked nose and feathers in his headband and holding a soil augur, appeared on orange and white hats with a Department of Agronomy logo and in the departmental newsletter, "Squanto Speaks" (Cook 1989). Chief Illiniwek paraphernalia includes license plate holders and stickers ("Illini Fan on Board!"), Monopoly game ("Illiniopoly"), toilet seats, toilet paper (no longer available), wallets, notebooks, stationery, gift-wrapping ribbon, envelope seals, mugs, soap, shot glasses, paper plates, cookie jars, coasters, wine coolers, socks, umbrellas, pillows, scarves, mittens, ski hats, earrings, mugs, Christmas ornaments, watches, garbage cans, diaper covers, baby bottles, rugs, afghans, boxer shorts, and navy blue silk panties (inscribed with "Illini Backfield in Motion" or "Illini Fanny"). Abbott's Florist markets orange and blue flower arrangements planted in an upside down Illini football helmet. Upscale Art Mart sells "Illini Mix" jelly beans, orange and blue jelly beans in a plastic bag (*Illio* 1983, 1988). Chief-themed local businesses include Chief Heating & Air Conditioning, Chief Illini Village mobile home park, Chief Paving & Excavating, Chief Windows Siding & Roofing, The Head Hunters barber, Head Hunters Beauty Salon, plus fifty-four businesses with "Illini" in name, ranging from Illini Christian Children Home and Illini For Christ to Illini Pest Control, Inc., and Illini Porta-Potty (*Ameritech PagesPlus* 1996–97 telephone directory). Other businesses use "Illini" in advertizing slogans. Kam's (campustown bar): "The Home of the Drinking Illini." Eisner's (now-defunct grocery store): "Eisnerland is Illini Country." Blossom Basket Florist: "The Fighting Illini Florist." Old Style billboard: "Illini, You've Got Style." A sampling of newspaper advertisements: "Me Tell 'Um World!" —caricature of Indian beating out Illinois Power Company ad message on drums and claiming, "One ELECTRIC BLANKET takes the place of *three* ordinary blankets!" (*Daily Illini*, 23 November 1950). "Aiming for excellent service at downtown Marathon [gas station]" —cartoon of Indian "princess" drawing a bow (*Daily Illini*, 7 October 1955). "Illinichecks. The Original Student Checking Account. Champaign County Bank & Trust Co." —figure of Chief Illiniwek with upraised arms (*Daily Illini*, 13 September 1960).

Settler colonialism entails and includes the formation of a distinctive settler colonial culture (Prochaska 1996). Historically, land is at the center of such colonial confrontations—expropriation of one group, settlement and colonization by another. Colonial culture refigures and renders these often violent transactions in historical narratives usually as a series of "absences" and "presences." "The land was vacant, we really didn't expropriate it." "We took the land, but mostly without bloodshed." These constitute "anti-conquest" narrative strategies of representation "whereby European bourgeois subjects seek to secure their innocence in the same moment as they insert European hegemony" (Pratt 1992:7).

What is distinctive about what could be termed the postcolonial culture in Champaign-Urbana is that it takes the form primarily of Chief Illiniwek (King 2000). Key in this regard is that in the heart of the heart of Chief Illiniwek country, there is literally nothing, a historical absence, a nonperson. Chief Illiniwek is a sign without a historical referent, a free-floating signifier in a prairie-flat land wiped clean, erased of Native Americans. This makes the literalness with which pro-Chief supporters invoke and refer to Chief Illiniwek—as if it were a part of them—all the more a conundrum.

To what extent does postcolonial theory help us make sense of Chief Illiniwek? Following Eric Hobsbawm and Terence Ranger, we can say that Chief Illiniwek is a classic case of an "invented tradition," a tradition "actually invented, constructed and formally instituted." As a social construction, an invented tradition consists of "a set of practices . . . which seek to inculcate certain values and norms of behavior by repetition, which automatically implies continuity with the past" (Hobsbawm and Ranger 1983:1). Thus, Chief Illiniwek is a tradition invented during halftime at an Illinois football game in 1926.

The origins of Chief Illiniwek are less important than the question, once the Chief was invented, why did it catch on? With Renato Rosaldo we can answer, "imperialist nostalgia." Imperialist nostalgia occurs when "people mourn the passing of what they themselves have transformed" (Rosaldo 1989:69). An unconscious or ideologized reaction, imperialist nostalgia was first applied by Rosaldo to anthropologists, missionaries, and other agents of change in the Philippines who denied to themselves complicity in changes occurring to the indigenous population that they themselves had been instrumental in bringing about. Similarly, those who consider Chief Illiniwek an "honored symbol" of the historical Illiniwek are displaying imperialist nostalgia.

The community to which Chief Illiniwek appeals is what we can call, *pace* Benedict Anderson (1983), an "imagined community." "At precisely such moments [singing the national anthem], people wholly unknown to each other utter the same verses to the same melody." Thus, the Chief standing with raised arms after his dance and the crowd singing the alma mater is an occasion "for the echoed physical realization of the imagined community" (132).

Finally, Chief Illiniwek exemplifies the much larger phenomenon of "playing Indian" (Deloria 1998; Root 1997; Springwood and King forthcoming). Boy Scouts, Eagle Scouts, Order of the Arrow. Order of Red Men. Campfire Girls. Woodcraft. Boston Tea Party. "White Indians" —white New Agers as Native American "wannabes."

> *At the conclusion of Dennis O'Rourke's film* Cannibal Tours *(1987), upper-middle-class Western tourists, who have journeyed up the Sepik River in Papua New Guinea, paint each other's faces, stage an onboard party, and playact for the camera in a slow-motion scene with a Mozart soundtrack.*

To pursue the argument a step further, what is "playing Indian," "playing Native," "playing an Other," all about? It is about play, for one thing, in the sense of dressing up, masquerade, the Bakhtinian carnivalesque (Bakhtin [1965] 1984). It is also about appropriation, in the sense of taking on, assuming an other's identity, taking another's identity. The implication here is replacing one with another, silencing another, speaking for another. Westerners playing New Guineans play to fellow Westerners; they do not play "Natives" in the presence of New Guineans. Such appropriation is ultimately predicated on power; power is the necessary prerequisite for appropriation. Cultural appropriation is often counterpart to physical expropriation. "Indian play . . . necessarily went hand in hand with the dispossession and conquest of actual Indian people" (Deloria 1998:182). Thus, Chief Illiniwek is the colonial ideology that corresponds to the experience of settler colonialism. But how exactly?

"It was, and is, appropriate that Chief Illiniwek, the embodiment of the
Red Men who had vanished before the overwhelming waves of White
Men, should return to the land of their fathers. It is fitting that he should
revisit the Illinois campus. In the name of his tribe and in memory of his
forefathers and of the warriors who had struggled and died both in pre-
historic and historic Illinois, it was proper and pleasing that the Chief
should strut his stuff and perform his ancient ritualistic dances, in the
lovely days of Indian Summer, while the Marching Band played weird
incantations before the packed Stadium of contemporary Palefaces"
(Burford 1952:407)

But Chief Illiniwek, never having existed historically, does not
actually return and "strut his stuff," "perform his ancient ritualistic
dances." Or does he? What exactly *is* going on with "the Chief," between the crowd and "the Chief"? Could there be some faint memory trace across the generations, some physiological synapse that is
triggered? Nonsense, and yet many commentators claim to see
some link, some connection between the crowd, "the Chief," and
Native Americans. Example: Chief Illiniwek's "physical body reminds us that we [Euro-Americans] can now remember and enjoy
that which we subdued, contained, dominated" (N. Anderson 1997:
3). Example: With the "Sioux costume and war bonnet, Borchers
succeeded in creating a powerful association between a football
team in Illinois, and the most-eulogized event in white-Indian history, the defeat of Custer at the Battle of the Little Bighorn" (Spindel
1997:230). Example: The 1926 halftime "event staged on the athletic turf served to effectively and *ritually* resolve the historical conflicts between the Indian and the EuroAmerican, while confirming
the dominance of the latter" (Springwood and King forthcoming;
emphasis in original).

The problem here is to link past and present in a historically sat-
isfying manner, to connect event and structure, to link the individual with a larger collectivity, to combine a social analysis with

a cultural interpretation. Look at it this way. The white conquest and defeat of Native Americans by whites during the nineteenth century, marked at the century's end by the closure of the frontier, which in effect undermined the raison d'être of Manifest Destiny, constitutes a historical break or rupture of paramount significance that can be viewed as an original or primordial trauma in the Freudian sense (Carter 1997; LaCapra 1983, 1989, 1992). Trauma, for Freud, is characterized by continual return, the "return of the repressed," which "acts-out" but does not resolve the original traumatic event until and unless it is "worked-through." Invented little more than a generation after the final defeats of Native Americans by whites, part of the cultural work Chief Illiniwek performs is staging this historical trauma.

In 1930 "an old Indian woman" from whom Borchers obtained his Chief Illiniwek costume told him "that she as a girl, had helped mutilate the dead of Custer after the battle of the Little Bighorn" (Borchers 1959).

Therefore, what is significant is not the invention of Chief Illiniwek in 1926 (production), but that he "took off," resonated with Illini fans then and now (reception). It is too pat, too easy to view the Chief's choreography performed to the "Three-in-One" as classic drama.

Two new marches written in 1928 for the University Band were added to the alma mater and telescoped together to form a trilogy, the "Three-in-One," still used today ("Chief Illiniwek" n.d.).

The Chief's dance reinvokes the once-threatening Indian as noble savage, and the resolution acts out white conquest as "anti-conquest," that is, as pacific conquest: smoking a peace pipe in 1926 and walking arm-in-arm off the field with Penn, singing the alma mater in communal unison today. Key, however, is that the Chief's acting out does not satisfactorily resolve the disjuncture between past Native American reality and present Chief Illiniwek myth.

"Playing Indian offered Americans a national fantasy—identities built not around synthesis and transformation, but around unresolved dualities themselves. Temporary, costumed play refused to synthesize the contradictions between European and Indian. Rather, it held them in near-perfect suspension, allowing Americans to have their cake and eat it too. . . . As it did so, playing Indian gave white Americans . . . a jolt of self-creative power" (Deloria 1998:185).

The Chief displaces but does not work through the original historical rupture or trauma; he can only continually return to play Indian over and over at halftime. This is why the Chief is a generic Indian rather than a historical individual. This is why he is "warlike" and the team is named the "Fighting Illini." This is why he wears Plains Indians Sioux regalia—the "noble savage" personified—rather than Woodlands Illiniwek clothing. This is why whites, preferably Eagle Scouts, and not Native Americans must play the Chief, for Chief Illiniwek is literally a story whites tell about themselves, part of their cultural construction of "whiteness" (Roediger 1991). For with the Chief the reality is myth, the myth reality. Uncomfortable thought: the Peorias of today may not be able to live up to the image of yesterday.

Humor constitutes one possible way of working through the historical trauma that the Chief stages. Yet the controversy over Chief Illiniwek today is taken so seriously that to propose such a resolution even in jest is outlandish.

We are not aware of any suitable substitute for the Chief, so we offer a solution. There are many faculty, staff, students and athletes with a Polish background. . . . I propose we adopt the Polish. Our hero could be the prince or princess of Poland. The loyalty song could be the Grand Polonaise or a Chopin piece, perhaps as played by Paderewski. The dance can be a mazurka or polonaise. . . . Poland has been conquered and overrun by Sweden, Russia, Prussians and Germany for many centuries so Poles can have a little empathy with our athletic teams. Poland rebounds. . . . Go Fighting Poles" —letter to editor (Dziul and Bamas 1997)

"Why should the University of Illinois even want a mascot that can't be fun? . . . I suggest calling our teams the Illinois Amaize'n because of the agricultural traditions of the school and the wordplay on amazing. I think a mascot that looks like a giant ear of corn on legs (similar to the beloved California raisin mascot) would be great to cheer on the teams" —letter to editor (Chassy 1998)

"I propose that our sports programs be represented by the Illinois earthworm. In the heartland of American agriculture what animal should be more appreciated? . . . Instead of one young gymnast in an 'authentic' costume, consider eight students in a costume slithering up and down the field at halftime. If we lose a game, who cares? How can you humiliate an earthworm? Better yet, when we win, what greater shame can the opponents bear than to have been beaten by a bunch of worms?" — letter to editor (Beberman 1999)

PRO-CHIEF AND ANTI-CHIEF: TALKING PAST ONE ANOTHER

One, if not the most, striking feature of the pro-Chief versus anti-Chief debate from 1988 to the present is the extent to which interlocutors on both sides talk past one another. "Mascot," say those who are anti-Chief; "honored symbol," say those who are pro-Chief.

Charlene Teters, the leading figure in the anti-Chief movement, has borne witness in both public statements and her art. "You say 'your Chief,' of course he's your Chief, you invented him" (Rosenstein 1996). In addressing the University Board of Trustees, she stated, "We are not mascots or fetishes to be worn by the dominant society. We are human beings" (Teters 1990).

Teters's art is political art; it turns the "performance art" of Chief Illiniwek back on itself. In one piece hang pennants of sports teams with their names and logos: "San Diego Caucasians," "New York Coons." In *Wiped Out* the names of Indian groups written in white on white are barely visible alongside rolls of Chief Illiniwek toilet paper, portraits of actual Native Americans are overlaid with graphics of Indians used in ads. In an installation piece the viewer must walk on a Chief Illiniwek rug in order to reach a bar that serves alcohol in bottles named after Indians.

Let us listen in on comments made by the pro-Chief side:

"I have been in the presence of students and alumni who watch the Chief perform his ceremony and I've seen tears go down their faces" — former University of Illinois president Stanley O. Ikenberry

The anti-Chief position is a "socialistic glop of political correctness" — letter to editor (Eden 1995)

Former Chief Illiniwek Tom Livingston described how as a freshman he went to a football game with an upperclassman, who disappeared around halftime. The Chief came out, did his dance, and stood while "Hail to the Orange" was sung. "It was something that moved me. It was something that inspired me. I got chills down my spine." When his friend returned, Livingston enthused, "Oh my God, you missed Chief Illiniwek!" "I didn't miss Chief Illiniwek—I am Chief Illiniwek," responded Bill Forsyth, son of a former university trustee (Rooney 1989)

"I was lucky. I made up my mind to attend the U of I when I first saw the Chief do his ceremonial dance, when I was six. I resent people trying to deny me enjoying the same experience with my children someday" — letter to editor (Gooding 1993)

"This [UI faculty senate voting 97–29 to retire the Chief] angered me. Why would it anger me, an 11-year-old kid? First, I have been going to Illinois basketball games since I was about 5 years old.... Second, I am a big fan of all Illinois sports.... People who are offended by Chief Illiniwek should not be. Doing so [eliminating the Chief] would be a terrible mistake" — letter to editor (Carpenter 1998)

"A couple weeks ago I returned to campus for the Ohio State football game. At halftime when Chief Illiniwek danced, I was shocked as there were audible boos in the stands. The Native American movement is being led by a group of misguided 'kooks' who bring dishonor and disrespect upon their people" — letter to editor (Hendricks 1993)

"My ethnic background and University of Illinois alumnus status compel me to express my opinion [on Chief Illiniwek]. I adore the graceful dances of the Chief, evoking special feelings of inspiration, dignity and delight. . . . Should the Shriners' rituals, jeweled costumes and red fezzes — all of Arabic origin — negate their noble philanthropy, or be viewed as an insult to the Muslim people? We copy because we admire — not mock" — letter to editor (Moushmof 1998)

"Minority rights are not always right" — Rick Winkel, Illinois state congressman representing Champaign-Urbana (Rosenstein 1996)

"God must be an Illini" — bumper sticker

"I bleed orange and blue" — bumper sticker

"Save the Chief, Kill the Indians!" — sign on Winnebago RV, pregame tailgate party (Springwood and King forthcoming)

The key question here is how can Chief Illiniwek be both a "positive" and "negative" representation — positive for some, negative for others?

Taken individually, the extraordinary artworks in The Age of Sultan Suleyman the Magnificent *exhibition certainly portray the Ottoman Turks in a positive light (Atil 1987). But considering the show's "absences" — the failure to display anything other than elite objects patronized by the palace, not to problematize the historical connection between Ottoman imperialist expansion and the development of this court culture — suggests a larger historical and cultural context which results in coding the show more negatively (Wallis 1994).*

So it is, too, with the Chief. Pro-Chief supporters emphasize the specific "text" of the Chief—the dress, the dance—and view it as a "positive" representation of Native Americans. Anti-Chief opponents, on the other hand, pay more attention to the "context" of the Chief. Thus, the "Chief" performs a secular dance but in primarily religious regalia; the Chief wears Plains Indian Sioux clothing in former Woodlands Indian Illiniwek country. Contrasting the "Chief" with the larger Native American context, anti-Chief opponents regard the Chief as inappropriate and inauthentic, a negative representation.

For those who are anti-Chief, pro-Chief supporters valorize a Chief that is wrenched out of context, decontextualized. But the issue that anti-Chief opponents do not engage is that if viewed in isolation, today's "Chief" is not a negative representation, not humorous or a caricature. It is a positive representation—solemn, serious.

Because each side accentuates certain aspects of the Chief but does not engage others—because they talk past one another—it makes it too easy, too simple to label Chief supporters "wrong" and Chief opponents "right." Politically, this makes good strategic sense; it is an excellent example of strategic essentialism, "a *strategic* use of positivist essentialism in a scrupulously visible political interest" (Spivak 1988a : 13). The Chief is essentialized as inauthentic and inappropriate, which leads to anti-Chief calls for this "mascot" to be retired. Intellectually, however, the issue is complicated by the fact that the Chief's decontextualized performance is more positive, more an "honored symbol" than it is negative, a mascot caricaturing Native Americans.

If human subjects are not essentialized, that is, considered intrinsically autonomous, authentic, bounded, but rather viewed as subjects continuously constituted, then the larger intellectual issue becomes that of appropriation, the power to appropriate. In this perspective, the key question is when, to what extent, under what conditions, is it all right to appropriate another's culture? If identity is malleable and culture continually constructed, then when is playing Chief Illiniwek mimicry and culturally derogatory, and when is it imitation, the sincerest form of flattery? "There is a very fine line between appreciation and appropriation, respect and self-aggrandizement, a line that is always shifting and impossible to decide in advance" (Root 1997:231).

> *The Boy Scout Koshare troop of La Junta, Colorado, performed Indian dances, made replicas of Indian material culture, and built a museum for Indian cultural objects. In 1953 they prepared costumes needed to perform the Zuni Shalako dance. The Zunis protested the Koshares' plans. "After visiting the Koshare kiva, however, the Zuni people changes their minds. They decided that the scouts' precisely copied Shalakos were authentic and real, and they took the masks back to Zuni and built a special kiva for them" (Deloria 1998:152).*

At the same time as New Age "white Indians" appropriate Native American culture, they valorize it as positive. Uncomfortable thought: such white New Age "wannabe" Indians are actually much closer to pro-Chief supporters, who regard the Chief as an "honored symbol," than either group would like to admit.

History helps here by establishing context rather than viewing today's Chief in isolation. A single synchronic snapshot of the Chief stilled in time may well be interpreted as "positive." But when viewed diachronically, tracing changes over time in the varied use of the Chief image—for example, just look at *Illio*, the university yearbook, year by year since the 1920s—lifts the curtain on a considerably more "negative" context. In recent years pro-Chief forces spearheaded by the university have had to engage in more or less continuous "damage control." The orange and blue "I" has been banned from the Chief's chin. In 1989 Squanto was "retired" as the Agronomy Department logo (Cook 1989). By 1990 cheerleaders and fans were prohibited from wearing "war paint" at games. In 1991 the Chief was banned from making appearances in the homecoming parade and pep rally. In 1993 Chief Illiniwek was banned from use on homecoming parade floats (Gehrt 1993). Changes over time in the Chief and related images also effectively undermine the fewer but still-heard pro-Chief claims to Native American "authenticity." "Is he [the Chief character] authentic? His costume is authentic twentieth century Sioux" (Spindel 1997:228).

To take the argument further and in a different direction, postcolonial theory fails to simultaneously address both anti-Chief and pro-Chief positions. To be sure, terms and categories such as "invention of tradition," "imperialist nostalgia," "imagined communities," and "playing Indian" are useful in elucidating certain of the issues at stake. Yet the contrast with Jay Rosenstein's film *In Whose Honor?* (1996), with all its rich ethnographic detail, is striking. Thus, when it comes to the most significant aspect of the Chief controversy, namely, the way Chief supporters and opponents literally talk past one another—that is, the fact that they inhabit different discursive fields—postcolonial theory is of limited use.

At the time of the Columbian quincentenary Coco Fusco and Guillermo Gómez-Peña toured a performance piece, The Couple in the Cage, *in which they presented themselves as part of a recently discovered Amerindian group, locked in a golden cage, and displayed for the public dressed in a hybrid mixture of feathers, grass skirts, face paint, studded leather, and sunglasses. Fusco and Gómez-Peña thought they were critiquing the historical display of indigenous peoples. Unsuspecting audiences frequently took the couple for "real." How strong must the psychic (Euro-American cultural) imprint of the "exotic primitive" be for such "play" to be viewed as "authentic"? (Fusco and Heredia 1993).*

What we have in the Chief Illiniwek controversy is mutually exclusive communicative communities. What we need is a way to account for different subject positions in a nonhierarchical way, one that does not "put down" those audience members who did not "get" Fusco and Gómez-Peña's satiric performance, one that does not reject with a knee jerk those who see "the Chief" as positive. We need some way, in other words, to acknowledge individuals as subjects imbued with agency and, at the same time, a position from which to comment critically.

In Jay Rosenstein's film In Whose Honor? *(1996), the camera zooms in and pans across a woman at a pregame tailgate party who is wearing a plethora of Chief paraphernalia—buttons, earrings. She points out her accessories to the camera, "and my Chief earrings here," and not missing a beat she continues, "And I honor the Chief." Her Chief identity is so elaborately articulated that it is clearly rich and meaningful for her, but it is not an identity I empathize with or agree with politically.*

The now-old "new social history" in the 1970s aimed to write history "from the bottom up," the history of peasants and workers; the Indian subaltern studies school in the 1980s similarly tried to represent, to give voice to, subaltern groups, especially women and peasants. Voice, agency, and subjecthood are fine so long as the academic representers do not speak for the subaltern represented, so long as those represented are "our" kind of subaltern or lower-class type (O'Hanlon 1989; Spivak 1988b). But the project of recuperation and recovery runs into trouble when we do not much like "them," for example, Chief Illiniwek supporters. "When the 'native' voice is evoked in support of the 'correct' ideology its validity is rarely challenged. However, in the case of the Chief there is a definite rupture between what is 'politically correct' [anti-Chief] and what is being said by the 'authentic native' [local white pro-Chief] voice" (Miller 1997).

Illinois. Illiniwek Confederation. Chief Illiniwek. Champaign-Urbana. Playing Indian. Appropriation. Power. Identity. In the end, it all comes down to identity. The absence in the presence of Chief Illiniwek and the presence in the absence of Native Americans demonstrate that far from a superficial issue of "political correctness," as pro-Chief supporters portray it, Chief Illiniwek in fact raises fundamental questions about identity: About the identity of those of us who live in Champaign-Urbana, but also in the surrounding region and beyond. About how a community is imagined, about who does and does not count as a member of a community. An "imagined community" is fine, but what does the already existing community stand for?

"That the community of the University of Illinois should choose to maintain the empty tomb of the dead Indian [the empty buckskin costume which any suitably athletic male candidate can wear] as its source of pride and honor speaks eloquently of the community's feeling of insecurity, its unwillingness to recognize its own margins and in doing so, debunk the mirage of consensus" (Kuntz 1997:9-10).

Playing Indian at Illinois has changed over time. When the "Chief" was invented in the 1920s, the final defeats of Native Americans and the closing of the frontier were still recent history. With the threat of the "savage" Indian eliminated, it became possible to express imperialist nostalgia for the "vanishing Indian." Today, pro-Chief supporters construct as part of their identity a feeling for, a bond with the "Chief."

"Playing Indian gave white Americans . . . a jolt of self-creative power" *(Deloria 1998:185).*

In the process pro-Chief supporters police the borders between those who agree with them and those who do not. Border patrol takes the form of pitting an "us" against a "them." Opponents of the Chief are regularly termed "foreigners" and "outsiders," people who come in from the outside to tell an "us" what to do. As outsiders, they just do not understand "our" Chief, say Chief supporters, yet they are trying to take something away from "us."

> *"Leave our Chief alone. . . . The very small group against the Chief should go to another state and stay out of Illinois. Charlene Teeters [sic] should stay out of our sight. . . . I have rights as an Illinois citizen to vote, but I can't go to the protesters' home state and vote. . . . Keep the Chief. He belongs to us, not them"* —letter to editor (White, 1998)

> *"I am of Cherokee descent and raised by a Pawnee uncle . . . the antagonists [of the Chief] are made up predominantly of whites, blacks, Asians, Indians who are not even native to Illinois and persons who are out for a cheap date"* —letter to editor (Norwood 1999)

> *"It is interesting to note that of the number of persons dissenting [against the Chief], many have little or no affiliation with our university and do not even live in our state. Many of the student dissidents are transients, in that they attend the University of Illinois, get the degree they want and move on. Many faculty could be considered transients"* — letter to editor (Mitze, 1998)

On the other side, many in the university community, especially faculty, are "anti-Chief." In 1994 a faculty inclusivity committee recommended banning the Chief (Puch and Wurth 1994). In 1998 the faculty senate voted 97–29 to get rid of the Chief; both the anthropology and history departments went on record as being anti-Chief. In spring 2000 the history department reiterated its anti-Chief stand and was joined by the English department. This is commented on in the local press. Yet my sense is that a far more pervasive attitude even among those nominally anti-Chief is "I'm embarrassed to be associated with a university with Chief Illiniwek as a mascot."

"Our school mascot is actively turning off more and more people, not just in our school but increasingly beyond our borders" — Alma Gottlieb (quoted in "Chief, Rhetorically Speaking" 2000)

White elite academics wish in the worst way that the Chief would just go away. Yet this attitude, too, tends to erase Native Americans. First, it disassociates the Chief issue from the actual lived situation of Native Americans. Second, this response prevents a connection from being made between whites playing Indian playing Chief Illiniwek and what this says in turn about Champaign-Urbana identity. Uncomfortable thought: wishing the Chief would go away, and the concomitant tendency to avoid engaging the larger context of the Chief, in effect erases the very Native Americans whom opponents of the Chief ostensibly support.

I, too, have played Indian. I am an Eagle Scout. Member of Order of the Arrow. Hiked the 50-mile Silver Mocassin trail. Danced with a bustle made of magenta and chartreuse feathers. At Stanford when they were still the "Stanford Indians," attended a football game where Chief Lightfoot performed. However, I was lucky (or unlucky, depending on your point of view), since I never became emotionally invested, and playing Indian was easy to shuck off. So I went in search of those Other Indians, Columbus's original ones . . .

ACKNOWLEDGMENTS

I thank Brenda Farnell, Fred Hoxie, Rich King, Debbie Reese, Charles Springwood, Carol Spindel, and students in my undergraduate and graduate seminars on history and postcolonial studies. Special thanks to Nicole Anderson, E. J. Carter, Richard Gringeri, Jane Kuntz, Jay Rosenstein, and Sarah Wenzel for stimulating conversations and background information.

REFERENCES

Anderson, Benedict. 1983. *Imagined Communities*. New York: Verso.

Anderson, Nicole. 1997. "Chief Illiniwek Remembered." Unpublished class paper, University of Illinois at Urbana-Champaign.

Atil, Esin. 1987. *The Age of Sultan Süleyman the Magnificent*. New York: Abrams.

Bakhtin, Mikhail. [1965] 1984. *Rabelais and His World*. Bloomington: Indiana University Press.

Beberman, Martin. 1999. Letter to editor. *Champaign-Urbana News-Gazette*, 10 Nov.

Bial, Raymond. 1993. *Champaign: A Pictorial History*. St. Louis: G. Bradley.
———. 1994. *Urbana: A Pictorial History*. St. Louis: G. Bradley.

Borchers, Webber. 1959. Letter. Chief Illiniwek reference folders, University of Illinois Archives.

Burford, Cary Clive. 1952. *"We're Loyal to You, Illinois": The Story of the University of Illinois Bands*. Danville IL: Interstate.

Carpenter, Michael. 1998. Letter to editor. *Champaign-Urbana News-Gazette*, 27 March.

Carter, E. J. 1997. "Loss, Trauma, and Transference: The Chief Illiniwek Debate." Unpublished class paper, University of Illinois at Urbana-Champaign.

Chassy, Carol. 1998. Letter to editor. *Champaign-Urbana News-Gazette*, 17 April.

"Chief Illiniwek Tradition." N.d. Manuscript. Chief Illiniwek reference folders, University of Illinois Archives.

"Chief, Rhetorically Speaking." 2000. *Champaign-Urbana News-Gazette*, 15 April.

Cook, Anne. 1989. "Squanto, Lacking Chief's Clout, Out as Agronomy Logo." *Champaign-Urbana News-Gazette*, 7 Dec.

Deloria, Philip. 1998. *Playing Indian*. New Haven: Yale University Press.

Dziuk, Philip, and Grzegorz Banas. 1997. Letter to editor. *Champaign-Urbana News-Gazette*, 5 Nov.

Eden, Paul. 1995. Letter to editor. *Champaign-Urbana News-Gazette*, 10 Nov.

Ewers, John C. 1964. "The Emergence of the Plains Indian as the Symbol of the North American Indian." In *Annual Report of the Board of Regents of the Smithsonian Institution*, 531–44. Washington DC: Smithsonian Institution.

Fusco, Coco, and Paula Heredia. 1993. *The Couple in the Cage: A Guatinaui Odyssey*. Film.

Gehrt, Trey. 1993. "Chief Banned from Floats." *Champaign-Urbana Daily Illini*, 29 Oct.

Gooding, John A. 1993. Letter to editor. *Champaign-Urbana Daily Ilini*, 8 Nov.

Hauser, Raymond E. 1976. "The Illinois Indian Tribe: From Autonomy and Self-Sufficiency to Dependency and Depopulation." *Illinois Historical Journal* 69: 127–38.

Hendricks, E. Charles. 1993. Letter to editor. *Champaign-Urbana Daily Illini*, 9 Nov.

Hickey, Timothy J. 1989. *Indian Lore of Champaign County*. Champaign IL: Prairie Provincial Press.

Hobsbawm, Eric, and Terence Ranger, eds. 1983. *The Invention of Tradition*. New York: Cambridge University Press.

Horsman, Richard. 1981. *Race and Manifest Destiny: The Origins of American Racial Anglo-Saxism*. Cambridge: Harvard University Press.

Hoxie, Frederick. 1994. "Exploring a Cultural Borderland: Native American Journeys of Discovery in the Early Twentieth Century." In *Discovering America: Essays on the Search for an Identity*, ed. David Thelen and Frederick Hoxie, 135–61. Urbana: University of Illinois Press.

———. 1998. "The Curious Story of Reformers and American Indians." In *Indians in American History*, 2d ed., ed. Frederick Hoxie and Peter Iverson, 177–97. Wheeling, IL: Harlan Davidson.

Hoxie, Frederick, and Peter Iverson, eds. 1998. *Indians in American History*, 2d ed. Wheeling, IL: Harlan Davidson.

Illio. 1983, 1988. University of Illinois at Urbana-Champaign Yearbook.

Iverson, Peter. 1982. *Carlos Montezuma and the Changing World of American Indians*. Albuquerque: University of New Mexico Press.

Kammen, Michael. 1997. *In the Past Lane?* New York: Oxford University Press.

King, C. Richard, ed. 2000. *Postcolonial America*. Urbana: University of Illinois Press.

King, C. Richard, and Charles Fruehling Springwood. Forthcoming. "Choreographing Colonialism: Athletic Mascots, (Dis)Embodied Indians, and EuroAmerican Subjectivities." In *Cultural Studies: A Research Annual*. Vol. 5, ed. Norman K. Denzin. Stamford CT: JAI Press.

Kuntz, Jane. 1997. "Remembrance (by Forgetting) of Things Past: Chief Illiniwek and the Imagined Community." Unpublished class paper, University of Illinois at Urbana-Champaign.

LaCapra, Dominick. 1983. "Marxism and Intellectual History." *Rethinking Intellectual History: Texts, Contexts, Language*, 325–46. Ithaca: Cornell University Press.

———. 1989. *Soundings in Critical Theory*. Ithaca: Cornell University Press.

———. 1992. "Representing the Holocaust: Reflections on the Historians' Debate." In *Probing the Limits of Representation: Nazism and the "Final Solution,"* ed. Saul Friedlander. Cambridge: Harvard University Press.

Lawrence, D. H. 1924. *Studies in Classic American Literature*. London: Secker.

Miller, Ian. 1997. "Authentic Ethnicity?" Unpublished class paper, University of Illinois at Urbana-Champaign.

Mitze, Bill. 1998. Letter to editor. *Champaign-Urbana News-Gazette*, 24 April.

Montezuma, Carlos. 1888. "The Indian of Yesterday: The Early Life of Dr. Carlos Montezuma Written by Himself." Unpublished manuscript. Chief Illiniwek reference folders, University of Illinois Archives.

———. 1907. "The Government, the Public, and the American Indian." *Alumni Quarterly of the University of Illinois* 1: 213–22.

———. 1921. "Indian Imposters." *Wassaja* 5: 3–4.

Moushmof, Milco. 1998. Letter to editor. *Champaign-Urbana News-Gazette*, 18 March.

Norwood, John. Letter to editor. *Champaign-Urbana News-Gazette*, 4 Nov.

O'Hanlon, Rosalind. 1989. "Recovering the Subject: Subaltern Studies and Histories of Resistance in Colonial South Asia." *Modern Asian Studies* 22: 189–224.

O'Rourke, Dennis. 1987. *Cannibal Tours*. Film. Los Angeles: Direct Cinema Limited.

Pratt, Mary Louise. 1992. *Imperial Eyes*. New York: Routledge.

Prochaska, David. 1990. *Making Algeria French: Colonialism in Bône, 1870–1919*. New York: Cambridge University Press.

———. 1996. "History as Literature, Literature as History: Cagayous of Algiers." *American Historical Review* 101: 670–711.

Puch, Dorothy, and Julie Wurth. 1994. "Group Want Chief Retired." *Champaign-Urbana News-Gazette*, 18 Oct.

Roediger, David. 1991. *Wages of Whiteness: Race and the Making of the American Working Class*. Boston: Beacon Press.

Rooney, Peter. 1989. "Tom Livingston: Current Chief Defends UI Athletic Mascot as 'Noble' Symbol." *Champaign-Urbana News-Gazette*, 26 Nov.

Root, Deborah. 1997. "'White Indians': Appropriation and the Politics of Display." In *Borrowed Power: Essays on Cultural Appropriation*, ed. Bruce Ziff and Pratima Rao, 225–33. New Brunswick: Rutgers University Press.

Rosaldo, Renato. 1989. "Imperialist Nostalgia," *Culture and Truth: The Remaking of Social Analysis*, 68–87. Boston: Beacon Press.

Rosenstein, Jay. 1996. *In Whose Honor? American Indian Mascots in Sports*. Videocassette. Ho-ho-kus NJ: New Day Films.

Slotkin, Richard. 1985. *The Fatal Environment: The Myth of the Frontier in the Age of Industrialization, 1800–1890*. New York: Atheneum.

Solberg, Winton. 1968. *The University of Illinois, 1867–1894*. Urbana: University of Illinois Press.

Spindel, Carol. 1997. "We Honor Your Memory: Chief Illiniwek of the Halftime Illini." *Crabtree Review* 3: 217–38.

Spivak, Gayatri. 1988a. "Subaltern Studies: Deconstructing Historiography." In *Selected Subaltern Studies*, ed. Ranajit Guha and G. Spivak, 3–32. New York: Oxford University Press.

———. 1988b. "Can the Subaltern Speak?" In *Marxism and the Interpretation of Culture*, ed. Cary Nelson and Lawrence Grossberg, 271–313. Urbana: University of Illinois Press.

Springwood, Charles Fruehling, and C. Richard King. Forthcoming. "Race, Ritual, and Remembrance Embodied: Manifest Destiny and the Ritual Sacrifice of 'Chief Illiniwek.'" In *Exercising Power: The Making and Re-making of the Body*, ed. Cheryl Cole, Michael A. Messner, and John W. Loy. Albany: SUNY Press.

Temple, Wayne. 1958. *Indian Villages of the Illinois Country: Historic Tribes*. Springfield, IL: Illinois State Museum.

Teters, Charlene. 1990. "Chief Illiniwek an Appropriate Symbol?" Presentation to the Board of Trustees. Manuscript. Chief Illiniwek reference folders, University of Illinois Archives.

Thornton, Russell. 1987. *American Indian Holocaust and Survival*. Norman: University of Oklahoma Press.

Tregillis, Helen Cox. 1991. *The Indians of Illinois*. Bowie MD: Heritage Books.

"University of Illinois Chief Illiniwek Auditions." 1993. Manuscript. Chief Illiniwek reference folders, University of Illinois Archives.

Veysey, Laurence. 1979. "The Autonomy of American History Reconsidered." *American Quarterly* 31: 455–77.

Wallis, Brian. 1994. "Selling Nations: International Exhibitions and Cultural Diplomacy." In *Museum Culture*, ed. Daniel J. Sherman and Irit Rogoff. Minneapolis: University of Minnesota Press.

White, Charles. 1998. Letter to editor. *Champaign-Urbana News-Gazette*, 26 March.

White, Richard. 1991. *The Middle Ground: Indians, Empires, and Republics in the Great Lakes Region, 1650–1815*. New York: Cambridge University Press.

Whitney, Ellen M. 1976. "Indian History and the Indians of Illinois." *Illinois Historical Journal* 69:139–46.

Wilentz, Sean. 1984. "Against Exceptionalism: Class Consciousness and the American Labor Movement, 1790–1920." *International Labor and Working Class History* 26:1–24.

Wolf, Eric. 1982. *Europe and the People without History*. Berkeley: University of California Press.

PART THREE

Activism

CHAPTER 8

Fighting Name-Calling

Challenging "Redskins" in Court

•

Suzan Shown Harjo

Most Native Americans despise the term *Redskins* and say that it is the worst epithet hurled at Native Peoples in the English language. The owners of Washington's professional football team say the name is not offensive and that it honors Native Americans. In 1999, a federal panel of judges ruled on the Native American side in the seminal lawsuit on the issue, *Harjo et al. v. Pro Football, Inc.* Now, the team's owners are fighting tooth and nail in court to preserve federal trademark protections for the name.

I am the Harjo in the lawsuit seven of us filed on September 10, 1992. We petitioned the U.S. Patent and Trademark Office for cancellation of federal registrations for "Redskins," "Redskinettes" (their cheerleaders), and associated names of the team in the nation's capital. The team's owners lost the important first round in litigation on April 2, 1999, before the cognizant federal agency that decides what material the federal government will protect against imitators. The Trademark Trial and Appeal Board found that "Redskins" was offensive historically and remained so from the date of the first trademark license, 1967, to the present. The three-judge panel unanimously decided to cancel the federal trademarks "on the grounds that the subject marks may disparage Native Americans and may bring them into contempt or disrepute."

On the heels of the announcement that the team was sold for a record-breaking $800 million, its owners appealed the decision to the federal district court in the District of Columbia. On June 1, 1999, the owners pleaded for a new trial to reverse the trademark agency. They want a new ruling that it is legally permissible for the federal government to protect the owners in the exclusive privilege of making money from the team's name. Our side defends the decision and hopes that, once the trademarks actually are canceled and commercially devalued, the disparaging name will be dropped. In short, the contest is between federal protection against racism and private profit from racism. It is a centuries-old struggle.

ORIGINS OF *REDSKINS*

The term *Redskins* has despicable origins in the days of Indian bounty hunting in the 1600s and 1700s. Bounties under a dollar were paid for Indian children, women, and men, dead or alive. For ease of commerce, few live Indians were delivered to the marketplace, and trade in dead bodies flourished. It quickly became too cumbersome for bounty hunters to transport wagon loads of bodies and gunny sacks of heads, and too bothersome for bounty payers to dispose of them. Thus began the practice of paying bounties for the bloody red skins and scalps as evidence of Indian kill.

In the 1800s, trade in dead Indians became more refined and "scientific," as soldiers collected heads for the U.S. Army Surgeon General's "Indian Crania Study." The Army and Smithsonian Museums advertised and paid for whole Indians and parts of Indians for study, and their extensive collections exist today in prominent museums and private collections in America and Europe.

Over the centuries, American politicians, soldiers, historians, and reporters used various wrongheaded names for Native Peoples, beginning with *Indians*—the name based on Columbus's notion that he had landed in India. The most common terms for us in the

English-language record were *Savages* and *Hostiles*. The one reserved for the nastiest name-calling was *Redskins*.

In reporting the Battle of Little Big Horn of 1876, headlines of the major newspapers of the day screamed *Custer's Men Lured into Trap by Wily Redskins* and *Major's Men Were Lured into Ambush by Fleeing Redskins*. The Sand Creek Massacre in 1864 was reported by a leading American paper under the banner *About Eight Hundred Redskins Killed in the Engagement—Savage Atrocities Which Provoked the Fearful Retribution*. Another scion of journalism headlined its account of the Wounded Knee Massacre of 1890, *Redskins Are Being Shot Down . . . without Mercy / Squaws and Bucks Treated Alike / No Quarter Being Shown to Any Hostiles*.

REDSKINS FOR RECREATION, REPRESSION FOR REAL INDIANS

The term *Redskins* first appeared as an American professional football team name in 1933, the *Boston Redskins*. The team moved to the District of Columbia in 1937 and became the *Washington Redskins*. In the team's fight song, *Hail to the Redskins*, fans urged their "braves on the warpath" to "scalp 'em" and "fight for old DC." In December of 1947, the team's owners advertised a "Redskin Pow Wow" for an upcoming game, proclaiming, "REDSKIN ROOTERS HAVE HEAP BIG TIME NEW YORK CITY . . . REDSKIN FANS HELP REDSKIN WARRIORS SCALP PALEFACE GIANTS."

Redskins was spawned in sports during a sorry period in American history. When the Boston team first used the name in 1933, there were fewer than 350,000 Native People alive in the United States. A debilitating and deadly state of federal repression of Indian religious freedom and civil liberties was in its sixth decade. Although the Native American population was up from 250,000 at the start of the twentieth century, most Native People lived in dire health and poverty conditions, and the future of many Indian nations and individuals was very much in doubt. Native Peoples were not in any position to lodge protests against their stereotyping in popular culture. These conditions continued for most American Indians and Alaska Natives during the years when the team's name and logos were first used and licensed, and until very recent times.

Native Americans in the first third of the 1900s did not enjoy the most basic civil, constitutional, or human rights. Indian religious practices were outlawed. For more than a century, Congress had funded Christian denominations to "civilize" the Indians. Native children were taken forcibly from their families and sent to federal boarding schools. There, the hostages/students were subjected to corporal punishment for speaking their tribal languages; barred from wearing traditional clothes, shoes, hairstyles, or religious symbols; and forced to adopt English and Christianity. These practices continued in all boarding schools until the late 1930s and in some schools until the 1970s.

Despite the enactment of the Indian Veterans Citizenship Act of 1919 and the Indian Citizenship Act of 1924, Indian people were barred by law from voting in Arizona and New Mexico until 1948. Most Indians faced informal but effective barriers to political participation until the mid-1970s, when the Voting Rights Act was applied to Indian Country.

In 1933, the "Civilization Regulations" of the secretary of the interior, which had been in effect since 1880 and reissued in 1904, banned all Native traditional religious activities, ceremonies, and dancing and imposed stiff incarceration, starvation, and, in many cases, open-ended penalties for those found guilty or suspected of "Indian offenses." Under the rules, an offender could be named as a "hostile," which was tantamount to a death warrant, and such leaders as Chiefs Sitting Bull, Big Foot, Crazy Horse, Geronimo, and Joseph were hunted down and killed or confined after being placed on the lists of "hostiles" or "fomenters of dissent" or "ringleaders."

Some of the "Indian offenses" included roaming off the reservation, possessing ponies, preventing children from attending the schools, conducting giveaways for celebratory or mourning ceremonies, and exhibiting or promoting "anti-progressive" behavior, "heathenish customs," or "practices of a so-called 'medicine man.'"

During this discredited era when the "Redskins" emerged in professional sports, Indian-related names and symbols surfaced in amateur athletics. Among these were the "Redmen" of St. John's University, the "Indians" at Dartmouth College and Stanford University, and the "Saltine Warrior" at Syracuse University. As documented by several of the essays in this volume, these names and mascots have been abandoned. "Redskins" has been dropped by Miami University in Oxford, Ohio, and Southern Nazarene University in Bethany, Oklahoma, and by high schools in Arvada, Colorado, Louisville, Kentucky, and Little River, Kansas. While nearly a thousand educational athletics programs have dropped their Native references since 1970, commercial sports businesses have resisted all calls for change.

WASHINGTON TEAM OWNERS UNRESPONSIVE
TO NATIVE AMERICAN CONCERNS

Native Americans have opposed the team's use of the name since its inception, but the team's owners and the National Football League—which has paid the Washington team owners' court costs—have been unresponsive. Since the early 1970s, the team's owners have "honored" Native Americans by refusing to meet with any who advocate a name change for the team. On January 18, 1972, a Native American coalition wrote to the team owners' attorney, asking him to "imagine a hypothetical National Football League, in which the other teams are known as the New York Kikes, the Chicago Polocks, the San Francisco Dagoes, the Detroit Niggers, the Los Angeles Spics, etc."

Making the case for the coalition of Native organizations, Harold M. Gross of the Indian Legal Information Development Service also wrote of the term's origins: "Born at a time in our history when the national policy was to seize Indian land and resources, and hunt down Indian people who stood in the way, the term 'Redskin' has been perpetuated through such media as western movies and television. Most often, the term is coupled with other derogatory adjectives, as 'dirty Redskin' or 'pesky Redskin' which is used interchangeably with the word 'savage' to portray a misleading and denigrating image of the Native American."

During the 1980s, I was head of the National Congress of American Indians (NCAI), the oldest and largest national Indian organization. We tried, to no avail, to meet with the team's then-owner, Jack Kent Cooke, but were not afforded the courtesy of a direct response. On January 15, 1988, he did write to the Concerned Indian Parents — a group in Minneapolis that had urged a team name change — saying, "I want you to know that I am totally out of sympathy with your project." A week later, Cooke answered us, indirectly, through reporter Paul Walsy, whose story ran on the UPI wire service on January 22, 1988: "Redskins owner Jack Kent Cooke has left no room for negotiation. 'There's not a single, solitary jot, tittle, whit chance in the world' that the Redskins will adopt a new nickname, Cooke said. 'I like the name and it's not a derogatory name.'"

It was clear that the team's owners had closed minds and would not change the team's name voluntarily. We explored various litigation options, rejecting the standard civil rights approaches as the least likely to prevail in court or to capture the attention of the most commercially successful team in sports. Without a viable litigation strategy, we focused on the court of public opinion, raising the issue at every chance in any available forum. One opportunity arose unexpectedly, in a hearing held by the U.S. Commission on Civil Rights on January 28, 1988. The subject was tribal courts, to which some commissioners were hostile, and their jokey chatter was about the prospects of the "Redskins" in the upcoming Super Bowl. I addressed the offensive name in my testimony, saying that such slurs in sports targeting others would not be permitted: "We have emotional scarring that is taking place . . . the highest rate of teenage suicide of any population in this country, which comes from low self-esteem, which comes from having those kids' elders . . . mocked, dehumanized, cartooned, stereotyped. That is what is causing the deaths of many of our children. We can't be polite about these problems anymore."

MAKING THE CASE IN THE COURT OF PUBLIC OPINION
Dismayed by the experience before the civil rights panel, I sought the counsel of an old friend, Howard Simons, then-curator of the Neiman Foundation at Harvard, on how to raise public awareness about the problem. Simons, who previously was managing editor of the *Washington Post*, wrote to one of the paper's top columnists, Richard Cohen, spelling out my position on Native-related names and images in sports and encouraging him to talk with me and to take a position on the topic. Cohen did, and his column, which ran on April 17, 1988, read in part:

> Indians have the highest suicide rate of all Americans. Their alcohol-related deaths are 459 percent higher. The number of accidents is 155 percent higher. Diabetes, 107 percent higher. . . . If the Redskins really wanted to portray the American Indian, their 'chief' would be a broken-down, sick old man. . . . Of course, there are many reasons for this sad state of affairs — not the least of them being the one-time policy of the government to destroy Indian culture and religion. But one current-day factor has to be self-image. . . . It hardly enhances the self-esteem of an Indian youth to always see his people — himself — represented as a cartoon character. And, always, the caricature is suggestive of battle, of violence —

of the Indian warrior, the brave, the chief, the warpath, the beating of tom-toms. . . . The National Congress of American Indians has asked the Redskins to change their name. That polite request has been rebuffed by the haughty Cooke. Other teams, though, have bowed to Indian wishes. . . . Little by little, we have learned that the pride of whole peoples is not a toy . . . there are few American Indians in the Washington area, so they have no clout. So I turn to the people who do — the celebrities who stock the owner's box at Redskins games. Would Cooke's Jewish guests attend if the team were called the Hymies? . . . It's time the Redskins changed their name. A rose by any other name would smell as sweet, but a team that insists on retaining an offensive name just plain stinks.

The leading sports columnists for the *Post* also called for the team to change its name. "Redskins, easily, is the most offensive nickname," wrote Michael Wilbon on October 19, 1991. "It needs to go (as do these stupid mascots). Would the Washington Palefaces fly? The Washington Darkies? Of course not. A black man running through the stands of RFK in that burgundy-and-gold Indian headdress is appallingly akin to a white man strutting around in blackface. Can't we get to the point of seeing that prejudice isn't isolated and isn't to be ignored by one group because it appears to affect someone else?"

On February 16, 1992, the *Oregonian* in Portland announced its policy to "immediately discontinue using sports teams' names and nicknames that many Americans feel are offensive to members of racial, religious or ethnic groups . . . this will include reference to Redskins, Redmen, Indians and Braves." Three other important media outlets soon adopted the Oregon paper's lead — the *Star Tribune* in Minneapolis, the *Salt Lake Tribune* in Salt Lake City, and WOL-*Radio* in Washington DC.

The following year, on March 5, 1992, the *Washington Post* spoke. Editorializing on "The Redskin Issue," the paper called for a name change, stating that "now is the time to do it." The editors opined that "the time-hallowed name bestowed upon the local National Football League champions—the Redskins—is really pretty offensive . . . to say that the use of the term 'Redskins' is well-intentioned or that it is not meant to be objectionable sidesteps the real issue. This is not a term fashioned by American Indians. The nickname was assigned to them, just as the pejorative designation 'darkies' was once imposed on African-American slaves. That was wrong then; this is wrong now. That the usage is common and innocently repeated out of habit makes it no less of an insensitive or insulting remark to those who are on the receiving end. We can do better."

NATIVE AMERICAN EFFORTS IN THE 1990S

The most visible effort to end anti-Indian racism in sports was launched by a project of the Morning Star Institute (a national Indian rights organization in Washington, DC, of which I have served as president since 1984), the 1992 Alliance, and the Elders Circle, which issued a declaration on October 12, 1990. It read, in pertinent part: "We call upon the entertainment and news industries, the sports and advertising worlds and all those with influence in shaping popular culture to forego the use of dehumanizing, stereotyping, cartooning images and information regarding our peoples, and to recognize their responsibility for the emotional violence their fields have perpetuated against our children."

Tribal governments also denounced the use of Native names and symbols in sports. The twenty-six members of the United Indian Nations in Oklahoma unanimously adopted a resolution on April 24, 1990, citing the "Washington Redskins" and "urging educational institutions, businesses and organizations to abandon caricatures of American Indians that promote negative images and racism." The resolution was endorsed by the National Congress of American Indians on December 6, 1991. Morning Star and NCAI joined forces with DC City Council member William Lightfoot on

March 3, 1992, to endorse his resolution calling for the Washington football team to change its name.

During the 1991–92 football season, the "Redskins" were dogged by demonstrators at their games. The largest protest, some two thousand people, took place outside the Minneapolis Metrodome site of Super Bowl XXVI on January 26, 1992. A newly launched group, the National Coalition on Racism in Sports and the Media, organized the demonstrators from a score of national organizations. They sported such banners as "Washington Rednecks" and called for the Washington team to drop its "racist name." A key player on the Washington team, Charles Mann, was asked by a network news reporter what he thought of the protest over the name. Mann responded that he did not know all the details, but that "if some Native Americans are offended, then the name should be changed."

DEVELOPING THE STRATEGY AND TEAM FOR LITIGATION
One of the people who was edified by the Super Bowl protest was a young patent and trademark lawyer with the prestigious Dorsey & Whitney law firm in Minneapolis. Stephen R. Baird was writing a law journal article on the 1946 trademark law. His research was keyed to Section 2(a) of the Lanham Act (15 U.S.C., Section 1052[2]), which states, in part, "No trademark . . . shall be refused registration on the principal register on account of its nature unless it—(a) Consists of or comprises . . . scandalous matter; or matter which may disparage . . . persons . . . or bring them into contempt, or disrepute."

Baird's theory was that the federal license registrations for the Washington "Redskins" were issued in violation of the trademark agency's operative legal authority. He wanted to learn why others had not used the mechanism to cancel the licenses and to force a name change. He did a Lexus search and found my name in various articles on the subject, contacted Morning Star, and talked at length with then-associate director, Gail E. Chehak (Klamath), who recommended a meeting. I balked at the notion of taking time from a taxing schedule to inform an attorney's research, but Chehak convinced me to meet with Baird and his wife, Debbie, at Morning Star in the spring of 1992.

Baird asked two questions for his research: Why did I reject the U.S. Patent and Trademark Office as a forum for getting the Washington team's name changed? Why did I reject Section 2 of the Lanham Act as a cause of action? The answers were simple. I never thought of the PTO as a forum and never heard of the Lanham Act. Baird took us to school on the PTO and the trademark law, and before the afternoon's conversation ended, I asked him to represent me for the purpose of developing a litigation strategy. Morning Star's board of directors readily agreed to pursue litigation against the Washington team's owners, to retain Dorsey & Whitney as legal counsel, and to have Morning Star serve as the sponsoring organization for the lawsuit and me as the lead petitioner before the PTO. Dorsey & Whitney agreed to represent us on a pro bono basis in a case seeking cancellation of the federal trademark protections for the Washington team's name.

The next important decision in crafting the litigation was who would bring the lawsuit against the Washington team's owners. We opted for a coalition of prominent Native American people, and I began considering people I wanted to stand with over the course of protracted litigation. Each person had to meet a set of subjective standards, which included a demonstrable record of taking principled stands, even if unpopular, and taking responsibility for the future generations of Native Peoples. They had to be citizens of Native nations. They had to have the maturity and stamina to withstand the rigors of public attention, much of it negative, and the patience needed for the long haul. They had to agree with our litigation approach and choice of legal representation. They had to

share the view that it was flat-out wrong for a team in the U.S. capital to be called "Redskins."

There were many Native People who fit the criteria. I made list after list, grouping possible candidates for tribal and professional diversity and a range of upbringings, life experiences, ages, and approaches to dealing with myriad problems in Indian country and in
popular culture. Because of the importance of the number seven in
Cheyenne cosmology, I made groupings of six others who might
embark on this journey or, if they could not, who would hold our
plans in confidence. The first group of six eagerly accepted the challenge and became co-petitioners in the case: Raymond D. Apodaca
(Ysleta del Sur Pueblo), Manley A. Begay Jr. (Navajo), Vine Deloria
Jr. (Standing Rock Sioux), Norbert S. Hill Jr. (Oneida); William A.
Means Jr. (Oglala Lakota); and Mateo Romero (Cochiti Pueblo).

BREAKING THE NEWS OF THE "REDSKINS" LAWSUIT

While Dorsey and Whitney prepared the complaint, the petitioners
worked on the statements and arrangements for the announcement
of the lawsuit. On September 10, 1992, we filed a federal administrative law action with the PTO against the Washington football organization, seeking to cancel federal registrations—and protection—
of the trademarked term "Redskins." It was our hope to remove the
federal government's imprimatur from the use of the name and to
convince the organization to drop the name in favor of one that
does not offend Native Peoples. We released the news simultaneously in Massachusetts, Minnesota, New Mexico, Texas, and Washington, DC. Deloria, Hill, Baird, and I met the press on Capitol Hill,
where the streets sport trash bins with the team's logo. Means spoke
for our coalition in Minneapolis, and Romero in Santa Fe. Apodaca
held forth in El Paso, and Begay in Boston.

The legal foundation of our case, as Baird explained to the media, is that federal trademark and related case law "clearly prohibit

trademark registration of words that are offensive or disparaging. Because the word 'redskin' has historically and is still commonly used as a pejorative, derogatory term, the challenged registrations of the Washington 'Redskins' should not have been granted and are subject to cancellation." My main message was that we hoped our lawsuit would convince the owners to change the racist name.

Deloria explained that the petitioners represent a broad cross section of American Indian culture and politics. "This is not just a disenfranchised few calling for something only a handful would agree with," he said. "While American Indians, like other groups, are diverse in their views, most share a deep feeling of offense at terms like Redskins. Enough is enough." Attorney, author of twenty-two books, and at that time professor in history, religion, and philosophy at the University of Colorado in Boulder, Deloria also said, "We don't want future generations of Indian children to bear this burden of discrimination."

"We are doing it to help the kids," said Hill, then-director of the American Indian Science and Engineering Society. "Our kids shouldn't have to adjust their lives and behavior to accommodate racism. That leads to low self-esteem and suicide attempts. At worst, it's life threatening. At best, it's an unnecessary barrier to positive achievement and opportunities." Hill is now a community builder fellow with the U.S. Department of Housing and Urban Development in Denver.

Senator Daniel K. Inouye (D-Hawaii) issued a prepared statement on the filing, saying, "Today, Native American leaders have taken what could prove to be the first step in eliminating offensive names and images from the sports world." Then chairman of the Senate Committee on Indian Affairs and now its vice chair, Inouye also stated, "The Native American people who have talked to me over the years about this problem have characterized it as a continuing injury. This demeaning portrayal of American Indian people, their appearance, their traditional dress, their ceremonial dances serves as a constant reminder of the injustices they have suffered at the hands of the non-Indians throughout the past five centuries. As we prepare to enter a new century, it is time to leave this era behind with the symbolic and substantive evolutionary act of changing offensive names and negative images in sports."

"A society which permits discrimination in the sports arena is going to overlook it in the marketplace," said Begay, who runs the Harvard Project on American Indian Economic Development of the John F. Kennedy School of Government. "That is precisely the situation of Native American people in society today. We should not be the poorest people in America, but we are. We should not be the only remaining targets of slurs in sports, but we are."

"If the 'Redskins' were doing this to any other ethnic or religious group or nationality, there would be a deafening outcry," said Apodaca, who was governor of his pueblo in El Paso and an NCAI area vice president. "Because we are Indians, with a small and invisible population and a small national voice, our outcry has not been heard. We are asking nothing more than what every other group of people in America has demanded and gotten—to be treated with dignity and respect." Apodaca now is the team leader for the needy tribal families program at the U.S. Department of Health and Human Services.

"We've just got to stop the perpetuation of these stereotypes," said Means at the Heart of the Earth Survival School he once directed. "Too many of our kids see that stuff and begin to believe it, begin to make fun of themselves as a defense mechanism, and begin to feel second rate or like they don't exist at all as real human beings." Longtime president of the International Indian Treaty Council, Means was joined at the press conference by representatives of the American Indian Movement and Native parents, students, and teachers.

"It is time for the younger Indian people to join their elders in open opposition to racist names, images and mascots," said Romero, who was twenty-five at the time of filing. A noted painter, he teaches at the Institute of American Indian Arts in Santa Fe, near his San Juan Pueblo residence and his Cochiti Pueblo home. As a Dartmouth College student, he confronted the fallout from those who wanted to return to the good old days before the school dropped its "Indians" name and mascot. Romero, who was joined at the 1992 press conference by other artists, students, and teachers, said, "We cannot project our own positive images through the generations and layers of stereotypes and negative images projected on us."

THE SIX-YEAR PAPER CHASE

Pro Football, Inc., answered our petition in December of 1992, asking the Patent and Trademark Office to dismiss the case as nonmeritorious. They asserted thirteen affirmative defenses, claiming that we were not the Native Americans who had legal standing, that we were not offended, and that we let too much time pass before filing suit. The PTO disagreed. In March of 1994, it declined to dismiss the suit and ordered the parties to proceed to a trial on the merits. Essentially, the PTO held that the case presented an important overriding public policy issue involving what material deserved the protection of the federal government.

A massive paper chase ensued. Each side inundated the other with discovery requests, and dozens of file-feet of archival materials were produced. The interrogatories seemed endless, and the responses taxed even those with the best memories and reference documents. Attorney Gerald Sullivan and others at Dorsey & Whitney had the daunting task of making order out of the thousands of papers and recollections. More than fifteen staff and volunteers were needed to carry out Morning Star's research, document production, and related work, including Jodi Archambault (Hunkpapa and Oglala Lakota), Chehak, Daryl Jennings (Seminole/Sac and Fox), Steven E. Watt (Seneca), Faye Wright (Klamath), and my children, who have grown up in the Indian rights struggle, Duke Ray Harjo II and Adriane Shown Harjo.

Scores of witnesses were grilled by opposing counsel in formal sessions recorded by court reporters. The aging and ailing Cooke did not testify. His son, John Kent Cooke, who was the team's owner until mid-1999, testified on the important tradition of the team's name, but he could not name the one Indian, a basket seller, he recalled meeting. Our side introduced in evidence many examples of Native and non-Native people and organizations who put their names behind our lawsuit and against "Redskins." Their side called us and our supporters names—"militants" and "fringe activist groups"—without seeming to notice that the entire case is about name-calling. Petitioners testified about being called names.

"In high school when I played football," said Hill, "I remember tackling [a player] for a two yard loss, and he called me a 'Dirty f***ing Redskin.'" Begay recalled an incident in his youth when a white man was "yelling and screaming at me" and calling him "dirty redskin, you stinky redskin . . . go back to your hogan." Experts in their professional fields testified on the history, meaning, and use of "Redskins." Our expert witnesses, who generously donated their time and expertise, were Frederick E. Hoxie in history, Arlene Hirschfelder in education, Teresa LaFrombroise (Turtle Mountain Chippewa) in psychology, Geoffrey Nunberg in linguistics, and Ivan Ross in surveys.

The Native American Rights Fund in Boulder filed a friend of the court brief supporting our position in 1997. The brief was submitted to the PTO by attorney Walter R. EchoHawk (Pawnee) on behalf of the National Congress of American Indians, National Indian Education Association, and the National Indian Youth Council. Pro Football lawyers fought to exclude the brief as prejudicial, calling the organizations our "amici cohorts." The PTO, which has no formal *amicus* process, excluded the brief. Pro Football then tried to argue that we lacked Native support.

The trademark judges heard oral arguments in our case on May 27, 1998. The team's attorneys maintained that "Redskins" was a neutral term, like "colored people" in the National Association for the Advancement of Colored People, although they could not come up with an example of "Redskins" in a Native organization's name. Our position was ably argued by attorney Michael A. Lindsay, who became managing partner for the case at Dorsey & Whitney in mid-1995. Lindsay took over as lead attorney in mid-1998, when Baird relocated his practice. Many other people at Dorsey & Whitney also worked on the case and deserve to be named: attorneys Minnie Alexander, Peter Beckman, Ronald Brown, Josh Burke, Michael Drysdale, Mike Gannon, Ken Levitt, Sara Gross Methner, Alan Wagner, Michael Wahoske, and Steven Wells, and legal assistants Laura Bjorkland, Tammy McCanna, and Laurie Scanlon, all in Minneapolis, as well as Virginia Boylan and Aldo Noto in Washington and Stewart Aaron in New York.

VICTORY AND BACK TO THE FUTURE

There was great jubilation in our camp on April 2, 1999, when we received the judges' 145-page decision. The bottom line of their unanimous ruling was that the "registrations will be canceled in due course." It was a stunning victory. Deloria said that the "federal government made the 'Redskins' let African Americans play on the team nearly four decades ago, and now it has taken another critical step toward ending the team owners' racism. The federal government was right then and it is right today."

The other side simply repeated its mantra that the name honors us and said they would appeal the decision. In May, a coalition of local and national religious leaders wrote to the National Football

League, asking the owners not to appeal. Native American leaders also wrote to the NFL, urging the owners "to change the contemptible name." The NFL announced its decision to sell the team to a new group of owners headed by Bethesda, Maryland, businessman Daniel M. Snyder. He announced that naming rights to the new stadium might be sold, but that the team's name would not be changed, saying that "Redskins" was a tradition and not offensive. The owners' lawyers appealed the decision in June.

On June 19, 1999, support for our position in litigation was evidenced in a broad-based event, *Change the Name! An Interfaith Gathering to End Racism in Sports*, in Washington's National City Christian Church. The gathering was sponsored by several hundred religious and social justice groups, unions, and Native American organizations, including such groups as the Leadership Conference on Civil Rights, the National Conference of Black Lawyers—DC Chapter, and the National Italian American Foundation. Native sponsors included the leading national organizations representing Native nations, tribal officials, and traditional leaders, as well as associations of Native artists, attorneys, activists, educators, journalists, and youth.

The passage of time between the filing and the decision in our case can best be traced in human terms in the lives of the Native American parties to the lawsuit. Deloria gained four grandchildren and published five more books, including the definitive work on federal Indian treaties. Begay earned his Ph.D. from Harvard, and his daughter, a high school student in 1992, graduated from college. Means became a grandfather three times. Romero gained three children, an MFA, and a professorship at his alma mater. Apodaca moved from Texas to Washington and launched a new career. Hill became the first Native person to chair the board of the National Museum of the American Indian. And I have lived to tell this story.

How long the lawsuit will last or how long the team's owners will hang on to "Redskins" is anyone's guess, but three things are certain at this time of publication. The Native American position is rock solid and will not change. The circle of non-Native support is wider, stronger, and more diverse. The time has come to consign "Redskins" to the history books and museums.

CHAPTER 9

Last of the

Mohicans, Braves, and Warriors

The End of American Indian Mascots

in Los Angeles Public Schools

•

Ann Marie (Amber) Machamer

On September 8, 1997, the Los Angeles Unified School District (LAUSD), the second largest school district in the nation, voted to ban the use of American Indian mascots and names by all public schools in the district due to the efforts of the Los Angeles American Indian Education Commission (AIEC). The commission, one of nine such entities devoted to gender and ethnic concerns, represented the needs of the Los Angeles American Indian community to the board. Throughout its twenty-five-year history, the staff of AIEC, its full-time director, administrative assistant, and volunteer commissioners (both elected and appointed), have served Indian and non-Indian students, parents, and teachers through advocacy, in-class presentations, textbook reviews, and teacher education. In 1995, shortly after I was elected to the commission, an American Indian parent of a student attending Birmingham High School filed a complaint against its mascot, placing the issue at the top of our agenda. Importantly, this was not the first time the issue had been raised; the minutes of the commission meetings indicate the intent to bring the mascot issue to the board nearly eighteen years before the LAUSD decision. Although this early attempt did little more than raise the issue, we consider it the genesis of our modern effort.

One of the most important ingredients in our success was having a strategic plan that was based upon our knowledge of the schools, school board, and district policies and politics, that was agreed upon by the American Indian community, and that was flexible enough to accommodate unforeseen changes. Throughout this two-year battle, we had many discouraging, false victories, including a lawsuit brought against the school district that challenged the jurisdiction of the board and asserted the plaintiffs' First Amendment rights to use American Indians as mascots. In achieving this ultimately successful outcome we employed many different techniques. These admittedly heuristic methods roughly fall into two rubrics: systemic activism and organizational culture. Systemic activism took advantage of existing mechanisms within the system and coordinated with more militant activists. The second category, organizational culture, focused on our need to understand and exploit the language and customs of schools and schools districts. The LAUSD decision has left a legacy that did far more than change local practices. It sent a message that was heard nationally by Indian and non-Indian communities alike. This chapter manifests many of the theories of the other contributing authors in a local, real-life context.

LEARNING FROM EXPERIENCE

During this effort we drew upon the successful battles of the past, such as the largely student-led effort at Stanford University a quarter-century earlier. My personal struggles against mascots began in the Fremont Unified School District in Northern California. Along with my two brothers and two sisters, I attended public schools in Santa Clara County (forty miles south of San Francisco), where my parents Milton (German) and Sylvia (Coastal Band Chumash) Machamer both taught. In 1991 the local Title IX parent group began to organize against the Fremont High School's mascot, the "Indians," and the Bay Area Indian community was locked in an emotional and frustrating two-year battle with the Fremont High School community.

At the beginning of this effort, Fremont Unified School Board members were unanimously opposed to the change. Like many Americans, they felt it was political correctness gone too far, and that the "traditions" of the "Fremont Indians" should be preserved. As a consequence, they stalled and blocked consideration of the issue. Two years later, after listening to and learning about American Indian people, most of them for the first time in their lives, and in spite of threats of recall, they voted unanimously to retire this outdated, harmful practice. Had the board taken that action earlier, they would have saved the community and themselves much strife. They hoped to avoid scrutiny and involvement by having both sides meet month after month even when it was clear they were at an impasse. In buying themselves time, the board hurt both Indian and non-Indian communities. Fremont High School should be seen by other school boards as both a precedent for change and an example of how not to go about it. As teachers, my parents had knowledge of district policies, politics, and personnel that proved to be valuable resources in gaining access, strategic planning, and communicating effectively. This is when we learned that activism within the system could accomplish what more militant activism did not.

PLAYING THE SYSTEM

Systemic activism takes advantage of existing mechanisms within the system. As teachers, commissioners, parents, and community members, we had access to the board and individual schools that more militant activists did not. Systemic activism is a slow process that requires planning, research, lobbying, and, most importantly, follow-through. Systemic activists also need to coordinate efforts with more militant activists. In Los Angeles, AIEC made it clear to officials that we were different organizations and that we operated independently of each other. If officials did not deal with AIEC, they would need to deal with the more militant activists. Officials clearly saw the commission members as a "safer" option. We found that this "good cop, bad cop" technique helped us to keep the attention of district officials. Of course, all independent groups were in constant contact and coordination.

Our strategies, which changed as needed, were based on the advice of friendly district insiders and our own instincts. Our first strategy was to request of the superintendent a task force that would examine the issue. It was implied that after we went through this process and made an honest effort to get the schools to change on their own volition, the outcome would be favorable for us, even if the schools refused. The superintendent would not be seeking to renew his contract and would be able to eliminate the mascots, a politically unpopular move. Although rare, there may be superintendents or principals in your area who have both the authority and guts to issue a directive to eliminate Indian mascots. Usually these are people who are retiring, relocating, or changing jobs. Finding these people and lobbying them can save much time and effort. Arriving at this strategy took us a few months of research and lobbying.

In the fall of 1995, John Orendorff (Cherokee), director of the AIEC, and the commissioners addressed the board to officially request a task force. Joanne Semon, a founding member of the commission, respected community elder, and member of the committee that drafted the district policy against discrimination and harassment, called attention to the fact that the use of American Indian mascots was clearly in violation of district policy. As expected, after our presentation, Superintendent Sid Thompson ordered the formation of a task force to examine this issue. This task force ensured us an audience with each school's top personnel. Without this mandate from the superintendent, it is unlikely the high schools would have taken our opposition seriously or met with us.

One of the difficulties with systemic activism is that it can be difficult to tell what are genuine delays and changes of plan and what are evasive actions. Oftentimes we were asked to attend numerous meetings with all kinds of people, students, faculty, and alumni. We were presented with hoop after hoop through which we were expected to jump. This had the effect of draining the energy and patience of our small community. Whether well intended or not, district officials often wanted our community to do most of the work for two reasons: this kept them removed from the controversy, and if we were continually engaged in "busy work," they hoped we might get tired and go away. This is one of the dangers of systemic activism. Knowing when and how to get out of this situation requires developing relationships with trusted insiders at both the school and district levels. It was important that the task force had a set amount of meetings and a deadline by which a report was to be submitted to the superintendent.

Representatives from the commission, the American Indian Movement, and other community members with a history of working on this issue met with representatives from the three schools (Birmingham Braves, University Warriors, and the Gardina Mohicans). The assistant superintendent served as moderator. The task force had four meetings held in district offices between November 1996 and May 1997 as well as six meetings with constituents of the three schools at their campuses. These task force meetings became quite redundant. Each time we met, school officials asked the same questions and made the same arguments. Insulting comments and offensive questions asked time after time revealed latent feelings of superiority and demonstrated an attitude of paternalism. These meetings tested our patience; however, we all agreed to maintain our composure, and we simply and calmly restated our position. We learned early on that as systemic activists, losing our tempers and raising our voices hurt our credibility and threatened our access.

Administrators and faculty represented the schools. Students attended only the first meeting. We were told one student felt that some of our members had dealt with her too harshly and chose not to attend further meetings. Although we do not concede this point, we did learn an important lesson: deal with students as gently as possible. Faculty and administrators are protective of their students and will deny access to them by any group or person they feel is intimidating. Regardless of whether this accusation had any validity, in future interactions with students (and faculty), we avoided angry or emotional arguments and framed the presentation around promoting tolerance and empathy for other cultures and religions and building critical thinking skills. Approaching students in this manner not only increased our access to students but also proved more effective than more confrontational methods.

The meetings at the schools were more interesting and productive. Here we had the opportunity to speak with different administrators, teachers, and students. Each school had different levels of resistance ranging from favoring change to begrudging resignation to outright resistance and hostility. Each school granted us different levels of access to students and faculty and worked with us in different ways. Two schools (University and Gardina High Schools) allowed us to meet with their student leadership classes. Initially resistant to the idea, many of the students came to see our point and changed their minds. Although no student wanted to change their mascot, many realized it was the right thing to do. Although not all students changed their minds, all displayed a willingness to listen and think critically, which made working with students one of the most pleasurable aspects of this entire effort. We found most to be thoughtful, articulate, and empathetic. Our nonconfrontational approach was extremely important and effective. A confrontational approach would have made these fence-sitting students hostile and defensive.

REORGANIZING CULTURE

Over the course of the year we developed a number of strategies to be more effective in these meetings with school personnel based on our understanding of their organizational culture. Knowing and exploiting their stated and unstated values as well as hierarchical structures are very important to gaining access and building support. First, we did our homework by researching the schools' histories through the Internet or yearbooks at the local library. We videotaped the antics at football games and tried to research the professional and personal histories of school administrators. This knowledge helped us gain the upper hand in meetings numerous times. During one meeting, a principal explained how, unlike other schools, their mascot was respectful of American Indians and not at all offensive. After his statement John Orendorff played a videotape of a football game he attended showing their mascot gyrating and doing the tomahawk chop. After this incident the school retired that particular mascot costume.

An unstated value of school administrators is their belief that organizations carry more credibility than individuals. We made sure that each of us in attendance represented a different organization to make it seem as though our community and therefore political power were larger than they actually were. It gave us more credibility to appear as though we represented six or seven local, state, and national organizations rather than presenting just our own individual opinions. If you do not belong to an organization, make one. In the case of my parents in Fremont, they created letterhead on their home computer and became an "organization" that has since spread statewide. Letterhead and a catchy acronym are enough to appear credible to most administrators.

Another strategy we used was to recruit the support of non-Indian organizations. The status of their names and resources can be very helpful. Lori Nelson of the Los Angeles National Conference for Community and Justice attended these meetings, collected information, and helped us devise strategy. Her skills as a facilitator and her contacts with other influential organizations were also invaluable assets. Due to her efforts, school board members were sent letters of support on our behalf from organizations with substantial influence. For a small minority with little political or economic influence, finding allies from other communities can be an important strategy for American Indian communities. We also collected the existing resolutions against American Indian mascots from national organizations such as the National Indian Education Association, National Congress of American Indians, California Indian Education Association, and the National Collegiate Athletic Association, to name a few. This diffused the argument that we were just a few local activists and proved we were part of a national movement supported by prominent state and national Indian and non-Indian organizations.

An important strategy we employed was to have a good mix of men and women, elders and youth, professionals and militant activists, at these meetings. This allowed us to exploit the most commonly stated and unstated values of school personnel. To schools, the academic and social education of students is of paramount importance. Our main argument in these meetings was that the mascot promotes intolerance and inaccurate impressions of American Indian cultures. Having a diverse group of Indian people highlighted the point that these mascots promote inaccurate stereotypes. The voices of American Indian students and the knowledge of elders helped to further illustrate this point. We maintained that schools, as the primary socializing agent of students, have a responsibility to change environments that promote intolerance, appropriation, and domination of other cultures as these mascots do.

Our most important strategy was to present a united front. We made sure everyone understood the overall plan and was kept informed as to the status of the effort. We agreed to do our part in making the task force productive. Individuals would not meet alone with district or schools officials or make any agreements without group approval by consensus. From the beginning we agreed there would be no compromise. Schools could not get rid of the mascot while keeping the names. The idea of this compromise deserves some discussion.

At the second task force meeting school representatives began to present the compromise, which we quickly declined. Institutional culture changes very slowly even when clear breaks are made with the past culture. Over twenty-five years after Stanford University eliminated both its Indian mascot and name, there remains an unofficial culture of alumni and current students who maintain their "tradition" of being "Indians" (see Springwood, this volume). Even when an institution removes all official vestiges of the mascot and name, an underground culture, determined to resist change, will persist. This transition is difficult enough when all vestiges of racism are removed, without complicating matters by retaining a major part of the prior culture. Retiring the mascots while retaining the names condones the use of the offensive images we are trying to eliminate. We clearly and calmly expressed our opinions and would not accept a compromise. We were, of course, accused of being unreasonable; at times some of those on our side would have been satisfied with a compromise. However, we all understood the importance of solidarity. This meant putting aside personal disagreements at least for the meeting.

Differences in opinion or personal rivalries might have made working in a diverse urban Indian population difficult, but without exception each person left these at the door. I cannot express the feelings of pride and gratitude we had when Indian people from all over the city and state came to school board meetings in support of our effort. Also, the support and encouragement we received from across the nation overwhelmed us. The American Indian community was an important source of motivation for those of us involved in the day-to-day frustrations and disappointments of the effort. Sitting through meeting after meeting and enduring offensive, racist comments and open hostility can damage one's spirit. Even the most determined and strong-minded person begins to experience feelings of isolation and self-doubt. It can become burdensome and can dampen your resolve. The support and prayers of community members replenished our spirits, revitalized our resolve, and reminded us of why we were fighting this battle.

FINAL SKIRMISHES

Toward the end of the school year the assistant superintendent submitted her report. She reported that there was no agreement between sides. The schools agreed to discontinue using the images but wanted to retain the names, a compromise we soundly rejected. Based upon the report and our lobbying, Superintendent Sid Thompson issued a directive on June 19, 1997, that mandated the elimination of American Indian mascots and names. Mr. Thompson was empathetic to our community, and because his term was ending, he was in the best position to issue such a controversial directive without political fallout. It is a little disturbing to think that a directive could have been issued eighteen years ago, but nonetheless we were overjoyed. AIEC ensured that the district would cover the associated costs to the schools, who had a full academic year for transition. This, we thought, was the end of our long battle. We were soon disappointed.

217

In August, the new board president (whose constituents included Birmingham High School) asked the incoming superintendent to put the directive on hold because the board did not have a chance to examine the issue. This was very misleading because during the past two years the commission had met with each board member numerous times and had kept all of them informed as to our progress; in addition, each board member received a copy of the task force report. The last thing we wanted was to open up the issues for public comment or debate again; nor did we want to give the opposition a chance to organize their resistance.

In order to avoid another lengthy public debate on the issue, we began to lobby the board to vote on a referendum immediately. The more time the parents and alumni had to organize their opposition, the more difficult it would be for our small community to counter their efforts. To avoid this situation, we arranged to have the board vote on the referendum at the next board meeting. By lobbying board members, we were sure we had at least five out of seven votes. Do not bring a vote to a school board unless it is assured of passing. If a motion fails, it will be more difficult to get another vote in the future.

The referendum was on the board's September meeting agenda. Members from both communities were present, but American Indians outnumbered Birmingham supporters three to one. American Indians and our supporters came from across the state. Each side was allowed just a few minutes to make a statement. Instead of spending our few minutes on debating the Birmingham representatives, we commented on what a historic day this was and commended the board for doing what was right, displaying true leadership, and setting a precedent for the nation. Perhaps giving a victory speech may have seemed like gloating, but our gratitude and elation were genuine. It is not often that our community is able to celebrate a political victory. After just a few minutes of discussion the board voted 6–0 with one abstention to pass the ban on the use of American Indian mascots. The drum in the middle of the district office courtyard helped us give thanks and celebrate. Again, the celebration would be short-lived, as the issue was not fully settled.

A group of parents and alumni of Birmingham High School sued the school board, superintendent, cluster leader, and principal. Their summons, served to the board on January 7, 1998, alleged the district overstepped its jurisdiction when banning their school mascot and violated their First Amendment rights. At this point the issue was out of the hands of the commission and Indian community since we were not named as defendants. The LAUSD lawyers would handle the defense. District lawyers moved the case to federal court because the plaintiffs raised First Amendment issues. In the meantime the schools began implementing the referendum. In August 1998, a federal court dismissed the case, confirming the jurisdiction of the district. Now we could consider the matter closed.

CONCLUSIONS

The LAUSD decision has left a legacy on both the national and local levels affecting both Indian and non-Indian communities. For example, the LAUSD referendum has been used as precedent by the Dallas Unified School District in its ban on American Indian mascots, effecting eleven schools. Locally, when we attend the football games of the dozens of schools in Southern California with Indian mascots, we have noticed major changes in the ways they use American Indian imagery. Gone are the grotesquely costumed mascots. Some schools have changed their official logos from Indian heads to objects they believe to be less overtly offensive, such as feathers or arrowheads. We see fewer tomahawk chops and less war paint. Most important, the LAUSD decision is something of which Indian people can be proud. It stands as another example of what we can do. Although the mascot issue may not be the most urgent problem facing American Indians, it is important as a symbolic issue. It reveals the latent attitudes whites harbor toward American Indians. These are symbols of dominance and superiority and expose feelings of entitlement not only to our land and resources but also to our religions and identities. In a way, it is the most fundamental issue facing Indian peoples.

An important factor in this success story was having a flexible overall plan that was based on our position within the district and our familiarity with school culture. Systemic activism gave us access to the board, superintendent, and school personnel, and with coordination with more militant activists we were able to maintain the attention of district and school officials. Our understanding of school values and culture helped us to be more effective in meetings and guided many of our strategies. The substantial support of the Los Angles American Indian community was an important source of strength and motivation over the years. Our most important strategy was agreeing on a plan and persisting until the end. This may not be the most urgent problem facing American Indians, but it is one we can solve.

CHAPTER 10

Escaping the Tyranny of the Majority

A Case Study of Mascot Change

•

Laurel R. Davis and Malvina T. Rau

In 1993, the sports teams at Springfield College (SC), Springfield, Massachusetts, were called the "Chiefs" and the "Maroons." By the end of 1998, all of SC's teams were known as the "Pride." From 1993 to 1998, the campus was a site of bitter struggle over this change.[1] The authors of this chapter were active participants in the struggle. Davis, a new faculty member and sport sociologist who had published an article about the Native American mascot issue, wrote a letter that set the SC administrators to work on the change. Rau, the SC provost, was the most active administrator in pushing through the change. Over the course of the mascot change, the coauthors learned a couple of important lessons: stereotypes of Native Americans are so deeply ingrained that only modest gains can be made from short-term educational efforts, and particular versions of democracy can stand in the way of social justice.

To understand the controversy over the mascot at SC, one needs to understand a bit about the college and the surrounding community.[2] Generally, students and faculty at SC are centrist liberals or moderate conservatives. Historically, there has been very little activism at SC, except for modest efforts during the 1960s and 1970s. Campus understanding of racial issues is minimal and is of the "people should just love each other" variety. Politeness, friendliness, and acquiescence are important campus norms, so activism is often perceived as impolite and threatening.

Another factor that affected the mascot change is the insular nature of the faculty. Many have little experience with other colleges and are not particularly bookish; thus many approach campus issues without much knowledge of efforts to address these same issues elsewhere. Most faculty who supported the change were recent arrivals from other institutions and/or were well read on the issue or on social justice issues more generally.

The percentage of Native Americans at the college, in the community, and even in the region itself is exceedingly small, even in comparison to national figures. In the vicinity, there are no recognized Native American nations and no Native American political organizations with an established public voice. Most of the SC students come from areas without sizable Native American populations.

SC was founded as a YMCA school in 1885 and nearly from the beginning emphasized physical education. A less central tradition at SC is interest in "Indian history and culture." For example, for many years a predominately Euro-American group called "Hosaga," named after an invented "Indian tribe," sponsored activities focused on "Indian culture." A building on a wooded part of campus was named "the Pueblo" and was associated with "Indian tradition." The college's "Indian traditions" are linked to Chief Massasoit, a leader of the Wampanoags during the 1600s, although he was not from the region where SC is located. A pond contiguous to the campus is called Lake Massasoit. References to Massasoit are replete in college newspapers, rites of passage, and so on. There are some indications that he is associated with the college because he is known as a "peaceful" leader. In fact, his nation was almost completely annihilated, so it would have been fruitless to pursue armed resistance (Loewen 1995). Thus in idealizing Massasoit, Euro-Americans are really idealizing their own dominance and a passive response to racial oppression. The generally conservative campus, insular faculty, interest in "Indian history and culture," and virtual absence of Native Americans were conducive to resistance to the mascot change at SC.

Early nicknames for teams at SC included the Stubby Christians, Gymnasts, Reds, and Maroons. At various times the teams were also known as the Indians, and the stereotypical image of a chief (that is, a face with feathered headdress; allegedly Chief Massasoit) was a frequent visage. In the spring of 1967, the sports information director and a committee of students ran a contest for a new nickname. The name *Chiefs* was selected, although the women's teams continued to be called the Maroons.

In 1975, stimulated by the athletic director, the student newspaper included an article, "'Chiefs' Need a Change," which suggested the need for a mascot change (Gibbons 1975:1). The central argument then was that the Chiefs mascot was inappropriate for the women's teams. The issue of using a Native American mascot was a secondary concern. In 1990, a different athletic director attempted to address the issue by working with the student government president and student newspaper sports editor. After a few meetings, however, the students lost interest.

The actual process of change began in 1993 when Davis urged the SC president to eliminate the Chiefs mascot. The president turned the issue over to Provost Rau and the athletic director, the same person who had raised the issue in 1990. The two formed a committee to examine the issue and make recommendations to the president. The committee included a female and male student, alum, and athlete; a graduate student; the NCAA faculty representative; the sports editor of the student newspaper; the president of student government; and a representative of the Alumni Council.

Many members of the Mascot Committee started with a neutral opinion of the issue. The committee developed six criteria to judge the current mascots and any new suggestions, one of the criteria being that "The nickname/mascot would not be offensive to any particular group or individual in regard to minority status or gender" (Mehan and Gibney 1994:1). The student newspaper informed the campus about the committee and the criteria and asked for suggestions.

Several months later, the Mascot Committee solicited ideas for a new nickname from the campus community, and about eighty names were suggested. The committee eliminated all suggestions that did not meet the six criteria, including the name Chiefs. Then they reduced the remaining suggestions to four: Athletics, Pioneers, Pride, and Spirit.

The president sent written communication to members of the campus community and alums in which he discussed the rationale for the change and the process to be followed. He stated, "It was the strong feeling of the [Mascot] Committee that gender equity should be a key consideration; thus, a common name should be selected that would represent both the male and female teams. Further, it was felt that although the College's use of the name Chiefs has always been intended to honor and respect Native Americans, there have been occasions where behavior at athletic contests has perpetuated offensive and stereotypical perceptions of Indians as warlike and violent. Given all that Springfield College stands for, changing the name was determined to be the right decision." The president announced a campus poll on the final four names and commented that "Responses to the poll, together with our solicitation of alumni correspondence . . . will provide important feedback to me" (SC president, letter to campus community, 28 October 1994).

Written reactions to the communications were relatively few but passionate. A few argued that the change was necessary to eliminate racial stereotyping and/or to create a single mascot for the women's and men's teams: "I think it is a good idea to change the name to a non-gender, non-discriminatory, non-violent one," wrote one former student to the provost (20 December 1994). A letter to the student paper stated: "For four years I have competed as a 'Maroon' while the men are the 'Chiefs.' I have never understood this distinction between the sexes. We all compete in the same maroon uniforms, with the same drive towards the same goal and for the same school, so why not under the same mascot?" (Druyor 1994, 2). Most argued against the change, stating that the Chiefs mascot honored Native Americans. One former student wrote to the president, charging that those advocating the change were left-wing extremists engaged in a ridiculous game of political correctness: "For decades the name Chiefs was used by our athletic teams, the chief appeared in full regalia and we all rejoiced and no one was offended. . . . I would guess that those offended are a handful of liberal left wing feminists and some radical ethnic minority whacos" (23 December 1994). Another alum wrote to the director of development, "I'm sick and tired of people striving to be what is currently termed 'politically correct.' . . . I believe that 'Chiefs' is not anti-native American, rather that it is intended as a title of admiration and respect" (26 December 1994).

The Alumni Council asked that the option of maintaining Chiefs be reviewed. The Student Government Association (SGA) requested that Chiefs be the nickname for both the women's and men's teams and that the college develop an icon that met the six criteria. The college president informed the SGA that the Chiefs name was not an option. He encouraged students to suggest additional names and said he would make the final decision by the end of the academic year.

The results of the poll were released. Approximately 14 percent of the college community voted. Among the voters, 28 percent wrote in Chiefs (38 percent of the students and 8 percent of the employees), 24 percent voted for Pioneers, 18 percent for Spirit, 16 percent

225

for Athletics, 7 percent for Pride, and 8 percent for another name or for none.

The Mascot Committee, disregarding the polling data, recommended Pride as the nickname and a family of mountain lions as the icon. The Alumni Council reacted by requesting that the president permit the alums and campus community "to vote on the mascot (with the Chiefs being one of the choices) and to make the result the final decision" (SC Alumni Council, minutes, 31 March 1995).

The president announced his final decision: the college would adopt the name Pride. He defended the process and linked the change to SC's philosophy of concern for others. Interestingly, it was only after the president's "final decision" that virulent activism against the change really began to flourish. After release of the Pride icon, the SGA requested a delay in icon development and organized an open forum on the issue. Provost Rau agreed to a student icon committee, which then solicited suggestions for the icon from students and sent recommendations to the president.

A small group of students, the Keep-the-Chiefs group, exhorted the president to retain the Chiefs nickname while reevaluating the icon. There was substantial overlap between the SGA and the Keep-the-Chiefs group, including two class presidents. This group was unofficially advised by an interim faculty member, a self-declared opponent of "political correctness" and "former chief of Hosaga" (St. Pierre 1997: 4). This faculty member's opinions were constantly legitimated by the facts that he had written two books about Native Americans, lived among Lakotas, and was married to a Lakota.

The Keep-the-Chiefs group rounded up supporters, and fifty students attended an Icon Committee meeting at which the committee members voted to halt progress on the icon design. The Keep-the-Chiefs group organized a rally (an unheard of event in recent years at SC). Approximately five hundred people turned up at the rally; most seemed to support the group's efforts, although others were simply curious. The Keep-the-Chiefs group carried their agenda to the Alumni Council, which voted to support the return to the Chiefs mascot.

The Keep-the-Chiefs group convinced the SGA to hold an all-student vote that included the option of re-adopting the Chiefs nickname (and adopting if for the women as well). At the same time, the SGA stated that "it would be inappropriate to have a mascot as a Native American because it is found to be offensive to many Indian groups" (SC SGA president, letter to SC president, 1 May 1996). Approximately 35 percent of the campus-based student body voted in the SGA poll: 92 percent for Chiefs, 5 percent for Pride, and 2 percent for neither. SGA passed a motion "that further use of the Pride be discontinued until research be done on the Chief nickname" (SC SGA minutes, 8 May 1996).

The following fall, two leaders of the Keep-the-Chiefs group began regular columns in the student newspaper. Soon, the group became an official ad hoc committee of the SGA. The Keep-the-Chiefs Committee pressed the college president for a new mascot committee and plastered the campus with a page from the 1923 SC yearbook, *The Massasoit*. The page discussed Chief Massasoit, stating that he "has come to mean to us here at Springfield what the Bulldog is to Yale, the Tiger to Princeton, and the Bear to Brown" (*Massasoit* 1923:148). The Keep-the-Chiefs Committee forwarded a proposal to the college president, made presentations to alums, and surveyed alums during homecoming. The committee reported that 480 alums supported keeping Chiefs while only 2 supported Pride (SC SGA minutes, 23 October 1996).

As part of a three-year social justice education effort, the college invited Ward Churchill, an author, professor, and activist regarding Native American issues, to speak to the campus. At his talk, Churchill demonstrated a point with a T-shirt produced by the Keep-the-Chiefs Committee that featured the stereotypical image of a chief (that is, a face with headdress) and the previously mentioned quote from the 1923 yearbook. Several students, mostly members of the Keep-the-Chiefs Committee, expressed their desire to keep Chiefs as a nickname but to drop any reference to Native Americans. Churchill explained that the word *chief* is not inherently a problem, but it would be too difficult to decouple the word from (problematic images of) Native Americans. In fact, to most non-Natives in the United States, the word *chief* (by itself) seems to connote not only Native American leaders but Native Americans more generally. Many Native American males have been addressed by the term *chief* simply because they are Native American. In response to student complaints about the process of change at SC, Churchill said, "You don't ask students before enforcing laws such as rape, sexual harassment, or physical assault" (Moriarity 1997:1).

Although many saw the talk as educational, many students were put off by Churchill's passionate and assertive demeanor. The talk unleashed a barrage of protests, particularly from the Keep-the-Chiefs Committee. One student accused the provost of calling the committee racist and lying about Churchill's topic, as he was billed to talk about stereotyping of Native Americans more generally but focused mainly on the mascot issue. Another charged faculty and administrators with laughing at some student speakers and applauding as Churchill "belittled the students" (LaGiglia and Junger 1997:3). Churchill was accused of making offensive comments at SC and being a fraud (that is, not Native American and not part of American Indian Movement/AIM organizations).

The Keep-the-Chiefs Committee staged a sit-in, where they demanded (1) a binding all-college vote, which would include the option of returning to the Chiefs name "with no Indian connotation or representation"; (2) a public apology from the provost; (3) library subscriptions to "all Indian Journals and papers"; and (4) funds for Vernon Bellecourt, a leader of AIM, to address the campus (Keep-the-Chiefs Committee, written demands, 11 March 1997). The last demand seemed like a strange request, given Bellecourt's opposition to Native American mascots. He was probably selected because he was critical of Churchill and because he suggested that there would be no problem with the Chief name if it could be disassociated from Native Americans. The president agreed to a nonbinding referendum (which never happened), a new mascot committee, acquisitions for the library, and funding for Bellecourt's talk. Provost Rau apologized for the misunderstanding.

Students on the Keep-the-Chiefs Committee continued to flood the campus newspaper with letters and articles. As usual, only a few publicly defended the change. A codirector of a small and relatively powerless local Native American organization accused the students of saying they would abolish references to Native Americans while at the same time promoting these references:

> The ... [Keep-the-Chiefs] Committee says ... they want to abolish all "Indian" connotations ... [yet] they state "... we intend to uphold the traditions of Native Americans." How could they uphold our traditions if they are not part of our culture? ... [The] student leadership is not totally accurate when they say [there] will be no logos, mascots or insignias that defame Native Americans associated with the defaming "Chiefs" nickname. Any logo or name that [is] used or has any Native American connotation is defamation. We noticed, in fact, at the rally on Tuesday, that [there] was a person(s) wearing a sports jacket that proclaimed the "Springfield Chiefs", complete with a logo depicting a bonneted Native American male. (Native Earth Education Project, letter to SC president, 14 March 1997)

The athletic director informed the college president that most of the coaches and team captains wished to remain the Pride and urged him to end the controversy.

The Keep-the-Chiefs Committee forwarded a proposal for the new mascot committee to the president, which included stipulations that the faculty "must have obtained tenure, must have no prior experience with the 'Mascot Committee,' must have an open mind and no biased opinions on this issue, and must have knowledge about the history of Springfield College." The proposed outcome was to "decide whether CHIEFS can be used by Springfield College athletic teams as a non-discriminatory name" (Keep-the-Chiefs Committee, written proposal, 25 March 1997). The president modified this proposal.

When Vernon Bellecourt spoke at SC, he told the audience the same thing Ward Churchill had told his audience: he criticized Native American mascots but stated that teams could be called Chiefs if there was no association with Native Americans, which would be difficult to achieve. Several members of the Keep-the-Chiefs Committee became inactive on the issue after hearing Bellecourt. Yet, a few days after Bellecourt's talk, the SGA passed a motion to stop use of the name Pride.

The New Mascot Committee met the following fall. At the first meeting only two of the eight student members attended, reportedly because they had not been notified by the SGA. During the meeting, a visitor from the Keep-the-Chiefs Committee questioned the process, including the selection of members. Ironically, only a couple of the mascot committee members were known as strong supporters of the change from the Chiefs. Subsequently, the SGA president unilaterally removed all students from the New Mascot Committee and stated that the SGA "will not accept any decision made by the committee until the . . . flaws are looked at and amended" (SC SGA president, letter to New Mascot Committee chair, 4 December 1997). The New Mascot Committee encouraged student participation but moved forward without them, eventually reaffirming the selection of Pride.

The Keep-the-Chiefs Committee continued to advocate for reversion to the Chiefs and to stymie resolution of the issue. One of the leaders called his newspaper column "A Chief's Column," while another included a picture of himself in a headdress with his column. At the same time as student support for the Chiefs began to dwindle, a small number of discontented faculty began to use the mascot issue for their own purposes. They cited the issue as an example of the authoritarian impulses of the administration and an agenda of run-amok political correctness that constrained free speech. A couple of these faculty began to serve as informal advisers to the remaining members of the Keep-the-Chiefs Committee. In one last effort, the SGA passed a motion for an all-college vote on the issue.

The SC president accepted the recommendations of the New Mascot Committee, including retention of the Pride nickname. Another committee was appointed to guide the icon development process. In the fall of 1998, SC teams were known as the Pride, and the icon was a stylized mountain lion. The campus community and alums (for the most part) have moved on to other issues.

Several aspects of the change at SC deserve comment. First, the change was initiated and pushed through by a very small number of predominantly Euro-American faculty and administrators, and the change was actively opposed by a small number of predominately Euro-American students. The majority of the staff, faculty, and administrators remained apathetic. Most students were apathetic as well, although given a choice, the majority would have selected the Chiefs. The presence of Native Americans in the process was extremely limited, and they were primarily employed to legitimate one position or the other. This case study demonstrates the lack of control that Native Americans have over discourse that is purported to convey their very essence. Although both sides in the struggle at SC illustrated this problem, those who resisted the change were

231

more willfully neglectful. How can one profess to be "respecting" Native Americans while ignoring the fact that most pan-ethnic Native American organizations have taken a stand against the mascots (Rosenstein 1996)?

Second, supporters of the Chiefs mascot were primarily driven by two motives: maintaining college tradition and (their mythical version of) honoring Native Americans. Interestingly, their early rhetoric highlighted both of these motives. As the controversy proceeded, they abandoned public articulation of the second motive. Their rhetoric shifted from "we want a Native American mascot to honor Native Americans" to complaining about the Pride mascot and lack of democracy in the process and advocating the name Chiefs while using an icon not associated with Native Americans. This shift enabled the Keep-the-Chiefs group to create alliances with the small group of faculty who were critical of the administration. Even though the rhetoric of the proponents of the Chiefs shifted, their desire for a Native American mascot did not disappear. This was evident through their continued reference to "Indian themes," such as mentioning Massasoit and displaying images of feathered headdresses. The students' inability to drop these references reveals what the resistance to change was really about. Much of the stereotyping of Native Americans is used as a foundation upon which many (mostly European) Americans build their (glorified) national identity (Davis 1993). And these stereotypes are so tightly woven into the social fabric that even conscious attempts to squelch their presence fail. When Native American mascots are critiqued, many (mostly European) Americans feel their own sense of identity challenged, and the latter challenge is what produces the strong resistance (Davis 1993).

Third, the members of the Keep-the-Chiefs group were very good at getting their voices heard and mobilizing other students. In fact, this group almost completely dominated campus discourse about the issue; the campus was inundated with keep-the-Chiefs rhetoric but only rarely heard arguments against Native American mascots. The group achieved their discursive dominance by getting elected to student government and joining the student newspaper staff, which was relatively easy due to the overall lack of student interest in these two organizations. During the period of controversy, both the student newspaper and student government shifted from neutrality and diversity of opinion to advocating for the Chiefs. Several previously mentioned factors also facilitated this discursive dominance. The generally conservative campus, lack of Native Americans, and insular faculty limited the number of people who actually understood the racism intrinsic to Native American mascots, and thus there were very few people who were able or willing to counter the dominant discourse. One consequence of this discursive dominance is that the vast majority on campus still do not understand what is problematic about Native American mascots.

Fourth, one major reason that the effort to eliminate the Chiefs mascot was successful was that most agreed that there should be a single mascot for the women's and men's teams. Due to the stereotype that all Native American chiefs are men, many did not think that Chiefs was an appropriate mascot for the women's teams. Many of those supporting the change at SC did so because of the gender issue, not because they objected to Native American mascots.

Some theoretical reflection about education and democracy is in order. There were few efforts to educate the campus about the mascot issue or Native American stereotyping more generally. At a college that emphasizes teaching and sport, it is surprising that few faculty used their classes to educate students about the issue. We speculate that this is because most of the faculty themselves did not understand the issue. The few educational efforts did enhance the understanding of a small percentage of the campus community, but most need much more extensive efforts. There are two main reasons why stereotyping of Native Americans is so difficult to understand for many in the United States. First, we have been deluged with stereotypical images of Native Americans since birth (Coombe 1996; Green 1988). Second, many stereotypes of Native Americans appear to be positive (for example, "they are all good fighters, spiritually enlightened, connected to nature"). Many do not view positive stereotypical ideas or images as stereotypes or as racist. (Of course, "positive" stereotypes are problematic for a variety of reasons, including that many from the category do not fit the stereotypes, and the stereotypes are often used to justify oppressive practices.) For these reasons, it takes more than a couple of talks or op-ed pieces to move understanding beyond these stereotypes.

Thomas Pettigrew (1994) argued that reduction of racism is more likely to emerge from behavioral change than from attitudinal change, and that change in attitudes often follows behavioral change. Certainly, attitudinal change of most members of the campus community at SC did not precede behavioral change (that is, a change in the mascot). We doubt that attitudinal change will follow the change in mascot. It may be ideal for widespread attitudinal change to precede, and even cause, behavioral change, yet many times we cannot afford to wait for attitudinal change when issues of social justice are on the line. At the University of Southern Colorado, it took over twenty years of ongoing educational programming before opinions shifted enough to eliminate their Native American mascot (Honor Our Neighbors 1995). Elimination of Native American mascots seems to proceed most often quickly and smoothly in communities where there are a sizable number of Native Americans who have been addressing issues of stereotyping for years. This activism lays the foundation for understanding the mascot issue and thus the change itself (Davis 1993). In these communities short-term educational efforts are probably very useful for facilitating a change in mascots. In communities where the Native American population is small or powerless, short-term educational efforts may not be especially useful.

The issue of democracy was raised continually by those opposing the change at SC. The basic argument was that any change in mascots should be voted on by the campus community and that majority will should prevail. The problem with this argument is what scholars of politics call "the tyranny of the majority" (Cain 1992; Guinier 1994; Madison [1787] 1999; Mill [1859] 1975). As James Madison ([1787] 1999) put it, " measures are too often decided, not according to the rules of justice, and the rights of the minor party, but by the superior force of an interested and overbearing majority" (678). Mill ([1859] 1975) added that the majority "may desire to oppress part of their number" (5). Guinier (1994) argued, "In an ideal democracy, the people would rule, but the minorities would also be protected against the power of majorities" (4). The danger is greatest when the numerical minority is unable to educate the masses due to their lack of power. This is the case for Native Americans in most parts of the United States. The majority of the population, non-Natives, for the most part do not understand and/or support the desires of Native Americans. Native Americans, therefore, suffer (in such ways as loss of land, lack of religious rights, and poor health, housing, and nutrition), partly because of the role a particular version of democracy plays in the United States (Guinier 1994).

One way that Native Americans, and sensitive non-Natives, suffer is living in a hostile discursive climate. Being continually surrounded by stereotypes of Native Americans, such as the case at schools with Native American mascots, is a form of racial harassment that affects people (Rosenstein 1996). Prior to the mascot change at SC, both authors of this chapter felt uncomfortable, offended, and insulted by the discourse associated with the Chiefs

235

mascot. At times, this discourse and related imagery gave us a sense that others did not care for our feelings, led us to feel as if we were unseen and unheard, strained our personal and professional connections, and limited our abilities to fully focus.

In situations where the oppressed category is the numerical minority (e.g., ableism, heterosexism), democracy may not be the appropriate strategy for reducing oppression. Simply put, authorities need to step in and create opportunities and a climate that allow numerical minorities to thrive, because the majority is unlikely to vote for all of the changes that make this happen. Most non-Natives do not understand the problems with Native American mascots and thus would not vote for elimination of these mascots (Sigelman 1998). In a case in North Carolina, majority-rule voting resulted in retaining the Warrior and Squaw mascots. As the North Carolina activists against these mascots point out, "one does not vote on racism and sexual harassment" (Honor Our Neighbors 1998, 11).

NOTES

1. The information presented in this chapter comes from a variety of sources: our own memories, the student newspaper, minutes from committee meetings, letters to administrators, and interviews with several individuals who worked on both sides of the issue.

2. Throughout this chapter, the term *nickname* refers to the verbal name for teams, the term *icon* refers to the pictorial representation of the nickname, and the term *mascot* refers to both the nickname and icon.

REFERENCES

Cain, Bruce E. 1992. "Voting Rights and Democratic Theory: Towards a Color-Blind Society?" *Brookings Review* 10(1): 46–50.

Coombe, Rosemary J. 1996. "Embodied Trademarks: Mimesis and Alterity on American Commercial Frontiers." *Cultural Anthropology* 11:202–24.

Davis, Laurel R. 1993. "Protest against the Use of Native American Mascots: A Challenge to Traditional American Identity." *Journal of Sport and Social Issues* 17(1): 9–22.

Druyor, Meg. 1994. Letter to the editor. *Springfield (MA) Student*, 24 March, 2.

Gibbons, Ed. 1975. "'Chiefs' Need a Change." *Springfield (MA) Student*, 9 Oct., 1.

Green, Rayna. 1988. "The Tribe Called Wannabee: Playing Indian in America and Europe." *Folklore* 99:30–55.

Guinier, Lani. 1994. *The Tyranny of the Majority: Fundamental Fairness in Representative Democracy*. New York: Free Press.

Honor Our Neighbors Origins and Rights (HONOR). 1995. "Indians: Two More Schools Drop Offensive Logos." *Honor Digest* 6(1): 5.

———. 1998. "Mascot Struggle Continues." *Honor Digest* 9(5): 11.

LaGiglia, Nick, and Brian Junger. 1997. "From the 'NI-EAR' Side!" *Springfield (MA) Student*, 7 March, 3.

Loewen, James W. 1995. *Lies My Teacher Told Me: Everything Your American History Textbook Got Wrong*. New York: Simon and Schuster.

Madison, James. [1787] 1999. "The Federalist, No. 10." Reprinted in *Politics in America*, 3d ed., ed. Thomas R. Dye, 678–80. Englewood Cliffs NJ: Prentice-Hall.

The Massasoit. 1923. Springfield College Yearbook. Springfield MA: Springfield College Junior Class.

Mehan, Adam, and Beth Gibney. 1994. "Mascot Committee Soliciting Input from SC Family." *Springfield (MA) Student*, 5 May, 1.

Mill, John S. [1859] 1975. *On Liberty: Annotated Text Sources and Background Criticism*, ed. David Spitz. New York: W. W. Norton.

Moriarity, Tom. 1997. "Churchill Calls Time-Out on Chief Controversy." *Springfield (MA) Student*, 7 March, 1.

Pettigrew, Thomas. 1994. "Intergroup Prejudice and Discrimination on the Campus." Paper presented at University of Massachusetts Racism Conference, Amherst, 22 Sept.

Rosenstein, Jay. 1996. *In Whose Honor? American Indian Mascots in Sports.* Ho-ho-kus NJ: New Day Films. Videocassette.

Sigelman, Lee. 1998. "Hail to the Redskins? Public Reactions to a Racially Insensitive Team Name." *Sociology of Sport Journal* 15(4): 317–25.

St. Pierre, Mark. 1997. "Letter from an Angry Alum." *Springfield (MA) Student,* 13 March, 1, 4–5.

PART FOUR

Interventions

CHAPTER 11

In Whose Honor?,
Mascots, and the Media

•

Jay Rosenstein

If Hollywood were to run out of Indians, the program schedules would be mangled beyond all recognition. Then some courageous soul with a small budget might be able to do a documentary telling what, in fact, we have done—and are still doing—to the Indians in this country.
—Edward R. Murrow

When I read those words in 1990, taken from a 1958 speech given by the legendary journalist Edward R. Murrow, it was as if he were speaking directly to me from the grave. Each word jumped off the page and filled my head; it was as though a huge neon sign were flashing before my eyes. The message was clear: Edward R. Murrow was telling me that I had to produce the television documentary that I had just recently begun to think about, a documentary about the use of American Indians as mascots in sports. Murrow himself was telling me that I had to be that courageous soul with a small budget. For the next seven years, as I struggled to make the documentary *In Whose Honor? American Indian Mascots in Sports*, I often returned to those words for inspiration.

What Murrow was referring to, somewhat indirectly, was the incredible power of the visual media to shape impressions, influence understanding, and even create and reinforce stereotypes about

American Indian people. But Murrow also recognized there was another side as well: just as the media can use their power to mis-educate and create false representations, they can also use that power to help fix those problems. That is exactly what I hoped to be a part of with *In Whose Honor?*

Although American Indian stereotypes are no longer as preva-lent in the TV and movie industries, the mainstream media still have a profound impact on the use of American Indian mascots. This essay discusses the history and significance of media coverage of Native American mascots and efforts to retire them. It stresses the entangled interests of the sports and media worlds and how those interests influence and impact coverage. At the same time, it directs attention to recent transformations, particularly the emergence of advocates within the national media for the elimination of Ameri-can Indian mascots in sports. I also add my personal experiences working within the media and the role that *In Whose Honor?* has played.

IN WHOSE HONOR?

In the fall of 1990, I attended an event that not only significantly changed my life but also eventually had a profound impact on the national media coverage and the public's understanding of the mascot issue. The handful of Native American students and faculty at the University of Illinois were giving a talk about their experi-ences as Native people at the university. Not surprisingly, the talk fo-cused almost exclusively on the school's mascot and its impact on their lives.

To this day, I have no idea why I was there. I certainly had not in-tended to go. But the result was significant. It was there that I first heard Native American graduate student Charlene Teters tell her story in person, and I was shocked and stunned by what she had to say. Part of my reaction was to the very moving story shared by

Charlene, about what happened to her children the first time she and they saw the university's mascot, Chief Illiniwek. Recalling the experience more than one year later, her voice was still filled with rage and anger. But the other part of my reaction was toward the media. Although I was a regular consumer of local news, I had never heard most of this information before. Despite Charlene and her mascot protests attracting much local coverage, including more than a few nasty editorials and hateful letters to the editor by Chief Illiniwek supporters, I was suddenly aware that the other side of the story—the Native American side—had hardly been told. And, what had been told was missing so much of the necessary historic and human context, it was practically meaningless. It was then that I began to think that this was a story that needed to be told, and told in a different way. "Someone ought to do a television documentary on this issue," I remember thinking. Little did I know that I would eventually be that someone.

My original goal in making *In Whose Honor?* was to change the nature of the local debate over Indian mascots both by correcting the false information that had been propagated by the local media and by allowing the American Indian people who objected to this mascot, for the first time locally (and one of the only instances nationally, it would turn out), to have extended time simply to tell their side of the story. Given how much media time is allotted to sports and the propagation of American Indian nicknames, it did not seem like much to ask. But in a way, it is, because the media and sports share a close relationship where a multitude of pressures helps discourage any criticism of sports-related issues in the media.

THE RELATIONSHIP BETWEEN SPORTS AND MEDIA

Over the last several years, the sports and media industries have become so entangled, they are practically one and the same. The relationship between sports and media begins with team broadcast rights. On the national level, television networks bid for the exclusive rights to broadcast certain sports, leagues, or high-profile events, such as the playoffs or the Super Bowl. These rights do not come cheap: Fox, CBS, ABC, and ESPN will pay $17.6 billion to broadcast the National Football League over the next eight seasons, Turner Sports and NBC will pay $2.64 billion to broadcast the National Basketball Association for the next four years, and the list goes on and on (Strauss 1998).

The bottom line is that these rights fees create a situation where the networks and the leagues are basically business partners. And just as it is in any business, it is rarely in one's best interest to criticize a partner. In this case, criticism may eventually lead to a network losing its broadcast rights. "Everyone (the media) is inhibited by the fear of losing these contracts," says Frank Deford, a *Sports Illustrated* writer and NPR commentator. Seth Abraham, the CEO of Time Warner Sports, agrees, saying "the leagues don't want to be embarrassed" by tough stories (Strauss 1998). Add to this the fact that some media companies are themselves sports franchise owners—for instance, Time Warner owns CNN and the Atlanta Braves—and it is easy to see why there would be pressure on the media to avoid any coverage of controversial sports stories.

In many ways, the situation is much worse at the local level. The competition for local broadcast rights—which include both radio and television—is just as fierce as it is nationally. But locally it is usually a winner-take-all situation; only one station gets to be the voice of the Washington Redskins, or the Florida State University Seminoles, or the University of Illinois Fighting Illini. These rights are highly coveted and usually very lucrative. But when a team selects a broadcast outlet, it can apply any standard it wants in making the choice, so a station that has been critical of the team in the past may find itself at a huge disadvantage. A station that has been criticizing the team's mascot or nickname, for example, is probably very unlikely to win a broadcast contract.

The financial pressures are not just limited to the broadcast media. Newspaper coverage of the local team draws a large readership. Newspapers often compete to provide the most extensive or in-depth local sports coverage, sometimes creating special sections dedicated entirely to this coverage, such as a season preview or a retrospective. But sportswriters depend on access to players and coaches in order to gather enough material to fill these sections. Cooperation from the team becomes vital. A media outlet that has been critical of a team might find itself getting less access than others, putting it at a great competitive disadvantage.

It happened in Ames, Iowa, where then Iowa State University basketball coach Tim Floyd became angry at a sports reporter who had written stories that were critical of the team's graduation rates and other issues. Floyd refused to grant the reporter any one-on-one interviews, "a strong sanction in as cozy a college community as Ames." A competing newspaper became the paper of choice for the die-hard fans, taking those readers and their associated revenue with them (O'Donnell 1998).

Being critical of the local team can hurt business in other ways, too. In St. Paul, Minnesota, a sports reporter uncovered evidence of academic cheating by the University of Minnesota basketball team. (He subsequently won a Pulitzer Prize for the story.) More than five hundred customers canceled their subscriptions in response to the story; even Minnesota governor Jesse Ventura criticized the paper for damaging the team's tournament chances, clearly more concerned about the sports program than the integrity of the state's largest university. As these examples show, reporters can easily save themselves—and their employers—a lot of money and grief simply by ignoring controversial issues and sticking to stories about the games.

In addition to broadcasting games, local television and radio stations bid on exclusive rights to air coaches' shows. Coaches' shows are meant to be publicity, not journalism, despite the fact that the stations that air them—and oftentimes the hosts—are called upon to cover the "news" of that same team. In Chicago, sportscaster Tim Weigel admitted his role as the host of the (former Bears' coach) *Dave Wannstedt Show* "was to console rather than confront." Weigel asks, "was it unprofessional to hold his hand rather than slap his face? Probably. But if forced to choose between being a pro and being a friend, I don't think there is a choice" (Weigel 1999). Weigel's comments clearly articulate the feelings of many in sports media: they would prefer to be friends with the players and supporters of the team rather than objective journalists. Conflicts of interest abound.

The line blurs further in promotional events. Especially in smaller communities, the media see themselves as part of the hometown community, and that usually means being fans of the local team. Sports and news reporters often participate in social events involving home games or the home team. In Champaign, Illinois, the town's only daily newspaper, a news-talk radio station, and a television news station all cosponsor pep rallies for the team. Clearly relationships—and allegiances—are tangled.

Yet many media outlets justify their conflicts of interest using a simple dividing line: sports is not news. Although news and sports share time during a station's "news"-cast and share part of what is collectively called a "news"-paper, the rules that govern news and sports are very different. Sports reporters are not held to the same standards of fairness, balance, and objectivity as news reporters. For instance, news reporters are forbidden from outwardly cheering for, or supporting, say, a particular political candidate or issue, yet it is completely acceptable—and, in fact, expected—for sports reporters to cheer for and support the local team. But unfortunately, it does not end there. In most cases, this fan mentality spreads to the serious news reporters, too.

In the isolated context of the home team winning or losing, this double standard is probably harmless. But when other issues arise from that same home team—violence against women, taxpayer-funded stadiums, racial stereotypes as mascots—can these so-called journalists suddenly turn from cheerleaders to objective reporters? Doubtful. For example, when a Champaign news anchor shouts on the air, "Go Illini!" in support of some good news from the University of Illinois Fighting Illini football team, can she then turn unbiased in reporting on the controversy over that same football team's Indian mascot, as she is often called upon to do? In these situations, the line that separates news and sports disappears.

It happens in other ways, too. While the news section of a newspaper normally would not advocate for an Indian nickname or logo, these nicknames and logos often appear on the front page, often as a promotion for a sports story inside. Of course, we expect and accept the use of the logo in the sports section, because sports is not news. But by allowing the logo to appear on the front page—without comment—the paper is already, in effect, taking a position on that issue: this logo is acceptable. In Champaign, the leading television news station has the Chief Illiniwek logo as a permanent part of its news set. So, when news reporters cover a story about the controversy over the use of the team's logo, they do so with that same logo looking over their shoulders. The news reporters may be trying to be fair and unbiased, but the station has already taken a clearly visible stand (the station has removed the logo since this writing).

In short, all of these situations play a part in the way in which sports issues are covered and, ultimately, what the public learns and believes about these issues. And the controversy over the use of American Indian mascots is no exception.

247

COVERAGE OF MASCOTS AND THE
ANTI-MASCOT MOVEMENT IN THE MEDIA

Despite the interdependent sports-media relationship, national media coverage of the anti-mascot movement has shown a great deal of progress. (For the purposes of this essay, the national media are defined as the *New York Times* newspaper, *Newsweek* magazine, the ABC, CBS, and NBC evening news broadcasts, and the national sports publications *Sports Illustrated* and the *Sporting News*.) The tone and point of view of that coverage has changed significantly in the past few decades.

From the time when the first anti-mascot protesters began in the late 1960s until the late 1980s, the mascot controversy got little attention. American Indian mascots were generally seen by the press as nothing but fun and games, and few writers made connections between these portrayals and actual living people. For example, the Atlanta Braves mascot "Chief Noc-a-homa" did a "victory dance" in front of his "lonely teepee" and shocked a *Newsweek* writer by speaking the phrase "public relations-wise" (Waters 1980). All this was written without a hint of irony. By the end of the decade, however, comments like these would rarely be written by the press.

By 1989, mascot controversies began to get more news coverage, especially in the *New York Times*. And as news coverage increased, reporters and columnists started to speak to and hear from American Indians about this issue, probably for the first time. A turning point came in 1990, when Franz Lidz, writing in *Sports Illustrated*, became the first national writer to pen an opinion piece that directly called for the elimination of American Indian mascots and nicknames. The piece, titled "Not a Very Sporting Symbol: Indians Have Ceased to Be Appropriate Team Mascots," details the struggle against the University of Illinois mascot by Charlene Teters and goes on to ridicule the conservative *Dartmouth Review* newspaper for calling for a return of the "Indian" nickname. Lidz neither sugar-coats the issue nor pulls any punches.

But this would prove to be just the beginning. The two major sporting events of late 1991 and early 1992, the World Series and the Super Bowl, thrust the Indian mascot and nickname issue onto the mainstream media's map. By some particular twist of fate, both events were held in Minneapolis, the original home of the American Indian Movement and a city with a large population of Indian activists. The World Series and Super Bowl became the perfect opportunities for some mass American Indian protests. And the press took full notice.

During the World Series, for the first time ever, the mascot controversy was covered on the national TV news. *ABC News* carried a story about the World Series protests, written and reported not by a news person but by sports reporter Dick Schapp (notice the blurring line). The two-and-a-half-minute segment, long by television standards, includes comments by former president Jimmy Carter of his intention to do the tomahawk chop and supporting remarks from former Atlanta mayor Andrew Young. Schapp also points out some disagreement among Indian people on the issue by speaking with a North Carolina Cherokee who manufactures foam tomahawks. Yet, like virtually every reporter who tackles that angle, Schapp never attempted to put this Indian disagreement in context. The question of whether the mascot protesters represent just a tiny minority of Native opinion is asked (as it often is) yet never answered (as it never is). A month later, NBC also aired a story about the protests.

But this major television coverage did more than just put the mascot issue in front of much of the American public for the first time. According to the *New York Times*, the television footage of fans doing the tomahawk chop (including Braves owner Ted Turner and wife Jane Fonda) provided many Native Americans around the country with their first glimpse of what was going on in some of these stadiums. The television media had unintentionally recruited many Native Americans into the anti-mascot movement.

Just three months later, the 1992 Super Bowl (which included the Washington Redskins) became a defining event. Protests ignited and inspired a flurry of coverage — especially anti-mascot columns — that lasted for years. After the Super Bowl, among national sports and news columnists who expressed an opinion on this issue, that opinion was virtually unanimous that American Indian nicknames and mascots had to go.

These columnists include *New York Times* sports writer Robert Lipsythe, who asked in the title of his column, "How Can Jane Fonda Be a Part of the Chop?" *Indian Country Today* publisher and Lakota Tim Giago was given a guest column in *Newsweek* and later in the *New York Times* to speak out against Indian nicknames and mascots. (A *Newsweek* staffer gave that column the unfortunate title of "I Hope the Redskins Lose," which no doubt contributed to the huge amount of hate mail Giago says he received shortly thereafter.) *Sporting News* columnist Mark Purdy noted that "if it's not such a big deal to have Indian nicknames, then it shouldn't be that big a deal to change them." *Sports Illustrated* editor Steve Wulf joined in with an editorial that used the *Portland Oregonian* newspaper's decision to stop printing stereotyped nicknames as a jumping-off point to call for teams with Indian nicknames to change. *Sporting News* columnist (and long-time advocate of racial equality in sports) Dr. Richard Lapchick wrote a column titled "Let's Chop Down the Remnants of Racism." And influential and nationally syndicated *New York Times* sports columnists George Vecsey and Ira Berkow each joined the growing chorus by calling for an end to American Indian nicknames and mascots.

Through all this, only one pro-mascot column appeared in the national media, one written by conservative George Will about the University of Illinois situation. In his column (1995), Will noted that "Chief Illiniwek probably will survive because the arguments against him are so strained and because many Native Americans recognize in his role a compliment from the university to their heritage." Like so many other writers and reporters, Will referenced this unnamed and unidentified mass of Native Americans that see mascots as a compliment. As always, these people are noted, yet never identified nor counted. Their existence in significantly large numbers is simply assumed and logged as truth.

But the effects of the 1991–92 World Series and Super Bowl were clearly demonstrated later, in 1995, when the Cleveland Indians and Atlanta Braves met in the World Series. Even before the games (and the protests) began, a number of writers, including *New York Times* columnist George Vecsey and former *Sports Illustrated* writer Rick Telander, started criticizing the teams' nicknames. Many in the press had been transformed from being reactive to proactive. Even some who had not expressed an opinion on the controversy before referred to the games as the "politically-incorrect" series. Although anti-mascot activists may not have won over a majority of the press (and certainly not a majority of the public), they had at least succeeded in educating the media—and through them, the public— that the use of American Indians as mascots and nicknames in sports is a controversial issue.

IN WHOSE HONOR?: COVERAGE AND REACTIONS

In the summer of 1997, I was thrown into the national media landscape as both a contributor and a source. My documentary *In Whose Honor?*—a critical look at the use of American Indian mascots in sports—was accepted by the PBS national television series *P.O.V.* for broadcast. *In Whose Honor?* is the first-ever documentary on the subject of Indian mascots to appear on national TV.

Although it is a national series, *P.O.V.* is no *CBS Evening News* or *NBC Nightly News*. The series runs only in the summer, basically because that is a "dead" time of year for programming and the only slot public television programmers were willing to give up for independent, and often controversial, films. *P.O.V.* is not always carried in prime time—in some markets, it airs at 10 P.M. or 11 P.M.; in others, not at all. Still, this was national television, and despite these handicaps, the program made a big impact.

That was helped considerably by the promotional effort done by *P.O.V.*, which landed articles and reviews in dozens of national newspapers and magazines. Unlike for many films, the articles and reviews concentrated almost exclusively on the issue of American Indian mascots, not the content of the actual film. So not only did my TV program express a voice on this issue within the media, but its existence also created a flurry of additional coverage about the mascot issue from other media.

Coverage of the film was overwhelmingly positive, with many writers using their reviews as a platform to criticize the use of American Indian mascots in sports. Some reviewers were incredibly outspoken. *Sports Illustrated* writer Jeff Pearlman provided the most memorable quote, calling the dance of the Illinois mascot Chief Illiniwek "sort of M. C. Hammer meets Richard Simmons meets Biff the town idiot." He also referred to mascot supporters as "white fans inanely dancing around dressed as Indians" (Pearlman 1997). The *Chicago Tribune, Virginia Pilot, Los Angeles Times*, and the Copley News Service all used their reviews as an opportunity to ridicule the University of Illinois for their continued use of an Indian mascot. In his review *New York Times* writer Walter Goodman criticized the Washington team, expressing hope that it might someday "recognize that Redskins is not a nice word" (Goodman 1997).

In response to *In Whose Honor?* not one single column or review appeared in a national publication that either defended or supported the use of American Indian mascots. In fact, *In Whose Honor?* received only one negative review anywhere. It was written for a small newspaper in Springfield, Illinois, by a University of Illinois alumnus.

The release of *In Whose Honor?* had more impact in the media than just its broadcast and the surrounding publicity. It helped to inspire similar anti-mascot news stories, many without a connection to any specific newsworthy event (known as a "news peg"). *ABC News* producer John Beattie saw *In Whose Honor?* and decided to make Charlene Teters the show's "person of the week" in October of 1997. Peter Jennings introduced the piece by nearly apologizing that not everyone will agree with the point of view. But the segment itself made no attempt at balance—it allowed supporters of the Cleveland Indians mascot Chief Wahoo to look especially foolish, while giving Charlene Teters the opportunity to state her case. It is a strong contrast to the ABC story done by Dick Schapp six years earlier.

But that was not all. Nickelodeon channel's *Nick News* created a segment about the issue, Court TV covered Vernon Bellecourt's trial—and acquittal—for burning Chief Wahoo in effigy, and the *Last Word*, a sports-talk show on the Fox Sports channel even discussed the issue. On that program, host Jim Rome debated former Kansas City Chiefs player Bill Maas, absolutely destroying and embarrassing Maas on the air as he tried to defend the practice of using Indian mascots. I was stunned by Rome's thorough knowledge and understanding of the issue. It would be difficult to imagine a sportscaster ten years ago defending Native American protesters with such passion and understanding. Much has certainly changed in the media.

Perhaps nowhere was that more evident than in January of 1999, when the Washington Redskins football team was sold. Immediately upon announcement of the sale, *Washington Post* staff writer Gene Weingarten wrote a column telling the new owners that this was the perfect time to change the name. Again, it is difficult to imagine such a column just ten years ago.

But the way in which *In Whose Honor?* triggered a flurry of media coverage also points out the ongoing problem faced by American Indians in trying to publicize their side of the story on this issue. It has to do with the basic framework in which news and sports exist. American Indians will always have to be part of a newsworthy event, such as a protest or the airing of a national documentary, in order to have their point of view included in the media. But the Washington nickname Redskins and Cleveland's Chief Wahoo can be propagated in the media almost daily, since they are considered acceptable parts of the sports world. Undoing this imbalance of power will be difficult, if not impossible.

CONCLUSION

So, where are we now? Since the World Series and Super Bowl protests of 1991 and 1992 and the airing of *In Whose Honor?* in the summer of 1997, much media attention has been focused on the mascot issue. Many in the national media seem to have been educated about the controversy, even becoming advocates for the removal of American Indian nicknames and mascots in sports. Yet, it is important to remember that none of these opinions are necessarily institutionalized. The media are, and always have been, nothing more than a collection of individuals. And as these individuals come and go, the stance on this issue by the media might begin to change. The process of educating and re-educating the media will have to continue.

REFERENCES

Berkow, Ira. 1996. "Sports of the Times: It's Time for Redskins to Exit." *New York Times*, Oct. 15.

Dunlap, David, and Susan Anderson. 1985. "Maskless Cheerleader." *New York Times*, Feb. 28.

Dunlap, David, and Sara Rimer. 1985. "The Redman, er, Woman." *New York Times*, March 30.

Giago, Tim. 1992. "I Hope the Redskins Lose." *Newsweek*, Jan. 27.

———. 1994. "Drop the Chop." *New York Times*, March 13.

Goodman, Walter. 1997. "Television Review: Feeling Unflattered by Imitation." *New York Times*, July 15.

Johnson, Allan. 1997. "Television." *Chicago Tribune*, July 15.

Johnson, Steve. 1997. "Channel Surfing." *Chicago Tribune*, July 15.

Kinsely, Michael. 1992. "NFL Comes under Protest." *Sporting News*, Feb. 3.

Lapchick, Richard. 1993. "Let's Chop Down the Remnants of Racism." *Sporting News*, April 12.

Leiby, Richard. 1994. "Bury My Heart at RFK." *Washington Post*, Nov. 6.

Lidz, Franz. 1990. "Not a Very Sporting Symbol." *Sports Illustrated*, Sept. 17.

Lipsythe, Robert. 1991. "How Can Jane Fonda Be a Part of the Chop?" *New York Times*, Oct. 18.

Molinaro, Bob. 1997. "On Warpath over Skins' Savagery of a Nickname." *(Norfolk) Virginia Pilot*, July 20.

O'Donnell, Jim. 1998. "Iowa Paper Feels Floyd's Wrath." *Chicago Sun-Times*, July 17.

Pearlman, Jeff. 1997. "Righting a Wrong." *Sports Illustrated*, July 14.

Penner, Mike. 1997. "The Hot Corner." *Los Angeles Times*, July 15.

Purdy, Mark. 1992. "If It's Not a Big Deal, Nicknames Should Welcome a New Tradition. *Sporting News*, Feb. 17.

Rose, Ted. 1998. "Root, Root, Root for the Home Team." *Brill's Content*, Sept.

Strauss, Lawrence. 1998. "Does Money Tilt the Playing Field?" *Columbia Journalism Review*, Sept.–Oct.

Vecsey, George. 1995. "Sports of the Times: This Series Could Prove Offensive." *New York Times*, Oct. 19.

Waters, Harry. 1980. "The No. 1 Fan." *Newsweek*, June 16.

Weigel, Tim. 1999. "Wannstedt Will Be Missed as a Friend and True Pro." *Chicago Sun-Times*, Jan. 3.

Will, George. 1995. "Chief Illiniwek and the Sensitivity Cavalry." *Washington Post*, March 9.

Wulf, Steve. 1982. "Not Home Free Yet." *Sports Illustrated*, Aug. 9.

———. 1992. "A Brave Move." *Sports Illustrated*, Feb. 24.

CHAPTER 12

Educators and Mascots

Challenging Contradictions

•

Cornel D. Pewewardy

Invented media images prevent millions of Americans from understanding the past and current authentic human experience of First Nations People.[1] My response to the usage of Indian mascots for sports teams has always been to argue that these trappings and seasonal insults offend the intelligence of thousands of Indigenous Peoples in this country. This chapter speaks to the American educator and discusses how, as educators, we are responsible for maintaining the ethics of teaching and for helping to eliminate racism in all aspects of school life. Therefore, the exploitation of Indian mascots becomes an issue of educational equity.

Why should educators be concerned at all about American Indian mascots, logos, nicknames, and the tomahawk chop? As someone who has spent his entire adult life teaching and administrating elementary schools for Indigenous children, I believe Indian mascots reveal a system of "dysconscious racism" and propagate a form of cultural violence, which operates at the psychological level. According to King and Ladson-Billings (1990), dysconscious racism is a form of racism that unconsciously accepts dominant white norms and privileges.[2] Dysconscious racism is "an uncritical habit of mind (that is, perceptions, attitudes, assumptions and beliefs) that justifies inequity and exploitation by accepting the existing order of things as given. It involves identification with an ideological view-point which admits no fundamentally alternative vision of society" (King 1991:5). With regard to racial inequity, this way of thinking encourages people to uncritically accept certain culturally sanctioned assumptions, myths, and beliefs that justify the social and economic advantages white people enjoy as a result of the historical and contemporary subordination of people of color (Wellman 1977). For example, constantly witnessing these racial antics and negative behaviors portrayed by Indian mascots and their supporters, day in and day out, one becomes absolutely numb to their presence.

A recent anecdote illustrates well the impact of dysconscious racism. In 1997, an eighth-grade student, writing an essay about his school's mascot, penned the following comment: "We simply chose an Indian as the emblem. We could have just as easily chosen any uncivilized animal" (quoted in "American Indian" 2000). Simultaneously innocent and racist, the sentiments expressed by this student are complex. In this essay, I aim to outline the relevance of Indian mascots for teachers and students. Ultimately, I want to argue that educators themselves frequently help to propagate racist, stereotypical images and that Indian mascots impact the psyches of young students—both Indigenous and non-Indian children—in untold and, too often, unforeseen ways. Teachers must examine the colonial legacies and asymmetrical relations of power that perpetuate the existence of these "maufactured Indians."

CHALLENGES

The challenge that we have today is to deconstruct a reality that has been manufactured by the American media and scholars. For many Americans there is something faintly anachronistic about contemporary Indigenous Peoples. Many people today look at Indigenous Peoples as figures out of the past, as relics of a more heroic age. Put somewhat differently, the contemporary presence of Indigenous

Peoples has been difficult to grasp for most Americans. Only recently have Indigenous Peoples begun to reclaim their own images and make their special presence known.

Teachers should research the matter and discover that Indigenous Peoples would never have associated the sacred practices of becoming a warrior with the hoopla of a pep rally, halftime entertainment, or being a sidekick to cheerleaders. Many schools, colleges, and universities around the country continue to exhibit Indian mascots and logos, using nicknames and doing the tomahawk chop in sports stadiums with inauthentic representations of Indigenous cultures.[3]

Many school officials claim they are honoring Indigenous Peoples and insist their schools' sponsored activities are not offensive, but rather a compliment. I would argue otherwise. There's nothing in Indigenous cultures that I'm aware of that aspires to be a mascot, logo, or nickname for athletic teams. It would be the same as a crowd of fans using real saints as mascots or having fans dressed up as the Pope (or Lady Popes or Nuns) at a New Orleans Saints football game and doing the "crucifix chop" to the musical accompaniment of Gregorian chants while wearing colorful religious attire in the stands. What would be the reaction of Catholics around the country if that happened?

This behavior makes a mockery of Indigenous cultural identity and causes many young Indigenous people to feel shame about who they are as human beings, because racial stereotypes play an important role in shaping a young person's consciousness. Subjective feelings, such as inferiority, are an integral part of consciousness and work together with the objective reality of poverty and deprivation to shape a young person's worldview. Beginning with Wild West shows and continuing with contemporary movies, television, and literature, the image of Indigenous Peoples has radically shifted away from any reference to living people to a field of urban fantasy in which wish fulfillment replaces reality (V. Deloria 1980). Schools should be places where students come to unlearn the stereotypes that such mascots represent.

So why do some teachers allow their students to uncritically adopt a cartoon version of Indigenous cultures through the use of a mascot portrayed by sports teams? Dennis (1981) contends that people engage in racist behavior because they are reasonably sure that there is support for it within their society. However, the cultural lens of many teachers may be highly ethnocentric and monocultural, yet no distortions are perceived in the field of vision (Aaronsohn, Carter, and Howell 1995).

To further understand why this is racist, consider how euphemisms and code words for ethnic persons and groups are used: *scalp, massacre, redskin, squaw, noble savage, papoose, Pocahontas, Cherokee princess.* Bosmajian (1983) contends that in addition to being subjugated by the church and state, Indigenous Peoples are dehumanized by society at large through the use of xenophobic-coded language. The English language includes various phrases and words that relegate the Indigenous Peoples to an inferior status: "The only good Indian is a dead Indian," "Indian giver," "drunken Indians," "dumb Indians," and "Redskins." [4] These words represent a new generation of ethnic slurs that are replacing the older, more blatant and abusive, nicknames (I. Allen 1990; Moore 1976).

MANUFACTURING IMAGINARY INDIANS

The portrayal of Indigenous Peoples in sports takes many forms. Some teams use generic Indigenous names, such as Indians, Braves, or Chiefs, while others adopt specific tribal names, such as Seminoles, Cherokees, or Apaches. Indian mascots exhibit either idealized or comical facial features and "native" dress ranging from body-length, feathered (usually turkey) headdresses to more subtle fake buckskin attire or skimpy loincloths. Some teams and supporters display counterfeit Indigenous paraphernalia, including tomahawks, feathers, face paints, symbolic drums, and pipes. They also use mock-Indigenous behaviors, such as the tomahawk chop, dances, chants, drum beating, war whooping, and symbolic scalping.

So-called Indian mascots reduce diverse Indigenous tribal members to generic cartoon characters. These Wild West figments of the white imagination distort both Indigenous and non-Indigenous children's attitudes toward an oppressed—and diverse—minority. The Indigenous portrait of the moment may be bellicose, ludicrous, or romantic, but almost never is the portrait we see of Indian mascots a real person (Stedman 1982). Most young children in America do not have the faintest idea that Indigenous Peoples are real human beings because of such portrayals.

Furthermore, the American racism we inherit today is connected with particular social constructions of reality. Racism is the primary form of cultural domination in the United States over the past four hundred years. Prior to Columbus, the New World, or America, functioned for millennia without the race construct as we understand it today (Stiffarm and Lane 1992; Mohawk 1992). According to Banton (1998), the pre-Columbian European explorers in the Pacific had only fleeting contacts with the islanders, who often received them in friendship. Their accounts were favorable. However, European writing inspired by these accounts went further and built the myth of the noble savage. This was of importance politically, for to believe that the savage is noble is to believe that humanity is naturally good. If evil does not have its origin in human nature, it must spring from the faulty organization of society.

In this context, Indigenous Peoples stood as the cipher for everything that was pristine and sublime. European intellectuals as an emblem that escaped the emotional and intellectual shackles of modernity used this fascination and its attendant desire for otherness. These notions of exotic innocence are no less stereotypical than the idea that Indigenous Peoples are less civilized and more barbaric. Solomos and Back (1996) contend that this kind of identification is locked within the discourse of absolute difference that renders Indian exotic and reaffirms Indigenous Peoples as a "race apart." It was this danger that Frantz Fanon outlined when he argued that those Europeans who blindly adore the difference of the other are as racially afflicted as those who vilify it (Fanon 1986).

Understanding hegemony is a key to understanding racism.[5] I concur with Hilliard (1997) and Kane (1997) that racism is a mental illness, because it is a socially constructed system of beliefs created by advocates and inventors of hegemonic systems. It is a precursor to mental illness, among ethnic minorities, because it requires that the individual function with the academic falsification of the human record (Guthrie 1998; Gould 1996), distortion of cultural identity (Bartolome and Macedo 1997, Pewewardy and Willower 1993), and delusions of grandeur about white supremacy (Novick 1995; Sleeter 1994). Tinker (1993) asserts that even many Indigenous Peoples have internalized this illusion just as deeply as white Americans have, and as a result they discover from time to time just how fully Indigenous Peoples participate today in their own oppression. At the ideological level, racism's link to mental illness requires continued systemic study, and at the applied level, massive financial resources for the deconstruction of the European colonial mind-set need to be devoted to the structuring of domination (Pine and Hilliard 1990). Conflicting ideological components, such as a defense of racial exploitation on one hand or an assertion of racial equality on the other, must depend in part for their effectiveness upon a degree of correspondence with that ongoing construction (Saxton 1990).

SPORTING PSYCHOLOGY

Authors disagree about the positive or negative affects of watching sports on the behavior of individuals and society. Wann and Branscombe (1993) contend that level of identification with a sports team is an important moderator of spectators' behavioral, affective, and cognitive reactions to events relevant to their teams. The results of Wann's (1994) study were consistent with Smith's (1988) study regarding the "noble sports fan." According to Wann and Branscombe (1993), persons who strongly identify with a specific sports team, relative to those spectators who are moderate or low in identification, report more involvement with the team, display a more ego-enhancing pattern of attribution for the team's successes, have more positive expectations concerning future team performances, exhibit greater willingness to invest larger amounts of time and money in order to watch the team play, and are more likely to believe that fans of the team with which they are identified possess special qualities.

A classic study of this misuse of imagery is the story of Louis Francis Sockalexis and the Cleveland Indians professional baseball team. Staurowsky (1998) examined how perceptions of historical accuracy have an impact on the legitimization of the Cleveland Indians' claim that the indigenous imagery used in the promotion of the franchise was chosen to honor the first Indigenous person to play in the major leagues, Louis Francis Sockalexis. An analysis was conducted of data gathered from Cleveland's own account of the naming of the franchise along with past and present renderings and antecedents of the story as they appear in a variety of publications and media sources over a hundred-year time period beginning in 1897 and ending in 1997. In light of the findings, Cleveland's professed organizational intent to honor Sockalexis was tested, and Staurowsky found their justification was based on faulty information.

Research on stereotyping has begun to benefit from studies of unconscious and automatic processes in human thought and behavior (Blair and Banaji 1996). Koomen and Dijker (1997) demonstrated that ingroup and outgroup information is differently processed. For an outgroup, target stereotype-consistent information was better encoded than stereotype-inconsistent information, whereas the reverse held for an ingroup target.

Fiske (1993) postulates that the impact of power on stereotyping is mediated by attention: the powerless attend to the powerful who control their outcomes, in an effort to enhance prediction and control, thus forming complex, potentially nonstereotypic impressions. Issues of power play a major role in the use of stereotyping. Sometimes the powerful have no clue that they have power. Therefore, the powerful pay less attention and so are more vulnerable to using or use of stereotyping (Fleming 1996). The powerful need not attend to the other to control their own outcome; they cannot attend because they tend to be attentionally overloaded; and if they have high need for dominance, they may not want to attend. Stereotyping and power are mutually reinforcing because stereotyping itself exerts control, maintaining and justifying the status quo.

According to Freeman (1993), children begin to learn the cultural stereotypes about race during the preschool years. These stereotypes provide the basis for race schemas that influence cognitive processing of social information. Virtually all research on race stereotypes and race schemas has confounded social desirability with race. More recently, psychologists have started to apply schema-based models of social cognition to the study of racial stereotyping in young children. In these cognitive models, schemas are thought to be cognitive structures that mediate the processing of information involved in person perception (Ashmore and Del Boca 1981; Dovidio, Evans, and Tyler 1986).

TRAUMATIC EXPERIENCE:

COLONIALISM, CULTURE, AND CHILDREN

Many accurate books about Indigenous Peoples have been written, yet misinformation abounds and inundates our children at an early age. Racist television cartoons, which were drawn in the 1940s and portrayed Indigenous Peoples as befeathered savages, continue to be shown today as entertainment (Pewewardy 1998, 1991; Huhndorf 1997; Mihesuah 1996; Reese 1996; Shively 1992; Vaughan 1988; Morris 1982; White 1979). Indigenous scholars such as Deirdre Almeida (1997), Paula Gunn Allen (1989), Rayna Green (1992), M. Annette Jaimes and T. Halsey (1992), Hauani-Kay Trask (1993), Ward Churchill (1994), and Philip Deloria (1998) have developed a body of academic research that delineates and links the appropriation and exploitation of Indigenous Peoples through television programming and movies. These media outlets help to shape children's values, their attitudes, and, subsequently, their behaviors.

Children learn by observation and readily imitate complex behavior patterns, even without reinforcement. According to Steele (1997), racism is the social-psychological threat that rises when one is in a situation or doing something for which a negative stereotype about one's group applies. This predicament threatens one with being negatively stereotyped, with being judged or treated stereotypically, or with the prospect of conforming to the stereotype. While these images help shape people's perceptions, stereotypes aid in the dehumanization and deculturalization of Indigenous Peoples (Bird 1996).[6]

As we enter into this new millennium, it seems clear that neither in theory nor in practice did the Europeans succeed in developing a universal point of view. The European nations themselves were built up largely as a result of a process of internal colonization in which a supposed trans-ethnic and trans-cultural nation was created by the extinction or assimilation of other cultural groups. External colonization was often a continuation of this process of internal colonization (Green 1995). Indigenous Peoples faced two such civilizing processes that arose from the Europeans. Furthermore, the linkages between colonialism and racism became evident throughout the late nineteenth and early twentieth centuries in the form of the articulation between nationalism and patriotism in the construction of the very definition of "Americanized."

Duran and Duran (1995:36) assert:

> When the colonization process is perpetuated in such a savage fashion as was done in the Western Hemisphere, there occurs a splitting of the personality that is consistent with the level of trauma. The feelings of helplessness and hopelessness are compounded to such a degree as to make the choice complete psychosis or splitting of the ego into at least two fragments. The split ego, then, will keep one aspect of the person in touch with the pain and one aspect identifying with the aggressor. It is a well known historical fact that some of the greatest Native American leaders were either betrayed or killed by Native American men who lost themselves in their identification with the aggressor.

According to Hutchinson (1996), a colonized mind-set is one in which there is arrogance, smugness, complacency, resignation, or believed necessary compliance with following a certain path or a settled ontology. It is commonly associated with feelings of helplessness, hopelessness, powerlessness, fatalism, or even the depths of despair and nihilism. These are the monocultures of the mind. People are negated as "beings of praxis" (Freire 1997).

As a teacher educator, I seek to convince future teachers that Indian mascots are an important cause for low self-esteem and self-concept in Indigenous children. This is the point where this issue becomes detrimental to the academic achievement of students in school. The

266

position statement of the American Indian Mental Health Association of Minnesota (1992) in support of the total elimination of Indian mascots and logos from schools clarifies this issue: "As a group of mental health providers, we are in agreement that using images of American Indians as mascots, symbols, caricatures, and namesakes for non-Indian sports teams, businesses, and other organizations is damaging to the self-identity, self-concept, and self-esteem of our people. We should like to join with others who are taking a strong stand against this practice."

Because the powerful messages from state and national organizations have been ignored, the question must be asked: why do racial slurs in the form of Indian mascots and logos remain?

I believe that the hidden agenda behind their use is about cultural and spiritual annihilation and about intellectual exploitation. Therefore, the real issues are about power and control. Those who want to define other ethnic groups and control their images in order to have people believe that their truth is the absolute truth drive these negative ethnic images. Furthermore, power and control are the ability to define a reality and to get other people to affirm that reality as if it were their own. Remember that media commercials are carefully designed and expensively produced to stereotype groups and to help us, as consumers, "realize" we are far less intelligent than we should be. This is an additive systemic approach to power and control.

MASCOT NAMES CHANGES

Through the politics of colonization, Indigenous Peoples were socialized into stereotypes of being seen as inferior, stupid, and lazy, thereby fulfilling the need to be everybody's mascot. This list of stereotypes of Indigenous Peoples is well known (for example, the University of Illinois mascot Chief Illiniwek, Oklahoma's Eskimo Joes, Crazy Horse Malt Liquor, Land of Lakes Butter, Jeep Cherokee, Pocahontas). Importantly, however, some large school districts across the nation, such as the Dallas Public Schools and the Los Angeles Public Schools (see Machamer, this volume) have eliminated Indian mascots from their school districts as the result of active advocacy parent and education groups wanting to work closely with school officials. Further, Wisconsin and Minnesota have recommended that publicly funded schools not use mascots, names, or logos that have been deemed offensive to Indigenous Peoples. But although various colleges, universities, high schools, and middle schools have dropped their racially insulting Indian mascot and logos, no professional sports team has felt enough heat or, perhaps, has enough conscience or respect to take a similar step.[7] One exception is the Washington Wizards, who succumbed to the political pressure to change their mascot from the Bullets to the Wizards, which suggests that changes are possible at this level. Change should be possible without the uninsightful alumni and student backlashes that smear Indigenous complainants as activists or militants—even as politically correct minorities. This is not the current fad of being "politically correct." Negative imagery of Indigenous Peoples has been around for more than a century and reflects the manner in which our nation treats an ethnic group. No other ethnic group is targeted and depicted in American sports as are Indigenous Peoples.

CONCLUSION

Most states make a commitment to provide the best public education for every student. The issue of equity is an important component of that commitment to educational excellence, ensuring access, treatment, opportunity, and outcomes for all students, based on objective assessment of each individual student's needs and abilities. Requirements and support for equity come from the state legislature, the federal government, the private sectors, community organizations, parents, school boards, and school district staff members.

Given this foundation, many of the issues pertaining to negative Indian mascots and logos displayed in all programs and activities in schools comes under the category of "discrimination." The discrimination prohibition applies to curricular programs, extracurricular activities, pupil services, recreational programs, and other activities (such as the use of facilities, food service). Although most states prohibit discrimination against students, many initial Indian mascot and logo complainants are dismissed as irrelevant by school officials. They then follow up through a process of filing an official complaint as an "aggrieved person" (that is, a student or parent of a student who has been negatively affected) who is a resident of the school district. Every pubic school district is required to have a complaint procedure adopted by the school board for residents to use. Some complainants objecting to Indian mascots and logos have additionally filed complaints with the U.S. Department of Education, Office for Civil Rights, Chicago Office, basing their discrimination suits on the student's sex, race, handicap, color, or national origin.

Understanding the contemporary images, perceptions, and myths of Indigenous Peoples is extremely important, not only for Indigenous Peoples, but also for mainstream America. Most images of Indigenous Peoples have been burned into the global consciousness by fifty years of mass media. It was the Hollywood screenwriters who helped to create the "frontier myth" image of Indigenous Peoples today. It was, moreover, a revelation that had gone largely unrecorded by the national media and unnoticed by a public that still sees Indigenous Peoples mainly through deeply xenophobic eyes and the mythic veil of mingled racism and romance. Each new generation of popular culture has, therefore, reinvented their Indian mascot in the image of its own era.

Those of us who advocate the elimination of mascots of Indigenous Peoples appreciate the courage, support, and, sometimes, sacrifice of all people who stand with us by speaking out and drafting resolutions against the continued use of Indian mascots in schools. When anybody, but especially an educator, advocates the removal of these mascots and logos, the local spirit of tolerance and social justice is enhanced, and a progressive model of pluralism for all children is conveyed. By taking a stand against mascots and other popular stereotypes, teachers create a powerful teaching moment that can help to deconstruct the fabricated images and misconceptions of Indigenous Peoples that most school-age children have had burned into their psyche by American public culture.

If a city's team name were the Pittsburgh Negroes, Kansas City Jews, Houston Hispanics, Chicago Chicanos, Orlando Orientals, or Washington Whities, and someone from one of those communities found the invented name, stereotyped labels, and associated ethnic symbols offensive and asked that they be changed, would people not change the name? If not, why not? Let us further "honor" these groups with demeaning caricatures of a rabbi in flowing robe, a Black Sambo image, a mascot who would run around in a Ku Klux Klan outfit. This tradition, I insist, is a mix of racism with sports enthusiasm under the guise of team spirit. Vickers (1998) asserts that Indigenous writers, artists, and activists on all fronts are sure to condemn all of the noxious stereotypes discussed herein.

In this essay I have tried to make several points in my message to educators. Educators need to educate themselves about Indigenous Peoples and their communities. Doing so will help them see that as long as such negative mascots and logos remain within the arena of school activities, both Indigenous and non-Indigenous children are learning to tolerate racism in schools. That's what children see at school, on television, and in the movies. This is precisely what sports teams with mascots and logos of Indigenous Peoples teach them — that it is "acceptable" racism to demean a race or group of people through American sports culture. Finally, I challenge educators to provide the intellectual leadership that will teach a critical perspective and illuminate the cultural violence associated with Indian mascots used in schools. Inaction in the face of racism is racism. As culturally responsive educators, we must understand that "enslaved minds cannot teach liberation." That's why educators cannot ignore Indian mascots.

NOTES

1. Previous research focusing on aboriginal peoples in the United States has used *American Indian, Indian,* and *Native American* as the nomenclature for this population. This essay subverts this tradition by instead using the terms *Indigenous Peoples* and *First Nations People.* These terms are capitalized because they are proper nouns, not adjectives. They are also capitalized to signify and recognize the cultural heterogeneity and political sovereignty of Indigenous Peoples in the western hemisphere (Yellow Bird, personal communication 1997).

In this respect, the consciousness of the oppressor transforms Indigenous identity into a commodity of its domination and disposal (Freire 1997). Ceasing to call Indigenous Peoples American Indians is more than an attempt at political correctness. It is an act of intellectual liberation and a correction to a distorting narrative of imperialist "discovery and progress" that has been maintained far too long by Europeans and Euro-Americans. Thus, *American Indian* and *Indian* are sometimes used interchangeably in this essay as a common vernacular only when trying to make a point in an attempt to liberate and combat linguistic hegemony, which is both a direct and indirect power block to the identity of Indigenous Peoples (Yellow Bird 1999).

2. *Racism* is defined as the unshared unilateral use of power that exploits, dominates, and tyrannizes people of color. The exploitation of cheap black, Hispanic, or Chinese labor to maximize profits within a capitalist system is a classic example of racism as defined by this mode of thinking (Terry 1996). Racism in America is rooted deeply in the very structure of society. It is not solely, or even mainly, a matter of personal attitudes and beliefs. Indeed, it can be argued that racist attitudes and be-

liefs are but accessory expressions of institutionalized patterns of white power and social control (Bowser, Hunt, and Pohl 1981).

3. The *tomahawk chop* is a social phenomenon that was created by those individuals who perceive the need for a supportive physical display of action (to cheer on one's favorite athletic team). It perpetuates an image of savagery and usually takes place in large crowds in sports stadiums accompanied by a so-called Indian war chant. This invented act of cheerleading plays on the transformation of Indigenous spirituality, knowledge, objects, and rituals into commodities and on commercial exploitation, as well as constituting a concrete manifestation of the more general, and chronic, marketing of Native America (Whitt 1995).

4. *Redskins* is a word that should remind every American there was a time in United States history when America paid bounties for human beings. There was a going rate for the scalps or hides of Indigenous men, women, and children. These "redskin" trophies could be sold to most frontier trading posts.

5. *Hegemony*, in this reading, becomes simply the establishment or preservation, by a ruling class, of identification between class and group (Saxton 1990).

6. The first method of deculturalization—segregation and isolation—was used with Indigenous Peoples. Indigenous Peoples sent to Indian Territory were isolated in the hope that missionary educators would "civilize" them in one generation. Indigenous children sent to boarding schools were isolated from the cultural traditions of their tribes as they were "civilized."

Forcing a dominated group to abandon its own language is an important part of deculturalization. Culture and values are embedded in language. Using a curriculum and textbooks that reflect the culture of the dominating group was another typical practice of state school systems and federal government programs. All these methods of deculturalization were accompanied by programs of Americanization (Spring 1997).

7. Resolutions to ban Indian mascots and logos from schools have also been drafted by American Indian organizations such as the National In-

dian Education Association, Kansas Association for Native American Education, Wisconsin Indian Education Association, and Minnesota Indian Education Association. Other groups that have passed similar resolutions include the National Education Association, Governor's Interstate Indian Council, United Indian Nations of Oklahoma, Great Lakes Inter-Tribal Council, Oneida Tribe of Wisconsin, National Congress of American Indians, and American Indian Movement. More recently, the National Collegiate Athletic Association has issued a statement supporting the elimination of Indian names and mascots as symbols for their member institutions' sports teams (Whitcomb 1998).

REFERENCES

Aaronsohn, E., C. J. Carter, and M. Howell. 1995. Preparing Monocultural Teachers for a Multicultural World: Attitudes toward Inner-City Schools. *Equity and Excellence in Education* 28(1): 5–9.

Allen, Irving L. 1990. *Unkind Words: Ethnic Labeling from Redskin to WASP.* New York: Bergin and Garvey.

Allen, Paula G., ed. 1989. Introduction to *Spider Woman's Granddaughters: Traditional Tales and Contemporary Writing by Native American Women,* pp. 1–21. Boston: Beacon Press.

Almeida, Dierdre A. 1997. The Hidden Half: A History of Native American Women's Education. *Harvard Educational Review* 67(4): 757–71.

American Indian Mental Health Association of Minnesota. 1992. Position Statement Regarding the Use of Team Mascots/Namesakes That Convey an Image of the Native People of This Land.

"'American Indian' Sports Team Mascots." 2000. <http://earnestman .tripod.com/> 29 March 2000.

Ashmore, Richard D., and F. K. Del Boca. 1981. Conceptual Approaches to Stereotypes and Stereotyping. In *Cognitive Processes in Stereotyping and Intergroup Behavior,* ed. D. L. Hamilton, pp. 1–35. Hillsdale NJ: Erlbaum.

Banton, Michael. 1998. *Racial Theories.* New York: Cambridge University Press.

Bartolome, Lilia I., and D. P. Macedo. 1997. Dancing with Bigotry: The Poisoning of Racial and Ethnic Identities. *Harvard Educational Review* 67(2): 222–46.

Bird, S. Elizabeth. 1996. *Dressing in Feathers: The Construction of the Indian in American Popular Culture*. Boulder: Westview Press.

Blair, Irene V., and Mahzarin R. Banaji. 1996. Automatic and Controlled Processes in Stereotype Priming. *Journal of Personality and Social Psychology*, 70(6): 1142–63.

Bosmajian, Haig A. 1983. Defining the American Indian: A Case Study in the Language of Suppression. In *Exploring Language*, ed. Gary Goshgarian. Boston: Little, Brown.

Bowser, Benjamin P., Raymond Hunt, and David C. Pohl. 1981. Introduction to *Impacts of Racism on White Americans*, ed. B. P. Bowser and R. G. Hunt. Thousand Oaks CA: Sage.

Churchill, Ward. 1994. *Indians Are Us? Culture and Genocide in Native North America*. Monroe ME: Common Courage Press.

Deloria, Philip J. 1998. *Playing Indian*. New Haven: Yale University Press.

Deloria, Vine, Jr. 1980. Preface to *The Pretend Indians: Images of Native Americans in the Movies*, ed. G. M. Bataille and C. L. P. Silet. Ames: Iowa State University Press.

Dennis, Rutledge M. 1981. Socialization and Racism: The White Experience. In *Impacts of Racism on White Americans*, ed. B. P. Bowser and R. G. Hunt. Thousand Oaks CA: Sage.

Dovidio, John F., N. Evans, and R. B. Tyler. 1986. Racial Stereotypes: The Contents of Their Cognitive Representations. *Journal of Experimental Social Psychology* 22 : 22–37.

Duran, Eduardo, and Duran, Bonnie. 1995. *Native American Postcolonial Psychology*. Albany: State University of New York Press.

Fanon, Frantz. 1986. *Black Skin, White Masks*. London: Pluto Press.

Fiske, Susan T. 1993. Controlling Other People: The Impact of Power on Stereotyping. *American Psychologist* 48(6): 621–28.

Fleming, Dan. 1996. *Powerplay: Toys as Popular Culture*. New York: Manchester University Press.

Freire, Paulo. 1997. *Pedagogy of the Oppressed*. Rev. 20th-anniversary ed. New York: Continuum.

Freeman, J. M. 1993. A Cognitive-Development Approach to Racial Stereotyping and Reconstructive Memory in African American Children. Ph.D. diss., University of Kansas, Lawrence.

Gould, S. J. 1996. *The Mismeasure of Man*. New York: W. W. Norton.

Green, Michael K. 1995. Cultural Identities: Challenges for the Twenty-First Century. In *Issues in Native American Cultural Identity*, ed. M. K. Green. New York: Peter Lang.

Green, Rayna. 1992. *Women in American Indian Society*. New York: Chelsea House.

Guthrie, Robert V. 1998. *Even the Rat Was White: Historical View of Psychology*. Boston: Allyn and Bacon.

Hilliard, Asa G. 1997. Psychology as Political Science and as a Double Edged Sword: Racism and Counter Racism in Psychology. Paper presented at the American Psychological Association Conference on Racism, Chicago.

Huhndorf, Shari. 1997. From the Turn of the Century to the New Age: Playing Indian, Past and Present. In *As We Are Now: Mixblood Essays on Race and Identity*, ed. William S. Penn, pp. 181–98. Berkeley: University of California Press.

Hutchinson, Francis P. 1996. Enhancing Our Foresight: Towards a Knowledge-Base for Creative Futures Teaching. In *Educating beyond Violent Futures*, ed. F. P. Hutchinson. New York: Routledge.

Jaimes, M. Annette, and T. Halsey. 1992. American Indian Women: At the Center of Indigenous Resistance in North America. In *The State of Native America: Genocide, Colonization, and Resistance*, ed. M. A. Jaimes, pp. 311–44. Boston: South End Press.

Kane, Eugene. 1997. Seeing Racism as a Mental Health Issue. Online—Milwaukee Journal-Sentinel. *www.jsonline.com/archive/autoarc/970511seeingracismasamental.stm* (May 2000).

King, Joyce E. 1991. Dysconscious Racism: Ideology, Identity, and Miseducation of Teachers. *Journal of Negro Education* 60(2): 133–46.

King, Joyce E., and Gloria Ladson-Billings. 1990. Dysconscious Racism and Multicultural Illiteracy: The Distorting of the American Mind. Paper presented at the annual meeting of the American Educational Research Association, April 16–20, Boston.

Koomen, Willem, and Anton J. Dijker. 1997. Ingroup and Outgroup Stereotypes and Selective Processing. *European Journal of Social Psychology* 27:589–601.

Mihesuah, Devon A. 1996. *American Indians: Stereotypes and Realities*. Atlanta: Clarity Press.

Mohawk, John. 1992. Looking for Columbus: Thoughts on the Past, Present and Future of Humanity. In *The State of Native America: Genocide, Colonization, and Resistance*, ed. M. Annette Jaimes. Boston: South End Press.

Moore, Robert B. 1976. *Racism in the English Language*. New York: Racism/Sexism Resource Center for Education.

Morris, Joann S. 1982. Television Portrayal and the Socialization of the American Indian Child. In *Television and the Socialization of the Minority Child*, ed. Gordon L. Berry and Claudia Mitchell-Kerman, pp. 187–202. New York: Academic Press.

Novick, Michael. 1995. *White Lies, White Power: The Fight against White Supremacy and Reactionary Violence*. Monroe, ME: Common Courage Press.

Pewewardy, Cornel D. 1998. Fluff and Feathers: Treatment of American Indians in the Literature and Classroom. *Equity and Excellence in Education* 31(1): 69–76.

———. 1991. Native American Mascots and Imagery: The Struggle of Unlearning Indian Stereotypes. *Journal of Navajo Education* 9(1): 19–23.

Pewewardy, Cornel D., and Donald J. Willower. 1993. Perceptions of American Indian High School Students in Public Schools. *Equity and Excellence in Education* 26(1): 52–55.

Pine, Gerlad J., and Asa G. Hilliard. 1990. Rx for Racism: Imperatives for America's Schools. *Phi Delta Kappan* 71(8): 397–407.

Reese, Debbie. 1996. Teaching Young Children about Native Americans

(ERIC Document Reproduction Service No. ED 394 744). Available on-line from *ERIC Digest*. <http://ericeece.org/pubs/digest/1996/reese96.htm> (2 April 2000).

Saxton, Alexander. 1990. *The Rise and Fall of the White Republic: Class Politics and Mass Culture in Nineteenth-Century America*. New York: Verso.

Shively, JoEllen. 1992. Cowboys and Indians: Perceptions of Western Films among American Indians and Anglos. *American Sociological Review* 57:725–34.

Sleeter, Christine. 1994. White Racism. *Multicultural Education* 39: 5–8.

Smith, Garry J. 1988. The Noble Sports Fan. *Journal of Sport and Social Issues* 12:54–65.

Solomas, John, and Les Back. 1996. *Racism and Society*. New York: St. Martin's Press.

Spring, Joel. 1997. *Deculturalization and the Struggle for Equality: A Brief History of the Education of Dominated Cultures in the United States*. New York: McGraw-Hill.

Stedman, Raymond W. 1982. *Shadows of the Indian: Stereotypes in American Culture*. Norman: University of Oklahoma Press.

Steele, Claude M. 1997. A Threat in the Air: How Stereotypes Shape Intellectual Identity and Performance. *American Psychologist* 52(6): 613–29.

Stiffarm, Lenore A., and Phil Lane. 1992. The Demography of Native North America: A Question of American Indian Survival. In *The State of Native America: Genocide, Colonization, and Resistance*, ed. M. Annette Jaimes. Boston: South End Press.

Staurowsky, Ellen J. 1998. An Act of Honor or Exploitation? The Cleveland Indians' Use of the Louis Francis Sockalexis Story. *Sociology of Sports Journal* 15:299–316.

Terry, Robert W. 1996. Curse or Blessing for the Elimination of White Racism? In *Impacts of Racism on White Americans*, ed. B. P. Bowser and R. G. Hunt. Thousand Oaks CA: Sage.

Tinker, George E. 1993. *Missionary Conquest: The Gospel and Native American Cultural Genocide*. Minneapolis: Fortress Press.

Trask, Hauani-Kay. 1993. *From a Native Daughter: Colonialism and Sovereignty in Hawaii.* Monroe ME: Common Courage Press.

Vaughan, Alden T. 1988. From White Man to Redskin: Changing Anglo-American Perceptions of the American Indian. In *Indians and Europeans: Selected Articles on Indian-White Relations in Colonial North America*, ed. Peter C. Hofter, pp. 287–323. New York: Garland.

Vickers, Scott B. 1998. *From Stereotype to Archetype in Art and Literature.* Albuquerque: University of New Mexico Press.

Wann, Daniel L. 1994. The Noble Sports Fan: The Relationship between Team Identification, Self-Esteem, and Aggression. *Perceptual and Motor Skills* 78:864–66.

Wann, Daniel L., and Nyla R. Branscombe. 1993. Sports Fans: Measuring Degree of Identification with Their Team. *International Journal of Sports Psychology* 24(1): 1–17.

Wellman, David. 1977. *Portraits of White Racism.* New York: Cambridge University Press.

Whitcomb, Charles. 1998. "'American Indians' Sports Team Mascots." <http://earnestman.tripod.com/ncaa_statement.htm> (2 April 2000).

White, John R. 1979. Playboy Blacks vs. Playboy Indians: Differential Minority Stereotyping in Magazine Cartoons. *American Indian Culture and Research Journal* 3(2): 39–55.

Whitt, Laurie A. 1995. Cultural Imperialism and the Marketing of Native America. *American Indian Culture and Research Journal* 19(3): 1–31.

Yellow Bird, Michael. 1999. Indian, American Indian, and Native Americans . . . Counterfeit Identities. *Winds of Change* 14(1): 86.

PART FIVE

Complications

CHAPTER 13

Uneasy Indians

Creating and Contesting Native American Mascots at Marquette University

•

C. Richard King

Increasingly, uneasiness haunts Native American mascots. Although opponents and supporters tend to simplify them, there is nothing simple about them. Indeed, these signs and spectacles of Indianness are complex, uncomfortable, and conflicted. They have evoked discomfort, promoted debate, and demanded defense. They have perpetuated ugly images, fostered counter-hegemonic interventions, and facilitated awkward alliances. Significantly, Native American mascots are uneasy in at least five ways.

First, they are problematic because they offer accounts of race, history, and culture that marginalize, terrorize, and injure Native Americans. In spite of important shifts in American public culture, these mascots continue to fashion inaccurate, exaggerated, and even hateful images of American Indians and, in turn, to fabricate spaces of terror in which the structural and psychological effects are all too real to Native Americans. The entrenched support and animated celebration that mascots enjoy among the general public only spread my sense of dis-ease, underscoring the articulations of ideology, identity, and imagined community.

Second, Native American mascots are difficult, perhaps increasingly difficult, because they center on playing Indian (Deloria 1998; Green 1988; Huhndorf 1997). Euro-Americans, and in some cases Native Americans, have actively assembled and enacted romantic versions of Indianness, juxtaposed beyond or against American colonial modernity. Indeed, they have often sought to mimic, if not simulate, authentic, original, or real Indians before the fall, prior to the cataclysm of conquest. This has been no small task. Instead it is an elaborate process of authentication, frequently piecing together clothing, dance, and demeanor understood to be Indian.

Third, mascots (and their supporters) are uneasy because they have become contested. Over the past thirty years, the practices, symbols, and identities once taken for granted by fans, players, alumni, and administrators have become debatable, questionable, and even negotiable. Employing protest, litigation, and public policy, sociopolitical coalitions in diverse locales have disrupted the means and meanings of playing Indian at half-time. They have done this, but perhaps more importantly they have reclaimed Indianness, destabilized white supremacy, and politicized the social as well. Together these disparate interventions and interruptions constitute an effective counter-hegemonic movement (see Winant 1994).

Fourth, spectacles of Indianness in association with athletics become even more troubled and troubling once we acknowledge the manner in which they have incorporated Indian actors and communities. In the early 1920s, Jim Thorpe—Olympic gold medalist, founding president of the National Football League, All American at Carlisle Indian school, and the Associated Press consensus selection as the greatest athlete of the first half of the twentieth century—not only played football for the Oorang Indians, a professional football teamed composed of all Native American players, but he also played Indian at halftime as well (Springwood this volume). More recently, the Seminole Nation has endorsed the Florida State University Seminoles, their mascot, Chief Osceola, and his antics (King and Spring-wood this volume). And members of the Huron Nation have asked Eastern Michigan University to reinstate the Hurons as the school symbol and mascot.

Fifth, the response of institutions, teams, and communities us-ing Native American mascots has exacerbated the difficulties and discomforts of Indians playing Indian. In many cases, they have de-veloped novel strategies to legitimate their use of Indianness. Some schools, such as the University of Utah and Bradley University, have softened their renderings, dropping their mascots while retain-ing names and symbols that play off of or encapsulate popular markers of Indianness. Alternately, other institutions, like the Uni-versity of Illinois, have sought support from Native American com-munities to authenticate their invented Indians (Springwood and King forthcoming).

These difficulties and discomforts at the heart of Native Ameri-can mascots occupy my attention in this chapter. To address the ironies and effects of producing and protesting Native American mascots, I examine the peculiar history of Indianness at Marquette University. At the Jesuit institution, named for the French mission-ary and explorer Jacques Marquette, Native Americans not only challenged and changed stereotypes but also played a central role in the reincarnation of the school symbol. Consequently, this essay af-fords a privileged understanding of the complexities and contradic-tions of (Indians) playing Indian at halftime. My analysis centers on four instances: the inauguration of the Warriors and the invention of their mascot, Chief White Buck, in 1954; the reinvention of the mascot as a more cartoonish figure, Willie Wompum; the retire-ment of Willie Wompum, following protests by Native American students; and Native American students' efforts to fashion a more dignified and accurate Indian symbol, known as the First Warrior.

In conclusion, I return to question the uneasiness haunting Native American mascots.

INVENTION

Among the first matters of business addressed in 1954 by the newly organized Student Senate of Marquette University was the creation of a new "fight-name," mascot, and symbol for the university and its athletic teams, the Warriors. Although the new icon received enthusiastic and unanimous support among student leaders, the student body, and the administration, it was not the sole option. In fact, some twenty-five possibilities were suggested, including Arrows, Apostles, Blackhawks, Black Robes, Hiawathas, Padres, Silver Foxes, and White Raiders. The Warriors won out for several reasons. First, the name was judged to be novel and distinctive. Indeed, Doc Erskine, assistant football coach, proposed that Marquette University adopt the Warriors as symbol and mascot after extensive research that indicated its uniqueness. At the time, only one professional franchise, the Philadelphia Warriors of the National Basketball Association, three small colleges, and a handful of high schools in Wisconsin were known as the Warriors (Sankovitz 1965). Second, the name played off the history of the institution. Marquette University was named for Jacques Marquette, who devoted much of his life to exploring North America and bringing the gospel to its indigenous peoples. Not surprisingly, students and staff construed his activities and the relationships he forged with these peoples in terms of enlightenment and friendship. Thus, the Warriors facilitated a process of remembrance, even commemoration, stabilizing safe versions of the past while energizing collective identity. Third, the Warriors complemented the professional sports franchises in the Milwaukee metropolitan area. Importantly, the Braves baseball team had arrived in Milwaukee a year earlier in 1953. Fourth, the name addressed nagging concerns about representing Marquette

University. Over the previous four decades the institution had been known, with alternating enthusiasm, as the Hilltoppers, so named because the original campus was perched atop a hill, and as the Golden Avalanche, so dubbed by a New York newspaper editor. The former was thought inaccurate, given that the university had moved from its original location, and the latter had fallen out of favor and was thought "not workable in a newspaper sense" (Sankovitz 1965). Happily, proponents argued, "The name warriors lends itself to pictorial representation and at the same time gives an indication of what all Marquette teams would like to be: a fighting band of athletes in the more friendly wars of athletic competition" ("A New Indian").

Initially and intermittently throughout the 1950s, the Warriors were personified by Chief White Buck, played by Marquette student Patrick Buckett. At the 1954 homecoming, he served as the grand marshall, orchestrated a number of public events, and introduced "Marquette's official Warrior dance, which he calls 'Marquette's Indian answer to the Bunny Hop'" (Burleigh 1954). Although it is not clear precisely how Buckett and his character were selected for the role of mascot, it undoubtedly had something to do with his involvement in the Indian hobbyist movement, his active participation in Boy Scouts, and his local popularity as the host of a children's television show juxtaposing cartoons with traditional Native American folktales (Thiel 1973). Even more important may have been the authentic air of Indianness exuded by the Irish American speech major. Indeed, Buckett referred to himself as Chief Wabi Abe, which he claimed was White Buck in Chippewa. His costume pieced together garments worn historically by Native Americans of the Great Lakes and Plains, and he skillfully performed a series of modern Indian dances, including the hoop dance. Most significant, Buckett not only played Indian, but he claimed to be an Indian, an honorary member of the Chippewa Tribe. A news article in the *Marquette Tri-*

bune described the initiation in romantic detail: "He was made an honorary blood brother in the Chippewa tribe at the ceremony. His blood and that of the Chippewa chief were mixed with dirt and thrown to the four winds 'to show that my bond with the tribe will last forever'" (Burleigh 1954). Assembling regalia, dance steps, and ceremonial gestures, Buckett declared, and the emergent Warriors of Marquette gladly understood, that he was an Indian. Framing his self-image and the university's collective identity in these well-worn clichés—buckskin, Boy Scouts, and blood brotherhood—he skillfully authenticated himself and a version of Indianness that gave new life to Marquette University. Importantly, Chief White Buck may have secured such effects precisely because he enabled safe excursions beyond the homogeneity of cold war America while remaining unquestionably familiar. Indeed, during this period, *white buck* was a colloquial term for a male college student and played off a popular song about white buckskin shoes by Pat Boone (Ray Fogelson, personal communication, April 1999). In essence, Chief White Buck confirmed that the Marquette Warriors was as much about whiteness as about Indianness.

Not surprisingly, then, Indianness became central to imagining Euro-American identities and shaping a white public culture in and around Marquette University. After 1954, the university represented itself through a changing set of Indian visages that set the limits of Marquette. Immediately after becoming the Warriors, students and administrators invoked images they associated with Native Americans to stage public events, dances, parades, cheers, pageants, and the like. Homecoming often showcased these strategies of self-fashioning. Floats played off of supposed Indian motifs. "The Sweethearts," the homecoming queen and her court, began wearing dresses and headbands adorned with a single feather. And the dances themselves were spectacles shaped by prevailing notions of Indians. The first homecoming dance in the Warrior era,

October 1954, introduced many of these features along with a twelve-foot replica of the Warrior—"The smiling Warrior is swinging his hatchet in true Indian fashion" ("University Mobile" 1954: 5). Later the same year, the harvest ball of 1954 had the theme of "Injun Summer." As one news article described it, "Split rail fences, a tepee, and cardboard Indians will create an atmosphere of Indian Summer and harvest time" ("Injun Summer" 1954:7). Beyond the confines of campus, businesses catering to students began marketing themselves through Indian motifs. The pervasiveness of using imagined Indians to fashion Euro-American selves and social relations between them is attested to by the visit of Chancellor Konrad Adenauer of West Germany to Milwaukee in 1956. To mark the occasion, university and civic leaders, including representatives of the Native American community, staged a grand ceremony in which Adenauer, who reportedly had a lifelong fascination with Indians, was given a feathered headdress by Milwaukee's Consolidated Tribes, named "Chief Layadaholu" ("wise leader of many"), and smoked a peace pipe. Later, he had dinner with university and government officials, before receiving an honorary degree from Marquette University in front of some five thousand spectators.

For Adenauer, Buckett, other students, and administrators at Marquette, the Indian, or more specifically the Indian warrior, was a mask to be worn on ceremonial occasions, a role to be played for pleasure and empowerment, a strategy intended to transcend the mundane elements of everyday life. Indeed, playing Indian operates as a mimetic technology, a form of mimicry through which its participants hope to materialize the power attributed to the Native American other. The various stagings of Indianness at Marquette in the 1950s simultaneously sought to use this force to satisfy individual longings and to construct a broader community of sentiment. In the process of imitating and incorporating signs of Indianness,

287

Euro-Americans hid, forgot, and otherwise erased the historical conditions and social structures that enabled them to name, represent, and assemble meaningful versions of self and other, society and history. In essence, students, fans, administrators, Buckett, and even Adenauer inscribed a romantic version of Indianness that glossed its racism as respect, submerging their appropriations and identity politics in terms of authenticity and honor.

REINVENTION

In spite of the popularity of Chief White Buck, the mascot was ultimately discontinued, primarily because subsequent students lacked the interest and expertise demanded by the role. In place of the Chief, the student body opted in the fall of 1960 to create a new mascot. The Student Senate voted unanimously for a warrior caricature, envisioning it, in the words of Bill Kaheny, as "a sort of focal point for student cheering" (Ford 1960:1). In February 1961, the new mascot, constructed by the Whitefish Bay, Wisconsin, design firm of Loucks and Loucks, made its debut. Heralded in the *Marquette Tribune* of 24 February 1961 as a "grinning, tomahawk-swinging caricature," the still-unnamed mascot was a huge fiberglass Indian head with exaggerated features, a ridiculous toothy grin, war paint, a headband, and a stylized buckskin shirt. The new icon was hollow, devoid of cultural reference, giving perverse physical expression to popular stereotypes. A male cheerleader wore the huge head and buckskin shirt and carried an oversized tomahawk, later complemented by buckskin pants and moccasins. The mascot appeared at Marquette football and basketball games, performing dances, leading cheers, menacing opponents, chasing their mascots, and otherwise entertaining the crowd. In March of 1961, the Student Senate sponsored a contest to name the mascot, awarding small cash prizes for the best suggestions ("Plan Contest" 1961:1). After reviewing nearly 150 submissions, a student committee strongly considered

"Reggie Redskin" and "Winalota," before choosing "Willie Wom-pum" as the name for the new mascot. Bill Schatz, captain of the cheerleaders and chair of the committee, explained that Willie Wompum was selected "because the 'womp' version of 'wampum,' an Indian word meaning money, dually signifies victory. . . . The catchy alliteration and its uniqueness were also factors" ("Willie Wompum" n.d.). Although some found the name "silly" and others had suggestions to improve it, students and fans largely responded with enthusiasm to Willie Wompum, supporting and cheering him for the next decade ("More Action" 1961).

Willie Wompum marked a profound shift in the fabrication of Native Americans at Marquette University. The longing for alterity, authenticity, and identity embedded within the Warriors and Chief White Buck gave way to parody, exaggeration, and folly. The new mascot did not simply make athletic events fun through the use of Indianness; it made fun of Indians at the same time. It enshrined a cartoon character, reducing the complex cultures and histories to a buffoonish icon that mocked the experiences and identities of liv-ing Native Americans. Indeed, with the emergence and elaboration of Willie Wompum, mockery supplemented mimicry.

RETIREMENT

In early 1971, as part of a larger social movement renewing American Indian ethnicity and exerting Red Power, Native Americans at Mar-quette University demanded sovereignty, seeking to regain control of Indianness. Spurred perhaps by the comments made by commu-nity activist Father James Groppi against such mascots and the editorial position of the *Marquette Tribune*, four students—Schuyler Webster, Patricia Loudbear, David Corn, and Bernard Vigue—peti-tioned the Student Senate to retire Willie Wompum a decade after his debut ("Whither Willie?" 1971; Deady 1971, Webster et al. 1971).

The mascot is definitely offensive to the American Indian. We as native Americans have pride in our Indian heritage, and a mascot that portrays our forefathers' ancestral mode of dress for a laugh can be nothing but another form of racism. Having a non-Indian play the part is just as degrading to the Indian. From the past to contemporary times there is little the white man has not taken from the Indian. About the only thing left is our pride, and now Marquette University threatens to take that away from us by allowing such a display of racism. . . . We did not give our permission to be portrayed for a laugh, and we are sure no other minority group would condone such flagrant degradation of their heritage and pride. We ask that the mascot be discontinued completely. . . . We are sure the absence of the mascot would not take away any of the effectiveness of the Number 1 basketball team in the nation.

By making visible the veiled presence of race animating the performances of Willie Wompum, the students' intervention had three effects. First, they articulated a powerful critique of racism, locating the dehumanization they experienced in a broader history of degradation and dispossession. Second, they endeavored to reclaim their heritage. Not only did they seek to champion ancestral practices, but they also demanded control over representations of these practices. Third, in word and deed, they asserted an energized, newly politicized Indian identity. In the process, they contributed to a national movement to re-create Indianness and public culture.

In response to these concerns, the Student Senate approved a resolution in which it "strongly urge[d] the administration to permanently retire 'Willie Wompum' . . . [and] investigate any other forms of institutional racism which may exist at Marquette" (ASMU Environmental Committee 1971). The *Marquette Tribune* actively supported the Senate's action and the sentiments of the Native American students. One editorial argued, "In a time of heightened racial pride, and in light of the history of American Indians, it would be an inexpensive and painless gesture—not an admission of guilt, but a recognition of the subtle, unintentional ways in which people can be insulted" ("Whither Willie?" 1971; see also "Willie Must Go" 1971). Although the understated tones of the editorial only faintly echoed the passion voiced by the Native American students, its emphasis on forging a humane, respectful public culture in which Indians could exercise autonomy marked a radical break with prevailing visions at Marquette.

Not surprisingly, the calls to retire Willie Wompum were greeted with vocal and vociferous opposition. Joel Jurkowski (1971), a sophomore in liberal arts, gave voice to many arguments against removal. Much like the protesters, the Student Senate, and the editorial board, Jurkowski frames his argument in terms of dignity: "To me, the name 'warrior' connotes someone brave, strong, and dedicated. This is certainly far from degrading." He continues by praising the namesake of the university, Père Marquette, and his "friendly" relations with the indigenous people of Wisconsin. Against this background, Jurkowski champions Willie Wompum, who "is supposed to be a representative of a warrior—this is not offensive. Willie is intended to be a mascot . . . nothing more than a mascot. He is not a hate symbol or piece of fiberglass for us to ridicule or take offense with." Beyond the university community, commentators echoed these sentiments, noting that Willie Wompum was just good fun, was not intended to offend, and could not be taken to be a racist icon. Daniel E. O'Connell (1971), president of the Shamrock Club of Wisconsin, suggested that the demands to remove Willie Wompum were "a lot of sour grapes." He proudly urged the university to revert to its former symbol, the Hilltoppers, and adopt a leprechaun for its mascot (O'Connell 1971). Like so many supporters of Native American mascots, defenders of Willie Wompum displayed a noteworthy inability to listen to the lives and experiences of marginalized others, substituting their dominant visions of dignity and appropriateness for mutual respect.

Over the opposition of the majority of the student body and the objections voiced in the surrounding community, on 1 April 1971, James Scott, vice president for student affairs, sealed the fate of the mascot: "it is my conclusion that Willie Wompum as he is currently known, named, and symbolized be retired now and the designation 'Warriors' be retained." He also charged the Student Senate with devising "an adequate replacement mascot, with the understanding that the recommended replacement not depict any person or group of people in a demeaning manner" (Scott 1971). Scott's decision brought to a close an important moment of dissension and reclamation. The four Native American students found their voices, challenged racist stereotypes, and successfully asserted sovereignty. In the process, they disrupted and reinterpreted the stories and sentiments giving life to Willie Wompum, as well as the identities and imagined community anchored in the mascot's performances. Importantly, this moment of removal and reclamation was punctuated with irony. Whereas Willie Wompum was demeaning and needed to be retired, the Warriors, which continued to take the form of imagined Indians, remained dignified and defensible and hence were to be retained.

RETURN OF THE REPRESSED

The ambivalent removal of Willie Wompum established a context in which Indianness continued to delimit the boundaries of identity and community at Marquette University. It cleared a space for the creation of a new explicitly dignified and implicitly Indian mascot that continued to embody the spirit of the Warriors. For some time, little action was taken to reimagine the Warrior in more "enlightened" terms. Then, in 1978, Native American students proposed the creation of an "American Indian Symbol as a symbol of dignity, not a mascot such as 'Willie Wampum'" (Baechle 1978). Supporters, as given voice by Vice President James Scott, hoped that the new symbol "could generate a great deal of excitement as a rallying or focal point at basketball games, while at the same time remaining a dignified symbol of a Marquette Warrior" (Baechle 1978). Dubbed the First Warrior, the new symbol made its debut in 1980. For much of the next decade, it appeared at home basketball games, occasionally at other athletic contests like soccer matches, and at a number of public events at schools, nursing homes, and scout meetings, serving as a symbol of the school, a public relations tool, and an educational medium, promoting understanding and respect for the native nations of Wisconsin.

In a seven-page proposal, the American Indian Students at Marquette University outlined the rationale, constitution, and implementation of a new American Indian symbol, the First Warrior, which they hoped the administration and community would accept as "a gift" (p. 1). Their presentation turned on autonomy and interpretation. Rather than propose a new mascot, as the administration had imagined when retiring Willie Wompum, they envisioned a symbol that would promote school spirit and cultural awareness. The First Warrior would not engage in the demeaning antics often associated with mascots but would perform traditional dances in authentic dress. As a consequence, it would not be "demeaning" but would affirm, and even preserve, Indian culture, heritage, and identity (p. 2). In addition, the Native American students sought to control the reception and significance of the First Warrior. They asked the media and Marquette community to refrain from referring to the First Warrior as a mascot. They carefully choreographed the public role of the new symbol, outlining the sorts of events, appearances, behaviors, gestures, and attire that would be acceptable and dignified. Also, they sought to limit the range of official or approved images: "Only photographs or accurate line drawings of the First Warrior are to appear in University publications. We must ask that the University not condone the use of cartoons or caricatures" (p. 3). In their proposal, the students reinvented Indianness at Marquette.

Oddly though, the students framed their reinterpretation in terms echoing those employed in 1954 to enshrine the Warriors. After noting that "the term warrior does not itself denote a relationship with the American Indian culture" (p. 1), they rapidly concluded "that the competitive and combative nature of this name can be best exemplified by an individual of American Indian heritage" (p. 1). Then, like the Euro-American student senators in 1954, they underscored that Native Americans were indigenous to the area around Marquette and that the namesake of the university had made contact with those peoples. They, moreover, were "very proud of our heritage, it will be an honor to have a dignified warrior symbolic of our culture identified with Marquette University's intercollegiate athletic teams, as well as the school itself" (p. 2). Finally, they endeavored to construct an imagined community. They were hopeful that "the sharing of the culture and traditions of the American Indian warrior" would create "a stronger relationship among all members of the Marquette Community" (p. 2). At the same time, they desired to strengthen the Milwaukee Native American community and were pleased to have received support from a majority of its constituents. For its part, the administration embraced the First Warrior as part of a broader effort to recruit and retain Native American students (Alice Kehoe, personal communication April 1999).

For both the university and the Native American students a concern for authenticity saturated discussions of the newly invented First Warrior. The shape of this reenergized preoccupation can be traced through the novel key words employed by supporters, who spoke of "culture," "heritage," "dignity," "tradition," "preservation," and "cultural awareness." Moreover, naming the First Warrior inscribed a desire for primacy, ingenuity, originality, which might transcend or at least counter the intervening time and tropes. Beyond rhetoric, the Native American students attended to fashion, style, and self-presentation, endeavoring to clothe Indianness in authentic dress. In their proposal the students had noted, "The style of the traditional dress is to be that of the Woodland Indian, which is most representative of the tribes of Wisconsin" (p. 2). A press release that heralded the initial appearance of the First Warrior offered even greater detail. The suit worn by the First Warrior was an amalgamation "representative of the six Wisconsin woodland tribes (Chippewa, Menominee, Oneida, Winnebago, Stockbridge-Munsee, and Potawatami)." The regalia, moreover, was designed by Lila Blackdeer, a Winnebago woman from Black River Falls, Wisconsin, which confirmed its organic accuracy. To obviate the faithfulness of their new Indian and to inform the general public, the press release lingered over each item, noting composition and function: "THE ROACH—is a decorative headpiece made of deer tail hair and porcupine quills, each sewn on separately. A deer bone holds one eagle feather in place, bearing spiritual significance." The student so attired would perform traditional dances. The students proposed, and the administration established, a complex selection process, concerned with grooming, appearance, and athletic ability, as well as "respect for traditional dress," competence at traditional dance, and understanding of Native American traditions. Appeals to the body further stabilized the version of authentic Indianness. "In striving for a genuine and authentic representation of an American Indian warrior, we feel we are compelled to request that this position be held only by American Indian students in so far as this is physically possible" (p. 3). If no Native Americans were willing or able to take on the role, then non-Indians could compete for the role, with "Some preference in the area of personal appearance [being] given to those students possessing physical characteristics typical of members of the American Indian race" (p. 5). In sum, they authenticated the First Warrior through naming, dress, performance, and body.

These longings to secure authentic Indianness began to crack and fissure almost as soon as the First Warrior stepped onto the basketball court. The first First Warrior, Clifford LaFromboise, did not perform exclusively traditional dances but often improvised. More troubling for Native Americans committed to the First Warrior, performances were accompanied by the Marquette Band, evoking, in the words of Greg Denning, the second First Warrior, a kind of "reverse culture shock" (Walker [1982]). Indeed, the spectacle of intercollegiate athletics, with its emphasis of entertainment, emptied the symbol of its spiritual and cultural significance, undermining its efforts and intention. Many spectators appreciated the First Warrior only as a show, or worse as a revamped, but failed, mascot (Denning 1982). Suggestions to salvage the imperiled authenticity embodied by the First Warrior either by bringing in Native Americans who could with confidence and competence perform authentic dances or by supplementing the traditional dances with modern forms, like the fancy dance, were rejected by the administration. The First Warrior became conflicted, even compromised, neither athletic mascot nor honorary symbol, neither a reincarnated white man's Indian nor a repossessed representation of Native America.

As a consequence of the Native Americans' refusal to soften, lighten, or otherwise play around with Indianness, the First Warrior never enjoyed great popularity. In fact, students, players, opposing teams, and color commentators were puzzled, bored, and even put off by the First Warrior. On occasion, fans turned their discomfort into aggression. During the 1984–85 basketball season, a spectator hurled a roll of toilet paper at the First Warrior, an action that elicited "the biggest cheers" during the game from fans in attendance

("Bring Back Willie" n.d.). Recognizing that the First Warrior failed to ignite the passion of fans, administrators devised a new mascot, named Blueteaux, who appeared at games alongside the American Indian symbol, performing standard antics and charades designed to rouse spectators. At the same time, the *Marquette Tribune* argued that both of these icons be replaced by Willie Wompum ("Bring Back Willie"). Making matters worse, segments of the Native American community in Milwaukee were troubled by the First Warrior. Some went so far as to "verbally harass" students portraying the First Warrior (Walker [1982]).

Although public sentiments were against them, as late as 1987 proponents of the First Warrior defended the merits of the symbol. In fact, the First Warrior Advisory Committee in a memo to Vice President James Scott argued for the establishment of a financial aid fund. Such an endowment, it was claimed, would enhance the status and attractiveness of the First Warrior, while increasing Native American recruitment and retention. Moreover, it would buttress the university's commitment to affirmative action. Finally, the fund would allow for the continuation of public programs designed to increase cultural awareness.

Despite the efforts of the advisory committee, the commitment of individual Native American students, and the apparent utility of the symbol, the university opted to retire the First Warrior formally in 1987. This decision was undoubtedly motivated by the disinterest of Native American students in playing the role and the lack of enthusiasm, and even the animosity, expressed by the student body toward the symbol. It had failed, moreover, to become the focal point for school spirit originally envisioned by supporters. Indeed, the administration felt that increasingly the First Warrior, in the words of Athletic Director Bill Cords, "was seen as more of a symbol of American Indians than of the school" (Russo 1991). Finally, the First Warrior had failed to become the recruitment tool the university had hoped it would be; retiring the symbol thus was part of a broader change in administrative policy as well (Alice Kehoe, personal communication April 1999).

The First Warrior must be understood as both an invention and an intervention. Much like previous mascots, the new Indian symbol was made up, literally stitched together from prevailing interpretations of Indianness. Discourse, dress, dance, and the racialized body helped to materialize the First Warrior as an authentic Indian. Importantly, these were the very terms and categories animating Chief White Buck. In contrast with its antecedents, the First Warrior was enlivened by an oppositional spirit. Indeed, it is a creative extension of the counter-hegemonic movement that ousted Willie Wompum. As such, it sought to counter popular prejudice, raise cultural awareness, and revitalize pan-Indian identity. In the end, the burdens imposed on this critical experiment proved too much for the First Warrior. The symbol could not reconcile romantic and resistant readings of Indianness, nor foster reverence where racist stereotypes prevailed; consequently, both Native Americans and Euro-Americans lost interest.

HAPPY ENDINGS?

In the fall of 1993, the administration opted to retire the Warriors nickname (Barnes 1993; Gillepsie 1993; Swierczak 1993). Significantly, the university decided to change its symbol or totem, not under pressure from Native American groups or in response to renewed activism, but rather in hopes of crafting a positive public image and a more inclusive learning community. At the press conference announcing the change, Bill Cords summarized the university position and vision, "I think this is a very proactive and progressive move because we are going into a new era. We feel this will get Marquette into the 21st century" (quoted in Barnes 1993:3). Although well received by many, the decision predictably spawned an intense reactionary response among fans, alumni, students, and pundits, who argued for tradition, supported the Warriors as an inoffensive symbol honoring American Indians, and damned the irrational rise of political correctness. In spite of these sentiments, in 1994, the university, retaining its colors of blue and gold, became the Golden Eagles, and thus ended its appropriations and incorporations of Indianness.

Is this a happy ending? Surely, it is a positive development; however, rather than undermining the difficulties and discomforts of mascots, it underscores their persistent significance. Indeed, from the start, the creation and contestation of Native American mascots at Marquette has been contradictory, complex, and conflicted. Initially, Euro-American students gave life to Indianness through romantic tropes, later reworking it in more overtly racist terms. Oddly, they sought to honor Native Americans in the process, and many students, alumni, and fans continued to advance a similar rhetoric of respect in defense of "their" Indians. At the same time, they hoped through these incarnations to escape the very legacies of colonial modernity that animated the forms and norms of playing Indian at halftime.

Later, Native American students challenged and re-created mascots in an effort to reclaim and revitalize Indianness. The struggle to retire Willie Wompum exposed the centrality of race and power, as it sought to exert control over Indianness. The initial intervention was a success, but it stopped short. It was incomplete. It is as if the students thought that removing Willie Wompum would undo racism. The invention of the First Warrior continued their opposition to stereotypes as well as their efforts to revitalize Indian identity and community. As resistant or creative as the new Indian symbol was, it was cut from old cloth. It was fashioned in terms of the dominant discourse. To play Indian at halftime, even in a more accurate and reverent manner, Native American students relied upon certain colonial categories, particularly authenticity, memory (heritage in place of nostalgia), culture as a flat, bounded object, Indian as a singular identity. In the process of speaking truth to power in its own terms, their project had much in common with counter-colonial projects more generally. Roger Keesing (1994; see also Kaplan and Kelly 1994; Kurtz 1996) has documented the ways in which anti-imperial interventions and inventions rely on and reproduce imperial idioms. As such, the history of mascots at Marquette might be read as a classic instance, not of false consciousness, but of the paradoxes and predicaments of postcoloniality (King 2000).

Throughout, institutional responses blunted and contained opposition. Willie Wompum was retired, but the Warriors were retained. The university maintained control of its imagined Indians, even as it acquiesced to the demands of embodied Indians. Encouraging and facilitating the re-creation of the Warriors as the First Warrior, the administration incorporated and co-opted Native American resistance. It turned creativity and contestation toward outreach and promotion, implicitly asking Native Americans to participate in a more enlightened form of marginalization. It endeavored to manage, even limit, the significance of the First Warrior, as it transformed the intervention animating it. The ultimate end of the Warriors was a culmination of these recuperative processes. The university once more set the terms, suggesting the decision was not about race, asymmetry, or harm, but rather about inclusiveness, diversity, and education. Consequently, as important as the eventual refusal to use Indianness was, it actually works to reinforce fields of power and does little or nothing to challenge prevailing stereotypes and sentiments.

A final form of dis-ease in addition to the difficulties and discomforts of race, incomplete opposition, complicity, and containment demands attention. The struggle over Native American mascots at the Jesuit institution turned on a particular understanding of the ar-

300

ticulations of representation and power in limited terms. Students and the administration negotiated control over Indianness through representation, not as a process of encoding and decoding, but as a fixed product. They neglected the importance of the conditions of production and the norms of reception. As a consequence, even as the stories changed, the structures remained unaltered. Perhaps, then, the end of the Warriors is not so much a happy ending, bringing closure, as much as it is an additional instance in an ongoing struggle over appropriation, autonomy, and asymmetry, one occasion in a more dynamic movement reformulating Indianness, identity, and history. The history of Native American mascots at Marquette University is not so much a happy ending as a hopeful beginning.

ACKNOWLEDGMENTS

This essay was made possible by the interest and enthusiasm of Mark Thiel, archivist at Marquette University, who first drew my attention to the subject. Raymond Fogelson and Alice Kehoe provided me with information not accessible in the archives. Charles F. Springwood and Marcie L. Gilliland offered valuable advice on earlier drafts.

REFERENCES

ASMU Environmental Committee. 1971. "Resolution #24." Marquette University Archives.

Baechle, Bea. 1978. "Committee Approves Indian as Symbol for Warriors." *Marquette Tribune*, 8 Nov.

Barnes, Brooks. 1993. "Logo Loses Fight: Warriors Laid to Rest." *Marquette Tribune*, 12 Oct., 1, 3.

"Bring Back Willie." N.d. *Marquette Tribune*. Marquette University Archives.

Burleigh, Bill. 1954. "Marquette Boasts of Real Indian Warrior: A Student in Speech." *Marquette Tribune*, 21 Oct.

Deady, Patrick. 1971. "Indians Petition Senate." *Marquette Tribune*, 10 Feb., 1.

Deloria, Philip. 1998. *Playing Indian*. New Haven: Yale University Press.

Denning, Mark. 1982. "First Warrior Defends Role." *Marquette Tribune*, 27 Jan.

Ford, Ray. 1960. "Senate OKs a Warrior Caricature." *Marquette Tribune*, 28 Oct., 1.

Gillepsie, Patrice. 1993. "The Last of the Warrior." *Marquette Journal*, fall, 38–45.

Green, Rayna. 1988. "The Tribe Called Wannabee: Playing Indian in America and Europe." *Journal of American Folklore* 99:30–55.

Huhndorf, Shari. 1997. "Playing Indian, Past and Present." In *As We Are Now: Mixblood Essays on Race and Identity*, ed. William S. Penn, pp. 181–98. Berkeley: University of California Press.

"Injun Summer Theme of Ball." 1954. *Marquette Tribune*, 28 Oct., 7.

Jurkowski, Joel. 1971. "Willie Wampum Called Not Offensive." *Marquette Tribune*, 10 Feb.

Kaplan, Martha, and John D. Kelly. 1994. "Rethinking Resistance: Dialogics of 'Disaffection' in Colonial Fiji." *American Ethnologist* 21(1): 123–51.

Keesing, Roger. 1994. "Colonial and Counter-Colonial Discourse in Melanesia." *Critique of Anthropology* 14(1): 41–58.

King, C. Richard, ed. 2000. *Postcolonial America*. Urbana: University of Illinois Press.

Kurtz, Donald V. 1996. "Hegemony and Anthropology." *Critique of Anthropology* 16(2): 103–35.

"More Action in Form of Full Outfit Suggested for MU's Warrior Mascot." 1961. *Marquette Tribune*, 8 March.

"A New Indian in the Neighborhood." N.d. (c. 1954). Anonymous document, Marquette University Archives.

O'Connell, Daniel E. 1971. Unpublished letter to *Milwaukee Journal*, 28 Jan.

"Plan Contest to Find Name for Mascot." 1961. *Marquette Tribune*, 24 Feb, 1.

"Proposal for American Indian Symbol." 1978. Marquette University Archives.

Russo, Erica. 1991. "Marquette Remains without Mascot." *Marquette Tribune*, 4 Dec.

Sankovitz, James L. 1965. Letter to Gale Brennan. 17 Feb.

Scott, James H. 1971. Letter to Samuel P. Sauceds. 1 April.

Swierczek, Wendi. 1993. "Students Clash over Change of Mascot." *Marquette Tribune*, 12 Oct., 1, 3.

Thiel, Mark. 1973. "In Pursuit of Dancing the Indian Way, Part II." *Whispering Wind Magazine*, March, 10–11, 13–14.

"University Mobile, Warrior Replicas Highlight Dance." 1954. *Marquette Tribune*, 21 Oct., 5.

Walker, Gail. [1982]. "Denning: First Warrior a Misunderstood Symbol." *Milwaukee Journal*, undated clipping, Marquette University Archives.

Webster, Schuyler, Patricia Loudbear, David Corn, and Bernard Vigue. 1971. "Four MU Indian Students Describe Willie Wampum as Racist Symbol." *Marquette Tribune*, 17 Feb.

"Whither Willie?" 1971. *Marquette Tribune*, 3 Feb.

"Willie Must Go." 1971. *Marquette Tribune*, 17 Feb.

"'Willie Wompum' Wins as New Name for MU's Mascot." N.d. *Marquette Tribune*. Marquette University Archives.

Winant, Howard. 1994. *Racial Conditions: Politics, Theory, Comparisons.* Minneapolis: University of Minnesota Press.

CHAPTER 14

Playing Indian and Fighting (for) Mascots

Reading the Complications of
Native American and Euro-American Alliances

•

Charles Fruehling Springwood

In this essay, I aim to highlight the complexity and contradiction that seem to characterize both the many exhibitions of Native American mascots and the efforts to eliminate or defend them. In particular, I foreground the perhaps unexpected forms of critique, resistance, consent, and alliance that have surrounded the relationships formed between Native Americans and non-Indian Euro-Americans in order to stage, protest, or defend these invented "team spirits." At the center of this essay is a portrayal of the 1922–23 Ohio football team named the "Oorang Indians," an all–Native American squad coached by Jim Thorpe, whose players may have enacted the first Indian halftime show. Prior to this, however, I open my discussion by briefly describing two much more recent occurrences that serve to frame the complicated, ironic nature of these relationships.

In the 1952 Rose Bowl, the University of Illinois "Fighting Illini" beat the Stanford University Indians in the first nationally televised college football game. As other essays in this collection reveal (Prochaska; Rosenstein), the resilient mascot of the University of Illinois remains, amid controversy. Stanford's mascot, however, did not experience the longevity enjoyed by Chief Illiniwek. The Stanford Indian became reality in 1930 when, on November 25, the university officially adopted the "Indian" name and a caricature of a feathered Indian, in silhouette. This 1930 action made formal what already, since the turn of the century, had been a traditional affiliation with "the Redman." The momentum leading up to this formal identification grew out of a traditional football rivalry with the University of California and its Golden Bear mascot.

At the center of this collegiate battle was an ax, the Stanford Axe, which was "stolen" by the University of California baseball team during a brief two-game series in 1899. "A number of abortive attempts to retrieve the Stanford Axe were made throughout the years, but it remained for an intrepid little band of 21 men living in Sequoia Hall . . . to accomplish the feat" (Liebendorfer 1972). The recapture of this "trophy" on April 3, 1930, inspired Stanford supporters to prepare for the bowl game that autumn by obtaining a large "beautiful prehistoric drum which was supposed to have been found in the Gobi desert" and preparing a war chant to be issued during the game:

Stanford Indian / Scalp the Bear
Scalp the Golden Bear / Take the Axe
To his lair / Scalp the bear / Stanford Indian

The Indian tradition at Stanford became embodied in 1952 when H. D. Timm Williams began appearing at football games in full Plains Indian regalia and headdress as Prince Lightfoot, to perform sideline Indian dances in celebration of touchdowns. On particular occasions, he would (mis)use a barely recognizable version of a Plains eagle dance to cast a "hex" or "spell" on the opponent. In 1972 Williams, identified by local media as a "full-blooded Yukon," was serving as the head of Governor Ronald Reagan's California Indian Assistance Project when his Stanford performances, as well as the university's Indian nickname and symbols more generally, came under intense criticism from Native American students. In fact, a petition to end Stanford's affiliation with Indian signs, symbols, and mascots was drafted and signed by all fifty-five Native American students on campus. In a move of support, the student senate agreed, by a vote of eighteen to four, to retire the Stanford Indian, much to the disappointment of many alumni as well as Prince Lightfoot. As Williams publicly resisted the movement to change Stanford's mascot, he was derided by Native American students and staff who labeled him "Uncle Tom Tom" (Riley 1972).

Intense local support is commonly generated in defense of Native American mascots that come under criticism. Since 1972, pleas for the return of the Stanford Indian have emerged from time to time in editorials and small protests. But in the late 1980s and 1990s, these voices have been supported, in particular, by a conservative student newspaper, the *Stanford Review*. The weekly publication, which took positions in favor of the controversial Western Cultures program at Stanford and against the Rainbow Coalition and its diversity platform, supported the return of the Indian name and mascot. Printed advertisements for unofficial Stanford Indian paraphernalia, identical to the old, official merchandise once available on campus, have appeared with regularity in the *Review*. In October of 1994, a special editorial column, "Smoke Signals," was introduced, ostensibly written by the "old Stanford Chief." "Banished from the Farm years ago, the last of the Stanford Indians has returned. The Chief's observations, insights, and opinions on campus events will appear weekly on page two." Against the wishes of the administration, the old Stanford Indian caricature accompanied the column.

While the Stanford case represents one of the earliest efforts to successfully retire an Indian mascot, occurrences at Eastern Michigan University in the early 1990s reveal newer forms of Native American–Euro-American alliances in defense of these team symbols. Since 1929, Eastern Michigan University, located in Ypsilanti, had identified its image and its athletic teams with the name "Hurons" and a logo bearing a feathered Indian face. On January 30, 1991, partly in response to a call from the Michigan Civil Rights Commission for schools to discontinue the use of Native American nicknames and mascots, the Eastern Michigan president, William E. Shelton, with the support of the Board of Regents, ordered that the Huron name and logo be removed from all university property and images. In a public statement read to the board, Shelton commented: "Numerous advocacy groups for Native Americans and human rights have long opposed the continued use of Indian symbols for sports teams, contending they are injurious and humiliating. In good conscience, we cannot dismiss these pleas without defying our own institutional values to promote respect, equity, and cultural diversity and sensitivity. To do so, I believe, would compromise our integrity" (Shelton 1991). A new identity for the school, the Eagles, was chosen to replace the old one. Shelton and those supporting this decision certainly expected strong emotional reactions of protest to follow in defense of the traditional Huron name and symbol.

Initially, the loudest voice of dissent came from alumni, who desperately wanted to rescue the banished Huron name and logo. A series of protest rallies were staged on campus, and a new group, the EMU Huron Restoration, Inc., was formed by various alumni. One rally debuted a new branch of the restoration group, the Student Huron Restoration Alliance. Members sang the old Huron fight song and marched over to the president's office, demanding a hearing. Later, they moved around campus in a van, accepting donations for "Return the Huron" shirts. Ultimately, the parent group—EMU Huron Restoration, Inc.—hoped to file a lawsuit against the university and Shelton.

Perhaps, however, Shelton and supporters did not anticipate the decidedly visible involvement of some Native Americans in these protests. The strategic emergence of key alliances between a few Native Americans and the restoration group is of greatest interest here. A number of Native Americans—both on and off campus—had spoken out against the Huron name in previous years, but once it had been removed by Shelton and the board, the restoration group began seeking new Native American voices with whom they might join in their efforts to restore the Huron tradition. One alumnus, David Kasper, contacted Bob Bennett, who was an elected spokesperson for the local Wyandotte Council, which represents about four hundred Wyandotte or Huron citizens. Bennett is the great-great-grandson of Chief Joseph White, the last Huron chief of the Anderdon Reservation. The EMU Huron Restoration group also initiated contact with Chief Leaford Bearskin of Oklahoma's Wyandotte Tribe. Both Bennett and Bearskin expressed disappointment that EMU dropped its affiliation with the Hurons and, subsequently, became extremely significant voices for the EMU Huron Restoration group. Native American voices, indeed Huron voices, lent an important contour of authenticity to the movement. These two men accepted invitations to appear at protest rallies and press conferences throughout 1991 and 1992.

The restoration group also gave a most provocative spin to their agenda. In a variety of instances, they claimed that the decision to retire the logo was a form of oppression that victimized the Huron people. The narrative that was constructed positioned the Huron people as somehow banished and forgotten as a result of the decision. In fact, during a public meeting of EMU Huron Restoration, a revision of a famous poem originally written by a Nazi death camp survivor was passed out. It read: "In Germany, the Nazis first came for the Communists and I didn't speak because I wasn't a communist. Then they came for the Jews and I did not speak because I was not a Jew. Then they came for the trade unionists and I did not speak because I was not a trade unionist. Then they came for the Catholics and I did not speak because I was not Catholic. *Then they came for the Huron Indians, and I did not speak because I was not a Huron Indian.* Then they came for me . . . but by that time there was no one to speak up for anyone" (cited in Tarkington 1991; the restoration group's revisions are emphasized). In essence, these protesters implied a comparison between the horrors of World War II and the ostensible harm the logo decision caused contemporary Huron people.

These alliances complicate prior visions of public culture and community in the context of support and criticism of Native American mascots, forcing us to rethink how identities are (re)constituted in these public dramas. In the case of Eastern Michigan University, the efforts of the restoration group to essentially enlist the support of some Huron representatives seems ironic given the prior history of the social relations between the restoration alumni and Native American peoples more generally. For example, no apparent efforts had ever been made by students or alumni to engage Native American people, let alone Hurons, before the logo was retired. Indeed, one restoration member confessed that he was not even aware that Huron people even existed anymore, admitting "I thought they were extinct." It is important to read these complicating alliances in a way that does not reduce any particular voices to mere instruments of power but similarly does not obscure the very tangible contours of power that structure opportunities for consent and dissent.

These portrayals of protest, alliance, and clashing experiences of community at Stanford and Eastern Michigan provide an opening to begin to understand and analyze the many occasions wherein Native Americans either vigorously support Indian mascots—frequently pitting them against other Native Americans—or even participate wittingly in the kinds of Indian performances that authors in this collection vigorously critique. Indeed, non-Indian mascot defenders commonly invoke mention of Native American voices of support to bolster their arguments that such signs and symbols are harmless (see Springwood and King forthcoming). Some cultural critics would argue that Native American support for, or even participation in, these halftime orchestrations of Indianness reveal a sort of cultural hegemony, in which people seemingly victimized by a particular form of oppression indeed express their enthusiastic consent for it. Undoubtedly, any nuanced appreciation of this consent will consider the relationship between power and culture, but to characterize Indian voices of consent as merely *duped* is not only patronizing but overly simplistic.

If we take power to be slippery, multiple, and vested in contradictory social practices, the sites of mascot controversy discussed here—when taken together—demand a reconsideration of the relationship between power, identity, and practice. A diversity of viewpoints among Native Americans regarding the issue of Indian mascots is not surprising. Cultural identity is constructed along multiple planes of existence, and one cannot really speak of *a* Native American identity in the singular anyway. Nevertheless, a nuanced critique of the intriguing, enthusiastic embrace by some Native Americans of these purportedly colonial, flattened, miscontextualized representations of Indianness is important. Perhaps the most spectacular alliance of Native Americans with Euro-Americans, in order to stage a white man's Indian mascot, was formed in obscure LaRue, Ohio, in 1922.

GRIDIRON INJUNS

LaRue, a town of fewer than nine hundred people and situated along the banks of the Scioto River some fifteen miles west of Marion, Ohio, is the smallest town ever to have been home to a National

Football League franchise. Walter Lingo was LaRue's wealthiest resident during the first several decades of the twentieth century, and in part, his prosperity resulted from his successful Airedale kennel business. Lingo specialized in raising and training this prized canine breed. In fact, his special strain of Airedales were known by the name *Oorang*, and Lingo's LaRue business was called the Oorang Kennels. His "class A" dogs sold for as much as $500 apiece, and locals claim that in one year he sold enough Airedales to gross more than a million dollars (Cass 1981). Thus, when Lingo decided to buy an NFL franchise in the early 1920s to help promote his Airedale kennels, it was a rather affordable purchase. Indeed, since the NFL was a relatively new and fledging league, Lingo had only to pay $100 for the franchise.

Lingo's boyhood love of dogs was equaled only by his fascina tion with the American Indian. An avid hunter of wild game, Lingo "considered American Indians to be mythic people and believed there was a supernatural bond between Indians and animals" (Borowski 1995:1). Further, he viewed them as masterful hunters. All of this renders the name he gave to his football team, the Oorang Indians, understandable. But Lingo went far beyond the tradition of a Native American moniker and mascot. He decided that his Oorang Indians would be composed exclusively of Native American players. To help make his vision a reality, he hired the internationally famous Jim Thorpe, a Sac and Fox Tribe member, to serve as the team's player-coach.

Thorpe and Lingo were already friends. Lingo frequently gave away Airedales to celebrities, including Ty Cobb and Gary Cooper, and he invited other famous people to hunt with him. It was one of these possum-hunting trips that brought Lingo and Thorpe together, and their mutual love of dogs and hunting laid the groundwork for a lasting friendship. In fact, Thorpe became a knowledgeable Airedale enthusiast. By the time Lingo purchased his football franchise, Thorpe, thirty-four, had entered the twilight of what had been a spectacular athletic career that included Olympic gold medals as well as tenures in both professional baseball and football. He agreed to play for and coach the Oorang Indians for their inaugural 1922 season at a weekly salary of $500. In order to hire players to field the team, Thorpe began scouting on reservations and using his connections with football alumni of the Carlisle Indian School in Pennsylvania. Soon, a full complement of players had signed, all Native Americans, including members of the Cherokee, Sac and Fox, Mohawks, Chippewa, Seneca, Winnebago, Penobscot, and Caddo tribes.

The role assumed by these players and their coach was not, however, a typical one for professional football players—not even in the 1920s. First, they were expected to help train the dogs. They resided in some boarding houses on Main Street, and in the evening, after dinner, they would take care of the canines, even taking them into the woods to exercise them. Lingo believed that his players demanded the best care, and as a result, they were cared for by the same dietitian and trainer who looked after the Airedales. Second, they played almost no "home" games in LaRue. In fact, the town did not even have a field, so the two home games they did host were played in nearby Marion. All of the other games, for two seasons, were played in the opponents' stadiums. For Lingo, the logic was simple. The Oorang Indians were a promotional spectacle, ultimately designed to sell his dogs. Appearances in tiny LaRue would have been pointless, and thus the team was essentially a full-time road team. Indeed, the Indians became perhaps the spectacle in the league, owing no doubt to their strategically choreographed Indianness. Third, the players were expected not only to play football but also to perform on the field at halftime.

While the other team rested and regrouped, the Oorang Indian players would return to the field in feathers and war paint, accompanied by a number of Airedale dogs. What ensued was a series of "Indian" dances, war whoops, and exhibitions of trailing and treeling the canines. The team also performed with racoons, coyotes, and a bear named Queen Mary, who sometimes wrestled with certain players. They also demonstrated how to throw the tomahawk, knife, and lariat and even held rifle-shooting contests, with the dogs retrieving targets (Whitman 1984:67). Local residents claim that sometimes mock battles were enacted, and the players would pretend to kill each other. Today, LaRue residents boast that the Oorang Indians were *the* original halftime show. Undoubtedly, such antics compromised the team's football performances, perhaps explaining why the team won a mere total of two games during its brief two-year existence.

One's imagination runs wild when musing about the various scenes and relationships possibly created by this unique arrangement in central Ohio in the early twenties. Nearly twenty Native Americans resided in an exclusively white, relatively isolated Midwestern town; a number of Amish homesteads were situated no farther than a mile outside of the town. Local reports of the behavior of the players ring of traditional Native American stereotypes. For example, stories about the players' drunken antics continue to circulate in popular lore, even today, and this narrative represented a dominant Euro-American impression of Native Americans as "violent, lawless, and impetuous" (Duran 1996:113). It was a common perception that these "Indians" would often stay up all night drinking. Robert Whitman, a local historian, based this description of the players' drinking on news reports:

> Jim [Thorpe] did not have the discipline of his players on or off the field, as one might surmise when reading of the many tales of the team's antics while on the road. For example, the Indians were clobbered by the Chicago Bears after they stayed up until dawn

drinking. An unfortunate Chicago bartender wanted to close up early, so the Indians tossed him into a telephone booth and turned it upside down, then helped themselves. . . . While playing in St. Louis they left a bar late, only to find that the trolley they wanted was headed in the wrong direction. The dilemma was easily solved. The Indians just lifted the vehicle off the tracks and turned it around to face the "right" direction. (Whitman 1984:67–69)

The player who left the most indelible impression in the minds of LaRue locals was Nick Lassa, known as Long Time Sleep, who, in fact, remained in the area long after the Oorang Indians disbanded. He lived at the Coon Paw Inn on North High Street. Resident Damon Leffler, who was fourteen years old when Lassa arrived in La-Rue, recalls: "He was quite a drinker, but he wouldn't hurt anyone. When he'd get drunk, he'd act like he was going to tear you all to pieces. . . . When he got drunk, he pulled his hair down over the front. It came just down to his eyes. It was blacker than coal. He looked real mean. Mostly, he bothered women at the telephone office. He'd go down there at night when he had a few drinks and peep through the window and scare them" (Cass 1981:13). On occasion, Lassa would be escorted to the town jail to "sleep" off the effects of the liquor. Of course, these reports are mediated through the memories and biases and discourses of largely non-Indian, white people. Their accuracy cannot be rejected outright, but the historical contexts in which these interactions and experiences unfolded must not be overlooked.

IMPERIAL IDENTITIES, AWKWARD ALLIANCES, AND POSTCOLONIAL SUBJECTIVITIES

How are we to make sense of a 1920s professional football team of Native Americans, playing football and performing at halftime as embodied Indian mascots? To be certain, such a thing could not — *would* not — occur in the present. Certainly most Native Americans—though perhaps not all—would cringe at the thought of it. Here, I intend to provide a theoretical context to better understand the voluntary partnership of the Oorang players with Walter Lingo and their adoring public. I do not pretend to invoke some set of theories to explain this or similar examples of Native American participation in performances and exhibitions of the "Indian" that many citizens—Native American and non-Indian alike—view as problematic. But it is important to articulate a conceptual framework that allows us to foreground how unexpected alliances between colonizer and colonized, or oppressor and oppressed, unfold within uneven fields of power, consent, and resistance.

There can be no easy explanations. It would be a gross oversimplification to merely claim that the social and symbolic hegemony of the imperializer is so overwhelming that its "subjects" are duped into consensual support of colonial performances and narratives that seem—from the cultural critic's perspective—stereotypical or even racist. Indeed, distinctions separating colonizer and colonized have become problematical and blurry. Nor would it be sufficient to reduce such alliances to economic opportunity, even though money cannot be overlooked as a significant motivator. Undoubtedly, as football players, Jim Thorpe and his teammates took advantage of an opportunity to play their game for money in a profession with especially few "openings" for Native Americans.

In recent decades, scholarly efforts to make sense of practices of resistance and consent, in the context of power, have drawn on one or another understanding of hegemony, a term originally formulated in the political writings of Italian Marxist Antonio Gramsci, particularly those included in *The Prison Notebooks* (1971; see also Kurtz 1996). Gramsci's original concept of hegemony as a particular form of power, ensuing from an intellectual and moral leadership of a society's predominant political bloc, opened conceptual space for viewing leadership as not merely a function of control, domination, and coercion but, more often, of consent, alliance, and support.

My approach in this essay is primarily informed by John and Jean Comaroff's "reading" of Gramsci (1991; see also Fiske 1993; Hall 1985). Within this Gramscian framework, social control and power are seen to reside within historically situated matrices of "signs and practices, relations and distinctions, images and epistemologies" (Comaroff and Comaroff 1991:21). Importantly, however, certain of these signs and practices tend to be located within the *dominant* conception of the world and its system of social relations, and the power of such a conception tends to "lie in what it silences, what it prevents people from thinking and saying" (21). Gramscian hegemony may clarify the emergence of unexpected support for colonial representations such as Indian mascots by allowing power to be conceptualized in largely cultural terms—though not at the expense of material constraints—such that it is embedded in social practices in a highly taken-for-granted manner. Hegemony is the dominant conception of the world and social relations, but unlike ideology, it is reproduced through more obscure modes, rarely articulated at the surface. In fact, as the Comaroffs have argued (29) "Hegemony, then, is that part of a dominant ideology that has been naturalized and, having contrived a tangible world in its image, does not appear to be ideological at all." This process of naturalization contextualizes certain practices and regimes of representation, rendering them absolutely normal, innocent, and even amusing.

But to complicate matters further, for the purposes of this essay, hegemony must be understood as unfolding within the context of Pierre Bourdieu's notions of *habitus*, position, and social field. Typically, people do not view the practices of popular culture to be analytically significant nor consider them to be linked to uneven relations of power. Generally, although not exclusively, a tendency to adopt such critical perspectives is part of the habitus, functioning as a form of knowledge or capital and shared among intellectuals and activists. This is not, however, to suggest that the intellectual somehow transcends the "constraints of social location" (see Swartz 1997:224). Rather, following Bourdieu, I contend that particular political agendas and identities, and the social relations they structure, are informed by participation within cultural fields (Bourdieu 1988; Swartz 1997). Empirically, we are confronted with the opposing orientations of various Native American individuals and groups to the public drama surrounding Indian mascots. Here, I attempt to sort out the contrasting historical experiences of these varying attitudes by clarifying their unique relationships to social space.

It is not difficult to locate historical examples in which people participated in performances or assumed roles that seemed, even during those particular eras, to do nothing more than exploit and demean their gendered, racialized identities. Perhaps the most conspicuous instance is that of the late-nineteenth-century blackface skits, which originally starred white performers masked in black makeup, staging enactments of African Americans as buffoonish clowns (Lott 1995; Lhamon 1998; Springwood and King 2000). Eventually, black actors assumed these roles, which seemingly served to reproduce demeaning stereotypes. How can we reconcile the ostensible complicity of African Americans in enacting narratives and images that denied their authenticity and humanity? Similarly, while the hardly implicit narratives of conquest and domination that characterized William Cody's Wild West Shows obviously turned on classic stereotypical tropes of the wild, bellicose Indian, many Native Americans voluntarily joined this once-renowned traveling spectacle. In fact, Geronimo, Black Elk, and Sitting Bull appeared as "celebrity Indians" in these programs, although one would have to cast serious doubt on any claims that they did so freely.

317

The first sustained critiques of Native American mascots occurred as early as the 1960s, with the movement assuming full momentum in the middle and late 1980s and continuing into the present. Such agendas, of course, did not emerge in a vacuum, but rather in tandem with a broader dynamic of American Indian ethnic renewal (see Bruner 1986; Nagel 1996). This emergence and resurgence of Red Power was connected to the larger matrix of political awareness, rebellion, and upheaval of the Viet Nam era of the 1960s. This is not to suggest that Native Americans were completely unaware of, or unaffected by, stereotypical representations of Indianness earlier than this time. But clearly a new narrative, in Bruner's words (1986), of "past oppression, present resistance, and future resurgence" characteristic of the 1960s and 1970s gave these postcolonial responses to neocolonial power new meanings and novel spaces from which to speak. Indeed, these narratives of resistance and resurgence provided not only structures of meaning but also new structures of power (144).

The Red Power movement was a particular mode for actively constructing new Native American identities and ethnicities, and these novel subjectivities unfolded in a larger social field of post-1960s America. But they articulated with different Native Americans in different ways. The variables of education, class, age, gender, and geography all had impact on the contrasting orientations to the narratives and habitus of American Indian ethnic renewal. The degree to which Native Americans shared versions of these narratives of resistance and spaces of Redness often depended on their historical, cultural, and socioeconomic location within the society of the United States. Indeed, there are undoubtedly conservative Native American spaces where certain political enactments of Indian identity would not only fail to convey cultural value but would, rather, be socially costly. No Native American has been unaffected by the new, politically charged forms of Indianness. But some have embraced and chosen to perform versions of their ethnic identity that rely very much on the prevailing, stereotypical understandings of cultural difference and Indian otherness produced by Euro-American discourses. Different social spaces are structured by contrasting economies of value.

It is nearly impossible to know for certain how members of the Oorang Indian football team viewed their identities and performances. We cannot know if they had misgivings about their enactments of stereotypical Indians. Yet, they undoubtedly were aware of the tension existing between their own cultures and histories and the pan-Indian one they were portraying. For example, Chippewa Leon Boutwell, the team's quarterback, expressed a genuine understanding of predominant stereotypes of Native Americans: "White people had this misconception about Indians. They thought they were all wild men, and even though almost all of us had been to college and were generally more civilized than they were. Well, it was a dandy excuse to raise hell and get away with it when the mood struck us. Since we were Indians we could get away with things and whites couldn't. Don't think we didn't take advantage of it" (cited in Whitman 1984 : 69). Significantly, Boutwell suggests the possibility that Native Americans might somehow playfully manipulate the existing colonial images of Indian people. I do not want to suggest, however, that such awareness reveals a large-scale moment of resistance. It is likely that those Native American football players did not think that their performances were as troublesome as most of their living descendants likely would. Indeed, Philip Deloria (1996 : 333) argued that the Oorang players, "of course, interpreted the game and the halftime show completely differently: both were part of the long tradition of Indians playing 'Indians,' a tradition with a certain bicultural sophistication and an array of meanings clustered around labor, adventure, and conviviality." The intersecting space of the Oorang Indians was extremely intricate, always under negotiation, and constantly transforming notions of whiteness, Indianness, and even discrimination.

But hegemony is never perfect, monolithic, and determining in the final instance. If it were, cultural revival and dissent might never occur. One hardly needs a set of social theories to understand that systems of power imbalance have always created relationships of exploitation, in which the victim of the system succumbed to it, either begrudgingly or indifferently. For example, leftist scholars generally would view the contemporary system of collegiate sport as exploitative, especially of young African Americans (Hawkins 1995/96), and yet, a highly sophisticated "Hoop Dream" culture inspires a significant number of black Americans. Likewise, it would be difficult to argue that patriarchy is not systematically linked to female prostitution, and certainly, many women embrace this location with varying degrees of freedom and enthusiasm (still others espouse the relationship because they have limited opportunities and are victims of abuse). Still, they are exploited.

Hegemony, and the consent and dissent surrounding it, are conveyed through narrative, myth, symbol, performance, popular media, and more, but hegemony's effectiveness is always tied in some way to its ability to create space, structure opportunity, and materially reward consent. But cultural fields cannot be reduced to one set of dominant actors and another set of subordinate actors. Hegemony might best be viewed as a negotiated matrix of social relations and identities, in which the *contrasting* interests of those occupying different positions within the field are transformed so as to appear mutually accommodating. The willing participation of Native Americans in the Wild West shows is indicative. With his Wild West shows, whose popular existence spanned from 1883 to 1916, William Cody, or "Buffalo Bill," created one of the most spectacular forms of traveling entertainment ever. The touring show employed human actors, musicians, U.S. Cavalry veterans of Indian wars and battles, and, indeed, many of the Native Americans whom they fought. The program typically enacted a series of live scenes, representing "epochs" of American history. Ultimately, the show performed a narrative turning on "how the west was won." Although Cody claimed that his show was largely educational, an enactment of American history, it often had very little in common with actual historical events. And although Cody seemed to know that the program was rife with certain inaccuracies, as Richard Slotkin (1993) points out, he also seemed to believe that these performances inscribed a poetic truth about the frontier, the colonists, and the Indians.

Why would so many Native Americans join the Wild West troupe? Clearly, money was an issue, and since there was little of it to be earned on reservations, the $25-a-month wage for traveling with the show was persuasive (Blackstone 1986; Russell 1960, 1970). At the fin-de-siècle, the Native American experience was undoubtedly a confusing, impoverished, and at times horrifying postcolonial existence. Sara Blackstone (1986:87) argues that many Native Americans joined the Wild West shows to keep themselves and their families from starving. Others, she suggests, sought "to learn more about the white man and perhaps help their people." Black Elk, who probably earned a higher wage of perhaps $75 a month as a famous chief, explained, "Maybe if I could see the great world of the Wasichu, I could understand how to bring the sacred hoop together and make their tree bloom again at the center of it" (Neihardt [1932] 1979:214–15).

In the 1980s and 1990s, many of the urban, working-class, and reservation Native Americans who were approached by mascot supporters and invited to become mascot allies had experienced very limited opportunities to be heard, represented, and acknowledged in public spaces. Thus, when a television camera crew or a representative from a major university came calling, and a temporary but *loaded* "stage" was erected, expressions of consent were understandable. Such was the case in 1993, when members of the Peoria Confederated, in Oklahoma, were approached by a local television crew from Champaign-Urbana in order to get the opinion of the *real* Illini Indians on the Chief Illiniwek controversy. Although previously representatives of the tribe expressed no interest in making a statement, with cameras in their faces and scholarship moneys apparently being slipped into their pockets, indeed they did come out in support of the University of Illinois mascot (Springwood and King forthcoming). The hegemony's potency results from complex constellations of power that conspire to shape opportunity, to advance discourse, and to dictate what counts as "common sense."

CONCLUSION

In part, my attempt to set Native American participation in mascot performances into theoretical relief is a response to a very typical defense of Indian mascots offered by non-Indian people. Repeatedly, supporters exclaim that *these* particular Indians or *those* Indians over there are not offended by the harmless images, and they insist that such opinions render moot all other criticism of mascots. Of course, they ignore, then, the fact that Indian voices of critique are the majority, but that is really beside the point. The point is, I believe, that the significance of this issue transcends a mere count of the raised hands of this or that group, and that we must strive to better understand the consequences of Native American mascots and appreciate the complex and complicated connections between "playing Indian" and the identities of Native Americans and non-Indian people alike.

During the height of the controversy over the Huron logo at Eastern Michigan University, Dave Donar (1991), a cartoonist for the student paper *Eastern Echo*, drew a humorous cartoon that encapsulates in a satirical image or two the argument that has taken so many words for me to develop. At the top is a Native American (shown from the waist up) with feathers and braided hair. He begins, "Hi! I am a Huron Indian and I'd be proud to be your mascot." In the next image, he waves an EMU flag with the old Indian caricature and says, "We have fought long and hard to get our name on T-shirts and underwear." Then, shown wearing an EMU football helmet, he adds, "and besides, I'd love to see my face on a football helmet." The final image, in the lower right corner of the frame, is a "view from a much wider angle," revealing that the Native American above is actually a puppet sitting on the lap of a white man (identified as "alumni") who is smoking a cigar. The man finally tells the puppet to say, "Very good! Now say good-bye chief." The Indian puppet complies.

This humorous cartoon more than implies a relevant critique of the efforts of the EMU Huron Restoration group. However, ultimately I cannot allow it to represent the theoretical crux of this analysis, which is clearly not an attempt to offer a flattened, reductionist conception of racial and ethnic identities and social space. Undoubtedly yet unwittingly, the foregoing discussion of hegemony and exploitation oversimplifies matters. The struggle of various social groups to shape their own representations of identity and history is never monolithic and is always radically variable, contradictory, and unpredictable. Because mascot performances and the social spaces of Native American and Euro-American subjectivities are multi-accentual and hybrid, they cannot be understood outside the context of history. For any given moment, because all social groups are uniquely positioned in relation to domains of *difference*, racial identities necessarily are "the product of encounters between and among differently located groups" (McCarthy and Crichlow 1994:xv).

There is no organic, essential Indianness; similarly, neither a singular European American subjectivity nor a monolithic whiteness exists. Homi Bhabha (1994:2) responds eloquently to this problem-

323

atic of understanding how conflict and consensus emerge in terms of practices of representation and experiences of community:

> It is in the emergence of the interstices—the overlap and displacement of domains of difference—that the intersubjective and collective experiences of *nationness*, community interest, or cultural value are negotiated. How are subjects formed "in between," or in excess of, the sum of the "parts" of difference . . . ? How do strategies of representation or empowerment come to be formulated in the competing claims of communities where, despite shared histories of deprivation and discrimination, the exchange of values, meaning and priorities may not always be collaborative and dialogical, *but may be profoundly antagonistic, conflictual, and even commensurable?* [emphasis added]

Indeed, Bhabha is able to anticipate the uneven experience of community emergent in the relationship between Jim Thorpe and Walter Lingo, between Geronimo and William Cody, and, especially, between H. D. Timm Williams—one-time Stanford Chief—and the Native American students who pressed for his removal. The argument that might unfold during a face-to-face encounter of the Huron-Wyandotte representatives—friends of the EMU Huron Restoration group—and many of the Native American contributors to this collection would likely reveal antagonism and conflict. Perhaps, though, it would also generate novel experiences of community and identity.

To suggest, as I have, that postcolonial power—as a particular vector of hegemony—helps us to better understand such awkward alliances as the one that brought Thorpe and Lingo together risks implying that conflict and consent are mere byproducts of ideological *manipulation*. Neither Gramsci nor neo-Gramscian scholars have implied as much. As John Storey (1998:129) explains, "To deny the passivity of consumption is not to deny that sometimes consumption is passive; to deny that the consumers of popular culture are not cultural dupes is not to deny that the culture industries may seek to manipulate." In closing, consider as emblematic the man who during the 1990s portrayed the Indian mascot (see Staurowsky, this volume) of the Cleveland Indians baseball team. During an exclusive interview with Cleveland sportswriter Larry Durstin in 1995, much to the dismay of the team front office, Chief Wahoo reflected on the controversy surrounding his continued existence and on whether or not his image was racist. "Of course it is. Any self-respecting native American would find it offensive. That's as plain as the nose on my face" (Durstin 1999). Contradictory existences such as the one embodied by Chief Wahoo are not surprising; rather, they compose the very fabric of postcolonial human subjectivity.

REFERENCES

Bhabha, Homi. 1994. *The Location of Culture*. London: Routledge Press.

Blackstone, Sarah J. 1986. *Buckskins, Bullets, and Business: A History of Buffalo Bill's Wild West*. New York: Greenwood Press.

Borowski, Sam. 1995. "Tiny LaRue Was Once an NFL Town." *Sunday (Portland) Oregonian*, January 8, Sports, 1.

Bourdieu, Pierre. 1988. *Homo Academicus*. Stanford: Stanford University Press.

Bruner, Edward. 1986. "Ethnography as Narrative." In *The Anthropology of Experience*, ed. Victor Turner and E. Bruner, 139–55. Urbana: University of Illinois Press.

Cass, Ron. 1981. "Long Time Sleep and LaRue's Oorang Indians." *Newslife*, 2 February.

Comaroff, Jean, and John Comaroff. 1991. *Of Revelation and Revolution: Christianity, Colonialism, and Consciousness in South Africa*. Chicago: University of Chicago Press.

Deloria, Philip. 1996. "'I Am of the Body': Thoughts on My Grandfather, Culture, and Sports." *South Atlantic Quarterly* 95(2): 321–38.

Donar, Dave. 1991. "Political Graffiti" [editorial cartoon]. *Ypsilanti, Michigan, Eastern Echo*, 4 September, 4.

Duran, Bonnie. 1996. "Indigenous versus Colonial Discourse: Alcohol and American Indian Identity." In *Dressing in Feathers: The Construction of the Indian in American Popular Culture*, ed. S. Elizabeth Bird, 111–28. Boulder CO: Westview.

Durstin, Larry. 1999. "Is Wahoo's Reign Near Its End?" *Cleveland Tab*, 29 March–11 April, 12.

Fiske, John. 1993. *Power Plays, Power Works*. London: Verso.

Gramsci, Antonio. 1971. *Selections from the Prison Notebooks of Antonio Gramsci*, ed. and trans. Q. Hoare and G. N. Smith. New York: International.

Hall, Stuart. 1985. "Gramsci's Relevance for the Study of Race and Ethnicity." *Journal of Communication Inquiry* 10(2): 5–27.

Hawkins, Billy. 1995/96. "The Black Student Athlete: The Colonized Black Body." *Journal of African American Men* 1(3): 23–35.

Kurtz, Donald V. 1996. "Hegemony and Anthropology: Gramsci, Exegeses, Reinterpretations." *Critique of Anthropology* 16(2): 103–35.

Lhamon, W. T., Jr. 1998. *Raising Cain: Blackface Performance from Jim Crow to Hip Hop*. Cambridge: Harvard University Press.

Liebendorfer, Don E. 1972. *The Color of Life Is Red: A History of Stanford Athletics, 1892–1972*. Palo Alto CA: Stanford University, Department of Athletics.

Lott, Eric. 1995. *Love and Theft: Blackface Minstrelsey and the American Working Class*. New York: Oxford University Press.

McCarthy, Cameron, and Warren Crichlow, eds. 1993. *Race, Identity, and Representation in Education*. London: Routledge Press.

Nagel, Joanne. 1996. *American Indian Ethnic Renewal: Red Power and the Resurgence of Identity and Culture*. New York: Oxford University Press.

Neihardt, John G. [1932] 1979. *Black Elk Speaks: Being the Life Story of a Holy Man of the Oglala Sioux*. Reprint, Lincoln: University of Nebraska Press.

Riley, Brendan. 1972. "Prince Lightfoot Says Indians Who Call Him Uncle Tom Don't Know Own Culture." *Palo Alto Times*, 17 April.

Russell, Don. 1960. *The Lives and Legends of Buffalo Bill*. Norman: University of Oklahoma Press.

———. 1970. *The Wild West: A History of the Wild West Shows*. Fort Worth, Texas: Amon Carter Museum.

Shelton, William E. 1991. "Shelton Explains Logo Decision." *Eastern Echo*, 11 February, 5.

Slotkin, Richard. 1993. "Buffalo Bill's 'Wild West' and the Mythologization of the American Empire." In *Cultures of United States Imperialism*, ed. Amy Kaplan and Donald Pease, 164–81. Chapel Hill NC: Duke University Press.

Springwood, Charles Fruehling, and C. Richard King. Forthcoming. "Race, Ritual, and Remembrance Embodied: Manifest Destiny and the Ritual Sacrifice of 'Chief Illiniwek.'" In *Exercising Power: The Making and Re-making of the Body*, ed. Cheryl Cole, John W. Loy, Michael A. Messner. Albany: SUNY Press.

———. "Race, Power, and Representation in Contemporary American Sport." 2000. In *Multiculturalism in the United States: Current Issues, Contemporary Voices*, ed. Peter Kivisto and Georgeanne Rundblad. Thousand Oaks, CA: Pine Forge Press.

Storey, John. 1998. *An Introduction to Cultural Theory and Popular Culture*. 2d ed. Athens: University of Georgia Press.

Swartz, David. 1997. *Culture and Power: The Sociology of Pierre Bourdieu*. Chicago: University of Chicago Press.

Tarkington, Jeff. 1991. "Alumni, Students Back for Round Two of Logo Dilemma." *Ypsilanti, Michigan, Eastern Echo*, 6 September, 4.

Whitman, Robert L. 1984. *Jim Thorpe and the Oorang Indians: The N.F.L.'s Most Colorful Franchise*. Marion OH: Marion County Historical Society.

Epilogue

Closing Arguments, Opening Dialogues

•

Charles Fruehling Springwood and C. Richard King

I

The chapters in this collection, taken together, represent a broad critique of Native American mascots. They make plain that such enactments of Indianness hinge on romantic, and frequently racist, renderings of Native Americans. Focusing on effects rather than intent, they further suggest that these invented icons harm embodied Indians. And although we hope many readers have gained a new appreciation of these controversial icons, the value of these essays rests not so much in their effectiveness in changing individual minds but in their propensity to problematize mascots and the cultural fields producing them. Indeed, the contributors refuse to see Native American mascots in simple terms, for as King argues in this volume, there is nothing simple about them. This refusal, in turn, unravels their complicated and conflicted nature. They demonstrate, moreover, that the tradition of playing Indian at halftime has assumed a variety of different meanings throughout the nineteenth and twentieth centuries and that such performances have always revealed much more about the non-Indian people and institutions that invented them than they have about Native American cultures and histories. Their interrogations also outline the ongoing strug-

gles—both the points of contention and the terms of engagement—
and hold out the promise of change.

2

As *Team Spirits* went to press, the patterns identified by contributors
recongeal with greater urgency and greater clarity, crystallizing in
classrooms and courtrooms, at athletic events and board meetings.
To clarify the shape of things to come, we present the most noteworthy instances.

During the winter of 1999, the civil rights division of the U.S. Justice Department decided to formally investigate Erwin High School
in Asheville, North Carolina, for its tradition of using the team nicknames "squaws" and "warriors." Lakota Sioux Pat Merzlak, a parent of
a student attending the school, filed a letter of complaint with the Justice Department, prompting the ongoing investigation. Erwin High
School, then, becomes the first publicly funded educational institution to be investigated by the U.S. Justice Department for discrimination resulting from "Indian" mascots and logos.

A majority of the student body at San Francisco's John Swett High
School voted to retire the school's seventy-year-old Indian mascot.
Then, at the request of the school district, the students conducted
a survey of district residents, ultimately revealing that 169 out of
333 residents (51 percent) opposed the mascot. However, on May 25,
1999, school board trustees voted 3–2 to keep the mascot.

In the spring of 1999, the Chief Illiniwek Educational Foundation
(CIEF), an organization supporting the use of Indianness by the University of Illinois at Urbana-Champaign, announced a $1,000 essay
contest, soliciting entries on the theme "How does Chief Illiniwek
best exemplify the spirit of the University of Illinois?" CIEF staged its
writing competition in response to a contest, sponsored by a group
opposed to Chief Illiniwek, to invent a new athletic mascot and team

329

name at the University of Illinois. CIEF sought not only to locate a defense of their beloved mascot but to link its defense of an imagined Indian with the struggles of embodied Native Americans. It planned to donate the prize money to a Native American organization that would support its cause. CIEF approached the Native American Women's Health Education Resource Center, a social service agency on the Yankton Sioux reservation in South Dakota, asking its director to support the contest, without explaining its pro-Chief agenda or the context of the embattled mascot. Ultimately, the resource center responded with, "Thanks, but no thanks."

During its biannual conference on January 27, 1999, the Society of Indian Psychologists issued a position statement calling for all Native American mascots to be retired. The three-hundred-member organization concluded that such icons inflict actual emotional harm on Native Americans while having a negative impact on the development of cultural and ethnic identities.

This sampling of brief descriptions represents a mere fraction of current sites of controversy and protest over Native American mascots across the nation. These instances serve to convey the broad, unfolding, and dynamic nature of the mascot issue in the United States.

3

Some claim that Native Americans should not be concerned with these mascots since Native American communities surely face more important problems, from drug and alcohol addiction to infant mortality and poverty. Such a view makes several important mistakes. We want to pause to reiterate what is at stake here, that is, why mascots matter.

First, the claim assumes that only Native Americans would challenge Indian mascots, when the situation is much more complicated. Undoubtedly, many object to mascots, some passionately enough to protest them. Practically all Native American organizations with a national constituency have taken a stand against them, and numerous others with local and regional memberships oppose them as well. Not only have some Euro-Americans, although surely a minority (see Sigelman 1998), along with African Americans and other peoples of color, expressed their distaste for such symbols, but they have also worked, often in concert with Native American individuals and organizations, to retire them. Still, some American Indians, probably a small number, as the essays by King and Springwood explore, have supported mascots.

Second, this argument suffers from a fundamental misapprehension of the significance of representation. Mascots are not trivial signs or flat performances. Instead, representation is an active practice in which individuals both encode and decode meanings. As a consequence, it has material effects. It is a productive nexus. It shapes the manner in which individuals understand and interact with themselves and others.

Third, because mascots frequently have been associated with educational institutions, mascots have profound consequences for the ways in which Native Americans (and others) learn about themselves. As part of deeper historical and broader cultural patterns of representation, they facilitate the formulation of negative self-concepts and impoverished self-esteem. In turn, these damaged selves have a greater propensity toward alcoholism, suicide, depression, and other social problems. Ironically, reactionary defenders of mascots commonly view these latter problems as more important.

Fourth, the traditional practice of Native American mascots, when viewed in the broadest historical context, opens an important window of understanding onto the history of the United States. Why have these mascots meant so much, in so many different ways, to non-Indian people? Indian mascots are interesting, even provoc-

331

ative, to anyone with an interest in better understanding American society, precisely because of the intensity with which their existences are defended. These essays have explored the sorts of histories, experiences, and patriotism that conspired to produce such passionate investments in (mis)representations of Native American peoples.

4

More basically, these symbols matter because they are intimately connected with everyday ideas, values, and worldviews—about Indianness. The contributors to *Team Spirits* would insist that such symbols are inseparable from these ways of thinking about life and people. Social identities are inseparable from performance, history, and power, and we believe that Native American mascots are engaged by the public in such a way that they produce knowledge about the imagined differences between Native Americans and non-Indian people. This is not to say that the tomahawk-chopping fans of the Atlanta Braves somehow gain a genuine understanding about the experiences and histories of Native Americans. Rather, the "knowledge" produced by these "team spirits" is a more subtle form of common sense. The non-Indian American citizen knows— as common knowledge—the categories implicit in mascot representations and already appreciates that Indians make for popular mascots while African Americans or Italian peasants do not. He or she already knows the stereotypical characteristics that seem to position the "Indian" as an "appropriate" athletic totem (see Springwood and King forthcoming). What are the consequences of such common sense? Throughout this collection, contributors have argued that such common sense interferes with the potential of many white Americans to engage Native American people as diverse, feeling, and thinking human actors with whom they share not only differences but also similarities.

5

The force of symbols and common sense is well illustrated with a comparative example that is both relevant and current. A significant majority of U.S. citizens support an amendment to the Constitution that would criminalize the burning of the American flag. Indeed, many react with a sense of horror at the very thought of someone burning Old Glory. This passionate perspective is often viewed as patriotic. Ironically, we suggest, a significant portion of those who oppose flag burning as a symbolic desecration are part of the non-Indian majority who fail to understand how Indian mascots could possibly convey anything harmful or distasteful. The point of this example is, of course, that symbols are made—by people and their social worlds—to matter very much. By appropriating a symbol, by transforming or disrupting its context, its meanings may not only be inverted but also denied or erased. Those who protest the existence of Native American mascots frequently argue that perhaps the most obvious, fundamental problem with them is context. It is difficult to understand how the heritage of an indigenous people can be appropriately celebrated in the context of big-time collegiate athletics. It is unlikely that images of Indians on the sweaters of football cheerleaders and choreographed halftime Indian dances honor Native Americans when, almost without exception, these manifestations offer relatively little to the lives and interests of most Native Americans. For example, what does a ceremonial Seminole headdress have to do with the football offense facing a-third-down-and-ten situation? It would be wrong to answer nothing, for obviously, this symbol has been made—by largely white Americans—to mean a great deal in the context of football.

We offer one final example of comparison. In the early 1990s, in Tokyo, Japan, Chuck Springwood observed a number of Santa Claus figures for sale. The Santa figures were intriguing because their arms—spread out—were pinned to little crucifixes. A devout Christian would possibly react in horror to such a "sacrilegious" juxtaposition of a commercial Christmas icon with a sacred symbol of martyrdom. But, in order to make this a more relevant analogy to Native American mascots, try to imagine the response of the Christian to the crucified Santa if the Japanese society that produced the provocative image had long ago conquered and colonized the Christian's own society.

6

Perhaps *Team Spirits* can serve best as conversation starter that will inspire people in communities with Native American mascots and, especially, in communities with ongoing Native American mascot controversies to thoughtfully reflect on the traditions and conditions that gave rise to the literally thousands of "Team Spirits" across the nation. Perhaps non-Indian people who have a great deal of emotional investment in one or another Indian mascot will take the opportunity to respond to Native American sentiment at face value. Commenting on Illinois state senator Rick Winkel's attempt to make Chief Illiniwek's existence a state law, University of Illinois graduate student Durango Mendoza, who is Creek-Muskogee, remarked, "My question to a person like Winkel is . . . 'What part of *ouch* do you *not* understand?' And I would tell him that you need to make sure that when you try to establish and legalize something that is hurtful, that you have second thoughts about it" ("Open Remarks" 1995).

REFERENCES

"Open Remarks to the Peoria Tribe from Native American Students, Staff, and Faculty for Progress." 1995. Unpublished videotape released by the Native American Students, Staff, and Faculty for Progress, Champaign, IL.

Sigelman, Lee. 1998. "Hail to the Redskins? Public Reactions to a Racially Insensitive Team Name." *Sociology of Sport Journal* 15(4): 317–25.

Springwood, Charles Fruehling, and C. Richard King. Forthcoming. "Race, Ritual, and Remembrance Embodied: Manifest Destiny and the Symbolic Sacrifice of 'Chief Illiniwek.'" In *Exercising Power: The Making and Remaking of the Body*, ed. Cheryl Cole, John Loy, and Michael Messner. Albany: SUNY Press.

CONTRIBUTORS

LAUREL DAVIS teaches sociology at Springfield College and is committed to eliminating Native American mascots. She has authored various articles on racism and sexism in sport and *The Swimsuit Issue and Sport: Hegemonic Masculinity in "Sports Illustrated."* She serves on the editorial boards of *Journal of Sport and Social Issues* and *Men and Masculinities*.

RICHARD CLARK ECKERT, of late deafened, is a member of the Bad River Band of Lake Superior Ojibwe, who enjoys participating in traditional activities. A doctoral candidate in sociology at the University of Michigan, he is also a lead singer on the Dream Star drum. His dissertation research concerns what he calls Deaf-American ethnicity.

DONALD M. FISHER teaches United States, European, World, and Native American history courses at Niagara County Community College in Sanborn, New York. He received a Ph.D. in history from the State University of New York at Buffalo in 1997. He is currently working on a cultural history of lacrosse in North America spanning the nineteenth and twentieth centuries.

SUZAN SHOWN HARJO (Cheyenne and Hodulgee Muscogee), mother of two grown children, is director of the Morning Star Institute. Her articles, commentary, and poetry have been widely published. She has developed federal Indian policy since 1975 to protect Native cultures and arts and has helped Native Peoples recover a million acres of land.

C. RICHARD KING, assistant professor of anthropology at Drake University, is the author of *Colonial Discourses, Collective Memories, and the Exhibition of Native American Cultures and Histories in the Contemporary United States* and editor of *Postcolonial America*. He is presently completing a book with Charles F. Springwood on the interplay of redness, blackness, and whiteness in college athletics.

MARY LANDRETH was lecturer of history at the University of Central Arkansas and a graduate student at Arkansas State University. Sadly, as this collection went to press, she was killed in a car crash. She will be missed.

PATRICK RUSSELL LEBEAU earned a Ph.D. in American culture from the University of Michigan with an emphasis in American Indian studies. He is an enrolled member of the Cheyenne River Sioux Indian Reservation, South Dakota.

ANN MARIE (AMBER) MACHAMER is a member of the Coastal Band Chumash Nation of California's central coast. She earned a B.A. in history (1993) and Ph.D. in education (1999) at UCLA. Currently she is Director of Research and Planning at Las Positas Community College in Livermore, California.

DAVID PROCHASKA teaches history and postcolonial studies at the University of Illinois, Urbana-Champaign. In 1990, he authored *Making Algeria French: Colonialism in Bône, 1870–1920*. He has published articles on visual culture in colonial Algeria, Senegal, Egypt, and India.

MALVINA RAU, professor in the School of Human Services at Springfield College, served as Provost and Vice President for Academic Affairs when the institution retired its mascot, actively advocating for the change.

JAY ROSENSTEIN is the producer/director of the award-winning documentary *In Whose Honor? American Indian Mascots in Sports*. He is an assistant professor of journalism at the University of Illinois, Urbana-Champaign.

Contributors

CHARLES FRUEHLING SPRINGWOOD, assistant professor of anthropology at Illinois Wesleyan University, is the author of *Cooperstown to Dyersville: A Geography of Baseball Nostalgia*. He is presently completing a book with C. Richard King on the interplay of redness, blackness, and whiteness in college athletics.

ELLEN J. STAUROWSKY is associate professor of sport sciences and coordinator of the sport communication program at Ithaca College. A former college athlete, coach, and athletic director, she has researched social justice issues in sport for almost twenty years. She has recently published, with Allen L. Sack, *College Athletes for Hire: The Evolution and Legacy of the NCAA Amateur Myth*.

INDEX

Aaron, Stewart, 205
ABC, 70, 244, 248, 249
ABC News, 249, 253
Academic Senate (CMU), 72, 77
activism, 222; Native American, 2, 117, 249; at SC, 228–29, 230–31; systemic, 210–11, 212–13, 220
Adams, Andrew, 116
Adams State College (Colorado), 4
Adara, 121, 124
Addonizio, Shari, 137
Adenauer, Konrad (Chief Layadaholu), 287
administrators, 212, 213, 214–15
Affirmative Action Council (CMU), 70–71, 72, 77
African Americans, 120, 149, 317, 320; and racial hierarchies, 150–52
AIEC. *See* American Indian Education Commission
Airedales: and Oorang Indians, 311, 312, 313
Alabama, 134
Alexander, Minnie, 205
Allen, William Harman van, 28
Alligator, 134
alligator wrestling, 147
All-Star Game, 100
Alpha Omicron Pi, 55
Alpha Tau Omega, 32
alumni, 77–78, 224, 225, 227, 307
Alumni Council (SC), 224, 225, 227
American Indian Center (Cleveland), 35
American Indian Education Commission (AIEC), 208, 211–12, 217, 218–19
American Indian Fellowship, 137

American Indian Mental Health Association of Minnesota, 267
American Indian Movement, 4, 12, 13, 83, 212, 249, 273 n.7
American Indian Students at Marquette University, 293
American League pennant race, 84
Ames IA, 245
Anderdon Reservation, 308
Anderson, Benedict, 9, 166
Angell, James B., 124
Anishinaabegs, 64
Apalachis, 133
Apodaca, Raymond D., 200, 202, 206
appaloosas: and FSU, 130, 131, 138–39
appropriation, 173–74
archaeological hoax: at Syracuse, 29–30, 35
Archambault, Jodi, 203–4
Arizona, 192
Arkansas: frontier image of, 49–50, 60; Native Americans in, 47–48
Arkansas State University (ASU): faculty resolution at, 56–58; "Indians" at, 50–56; Native American representation at, 61–62; stereotypes at, 57–59; team nicknames at, 46, 48
arrests: of protestors, 83, 84, 101
art, 83; political, 170–71
Arvada High School (Colorado), 193
Asheville NC, 329
assimilationism, 59–60, 152, 192, 272 n.6
ASU. *See* Arkansas State University
athletics, 66, 136, 193, 229; African Americans and, 151–52, 320; at ASU, 46, 51–53, 54–55, 56; playing Indian

346